INTERVENTIONS: NEW STUDIES
IN MEDIEVAL CULTURE

Ethan Knapp, Series Editor

POLITICAL APPETITES

Food in Medieval English Romance

∾

AARON HOSTETTER

THE OHIO STATE UNIVERSITY PRESS
COLUMBUS

Copyright © 2017 by The Ohio State University.
All rights reserved.

Library of Congress Cataloging-in-Publication Data
Names: Hostetter, Aaron Kenneth, 1971– author.
Title: Political appetites : food in medieval English romance / Aaron Hostetter.
Other titles: Interventions: new studies in medieval culture.
Description: Columbus : The Ohio State University Press, [2017] | Series: Interventions: new studies in medieval culture | Includes bibliographical references and index.
Identifiers: LCCN 2017022099 | ISBN 9780814213513 (cloth ; alk. paper) | ISBN 0814213510 (cloth ; alk. paper)
Subjects: LCSH: Food in literature. | Food habits in literature. | Cooking in literature. | Romances, English—History and criticism. | English literature—Middle English, 1100–1500—History and criticism.
Classification: LCC PR149.F66 H67 2017 | DDC 820.9/3564—dc23
LC record available at https://lccn.loc.gov/2017022099

Cover design by Susan Zucker
Text design by Juliet Williams
Type set in Adobe Minion Pro

♾ The paper used in this publication meets the minimum requirements of the American National Standard for Information Sciences—Permanence of Paper for Printed Library Materials. ANSI Z39.48–1992.

9 8 7 6 5 4 3 2 1

CONTENTS

Acknowledgments		vii
Abbreviations		xi
INTRODUCTION	Romance and Repast	1
CHAPTER 1	*Andreas*: Cannibals at the Edge of History	32
CHAPTER 2	*The Roman de Silence*: Crossing Categories	66
CHAPTER 3	*Havelok the Dane*: Food, Sovereignty, and Social Order	98
CHAPTER 4	*Sir Gowther*: Table Manners and Aristocratic Identity	133
CONCLUSION	Cheese and Cannibals	167
Bibliography		174
Index		188

ACKNOWLEDGMENTS

WHILE WRITING a book on medieval food and food practice, I often hear, "You must like to cook." It would be more accurate to say that I love to eat, and I am especially grateful for all the delicious meals I have been served by family and friends. What I have been able to cook was shared with these loved ones in turn. The payoff is the lovely conversation one has while eating together, lingering over wine and dessert while it grows dark outside, affectionately partaking of each other's company. Kant believed that prandial exchange was what made dining civilized, and Brillat-Savarin affirmed that "at the end of a well-savored meal both soul and body enjoy an especial well-being." My friends and family have fortified me in both body and soul for these past forty-some-odd years, and definitely opened my eyes to the possible glories of living in the edible world.

 Nothing of this book would have been possible without the support of my faculty advisors throughout the years. During my stay at the University of Colorado at Boulder, Katherine Eggert provided much-needed encouragement to the undergraduate Aaron, blowing up my critical world by introducing me to the poetry of Edmund Spenser. Bruce Holsinger introduced me to the medieval applications of Karl Marx in a fantastic seminar called "The Marxist Premodern." Most important was the influence of Beth Robertson, who basically conscripted me to become a medievalist way back in the early

1990s—brooking no denials or resistance—and introducing me to poetry in general and later to Chaucer's *Troilus and Criseyde*, and then inviting me to return to school for my very first graduate class after five years away working in the real world. My academic life would have been much different if I had not been exposed to medieval studies and its modern usefulness due to her diligent, imaginative scholarship and patient, warm, and powerful teaching. She basically has made my entire career possible with her support and intervention.

I would also like to recognize the many professors at Princeton University who were of material assistance during my stay there. Professor John Fleming was helpful during my first year, giving me much inspiration through the three seminars I had with him and providing me with many insights about how to be an effective teacher. Oliver Arnold and Bill Gleason were both vital supports during the dark middle point of my studies there, bolstering me when everything else seemed to be falling down. Andrew Cole proved to be a cheerful and thoughtful leader of my final seminar. Susan Wolfson also has given me unselfishly a great deal of professional advice since my graduation, especially in relieving my angst about the publication process.

Vance Smith and Kathleen Davis deserve a great deal of thanks, both for recognizing my potential as a medievalist and agreeing to train me further. The path was never easy, but they always supported me and believed in me, and gave their best. Vance was a capable hand at the tiller of my studies, both loosening my imagination and reining it in. His research and teaching have always inspired me to dig deeper in the texts I was studying, searching for the key question that relates the medieval world to ours. I will always remember his admonishment to recognize that medieval texts work through similar philosophical problems to those that engage and perplex us in the contemporary moment. Kathleen proved to be a guiding light and a life preserver in my studies, not only by introducing me to the glories of Anglo-Saxon literature but also by being a teacher, scholar, mentor, and friend to me as this project developed over the years. Through her example, she has single-handedly expanded for me the possibilities for one's critical labors.

I owe everything to my parents, Dan Hostetter and Janet Larson, who taught me how to appreciate good food, good books, and good music. They have been unswervingly supportive during the many twists and turns I have taken to get to this point in my career. Thanks also to my many sisters and brothers, grandparents, and step-parents for their love and kindness over the years.

Thanks also goes out to Ed and Terrie Plumer, who have graciously provided key editorial help during the process of finishing and marketing this book.

Most thanks of all must go to Lyra Plumer. She has proven to be essential to the compilation of this book, whether editing, critiquing, conversing about ideas, or making many other valuable suggestions. She was strong when I was scared and direct when I needed guidance. I'll always be grateful for your help.

I would like to extend my appreciation to my colleagues and fellow travelers during my various graduate degrees, for their challenging comments, inspiring conversations, and sometimes inebriated debates through the years: Brodie Austin, Sand Avidar-Walzer, Oscar Bettison, James Bickford, Hannah Crawforth, Benjamin Deneault, Renee Dickerson, Renee Fox, Jennifer Garrison, Melanie Haupt, Hannah Johnson, Erik Kennedy, David Lennington, Daniel Moss, John Reuland, Alana Shilling, Eric Turner, Dave Urban, Casey Walker, Andrew Young, and Wesley Yu.

Much gratitude goes out to my colleagues at Rutgers-Camden, who have welcomed me into their fold and challenged me to grow as a professor and researcher: Joe Barbarese, Holly Blackford, Jim Brown, Rich Epstein, Chris Fitter, Bill Fitzgerald, Keith Green, Lauren Grodstein, Rafey Habib, Tyler Hoffman, Ellen Malenas Ledoux, Paul Lisicky, Howard Marchitello, Patrick Rosal, Jillian Sayre, and Carol Singley. I would especially like to recognize Rich Epstein and Richard Hyland for their long-standing participation in our Anglo-Saxon translation group, which grew out of their participation in my very first Old English language class in Fall 2013. *Beowulf* will never be the same! A special shout goes out to Dee Jonczak, the English Department secretary, who has helped make my life at RUC so much easier and definitely more pleasant!

The students in my several graduate seminars have been especially helpful in the formation of these ideas, often making my first attempts to articulate these ideas into part of the conversation. Special gratitude goes out to the participants in my Spring 2012 "Studies in Medieval Romance" seminar and my Spring 2016 "Anglo-Saxon Poetry" class. Your intellectual bravery and flexibility have been inspirational!

Several of my department chairs were extremely helpful in the preparation of my book proposal and manuscript this past year. Tyler Hoffman, Howard Marchitello, and Lisa Zeidner all contributed a great deal in the way of advice, suggestions, and drafts as I was preparing both tenure and book materials this past year.

The work that appears in this book has been elaborated in many different venues over the years. A shorter version of chapter 3 was published in the *Journal of English and Germanic Philology*, volume 110, in January 2011. Material from chapter 4 appeared in *Studies in Philology*, volume 114.3, in Summer 2017.

ABBREVIATIONS

ANTS—Anglo-Norman Text Society

BOSWORTH-TOLLER—*An Anglo-Saxon Dictionary,* edited by Joseph Bosworth and T. Northcote Toller (1898)

CA.—circa

EETS—Early English Text Society

E.S.—extra series

JEGP—*Journal of English and Germanic Philology*

JMEMS—*Journal of Medieval and Early Modern Studies*

MED—*Middle English Dictionary*

MLN—*Modern Language Notes*

N.S.—new series

OED—*Oxford English Dictionary*

O.S.—original series

NM—*Neuphilologische Mitteilungen*

PMLA—*Publications of the Modern Language Association*

SATF—Société des Anciens Textes Français

S.S.—supplementary series

YLS—*Yearbook of Langland Studies*

All quotes of the Bible in English are from the Douay-Rheims translation. All translations are mine, unless otherwise noted.

INTRODUCTION

Romance and Repast

All social life is essentially practical. All the mysteries which lead theory towards mysticism find their rational solution in human practice and in the comprehension of this practice.
—Karl Marx, "Theses on Feuerbach"

The material world is not merely a vehicle for expressing the immaterial, but on the contrary contains the heart of its meaning and its mystery.
—Jill Mann, "Eating and Drinking in *Piers Plowman*"

Res condita tota / Est condita.

An object described in its entirety is a dish well-seasoned.
—Geoffrey of Vinsauf, *Poetria Nova*, trans. Margaret Nims

1. OUR EDIBLE WORLD

WHO KNEW that political supremacy could stick to the ribs? In the course of our brief planetary reign, our appetites have surpassed all bounds into a surfeit that modernity seems unwilling, even unable, to renounce. It is tempting to conceive human dominance of the world's resources as a kind of manifest destiny stretching across the millennia. Content to keep eating, we are loath to reconceive our sense of entitlement even in the face of rapidly approaching global food crises. Human history is an unending appetitive contest with our environments, as we chase down whatever we believe we need to survive. Consumption is not only the collective human fate but also its empowering practice—we eat because we rule, and we rule because we eat.

The foundational social mythology of the Bible alternately unleashes these sovereign human appetites and imposes stern limits upon them. God's instructions to Noah after the Flood are dietary empowerments. The survivors may now devour "every thing that moveth and liveth" in a reign of terror with God's blessing: "And let the fear and dread of you be upon all the beasts of the earth, and upon all the fowls of the air, and all that move upon the earth" (Genesis 9:2–3). Human ascendancy over the natural world is consumptive, becoming a toothy domination of every creature. The antediluvian vegetarian bill of fare is thrown open; sanctified subjugation makes every living thing a potential meal.

Moses's covenant to the Israelites brings this era of unbridled predation to an abrupt halt, with a host of complex, interlocking food restrictions that elevate the power of the edible to distinguish nation and nature (Leviticus 11). Nervous negotiation of dietary taboos becomes the gustatory norm for the rest of the Bible, especially as the food miracles of Jesus benefit the faithful. Yet God eases these proscriptions once again after the Resurrection. The Acts of the Apostles, a collection of miraculous missionary stories, throws open the realm of incipient Christianity even as it projects the renewed subjugation of the world into a nutritive object. Peter's visionary injunction to "kill and eat" (Acts 10:13) prophesies a new political relationship to the earth and its commodities, and God again authorizes the exploitation of every living thing.[1] Nothing is off-limits—*immundum* or unclean—to the restless taste buds of hungry humanity.[2] There is no longer any limit placed upon the appetite of a world redeemed by Christian grace, satiated bodily yet hungry for resurrection.[3]

Eating is the fundamental metaphor of the Christian's individual and corporate connection to the divine. The Eucharist, the ritualistic consumption of Christ's body held every mass, is a powerful symbolic appropriation of the act of nutrition, linking the body of the believer to a universal, infinite grace,

---

1. This necessity of violence against animals as a foundation of definitions of humanity is a fundamental question of the burgeoning field of animal studies. Although I do not engage this work more explicitly in this book, I acknowledge its relevance to many of the questions that drive my study, especially as I argue that the practices of eating (animals) forms an authorizing metaphor for the political ambitions of medieval romance.

2. The usefulness of such unrestrained consumption has other political benefits for the developing Christian church. By renouncing ancient Mosaic dietary prescriptions, the Christian apostles use appetite to transform their bodily identity from Jews to something new, transcending the national boundaries of Judea (see chapter 1 on Jesus' anticipation of this expansion of identity in Luke 10:3–8). Additionally, the relaxation of culinary strictures (as well as abandoning the practice of male circumcision) was a strategic move for a church desperately trying to win converts throughout the Mediterranean world, by allowing new adherents to continue practicing their own familiar customs.

3. See Giorgio Agamben for a discussion of medieval theories of bodily resurrection, especially whether these bodies will need to eat (*The Open: Man and Animal*, trans. Kevin Attell, 17–19).

an overflowing treasury of perfect spiritual satiation. The Host is a formidable resonance of medieval Christianity to issues of food and eating, and an avenue often explored in the modern understanding of medieval food practice, especially in the wake of Caroline Walker Bynum's *Holy Feast and Holy Fast* (1987), which links Eucharistic enthusiasm in late medieval Europe to practices of fasting and *inedia* often performed by female saints and mystics. Unfortunately, matching the obsession of the Middle Ages with our own theological preoccupations, the examination of food and foodways in medieval culture too often proceeds no further, and every secular meal becomes a dim reflection of religious metaphor. This book is a deliberate attempt to move beyond theological parallels, to interpret eating as a cultural practice with political and social import, and to reclaim a world of quotidian fascination and interest. Just as literary criticism has moved beyond an allegorical basis of understanding, so should the critique of food practice proceed past its strictly religious valences.[4]

We still live in an edible world, rendered even more digestible by the technological domination of the environment that renders all possible commodities "cleansed." Few things are forbidden to our appetites where consumption is the fundamental activity of large swaths of the global middle class. Labor—the physical manipulation of natural resources to serve human needs—no longer describes the daily activity for many planetary citizens. Marx argues that labor is "an eternal natural necessity, which mediates the metabolism between man and nature"; forming a sort of productive digestion of the world and its many useful objects.[5] Hannah Arendt further elaborates this basic definition: "Labor is the activity which corresponds to the biological process of the human body. . . . The human condition of labor is life itself."[6] She affirms the somatic function of labor: life is a struggle to render the world useful to our particular corporeal needs. Yet twenty-first-century technocratic capitalism preserves the metabolic act without its physicality, with former laborers folded

---

4. However, intriguing work on the Eucharist continues to be produced and should not be ignored. See most recently Jennifer Garrison's *Challenging Communion: The Eucharist and Middle English Literature*.

5. Karl Marx, *Capital: A Critique of Political Economy*, vol. 1 (1867), trans. Ben Fowkes, 133. Marx's fundamental concepts, such as labor-power, commodity formation, and fetishization are applicable to any given economic system, and so therefore, his observations are not limited to just industrial capitalist societies. Furthermore, the Middle Ages form a generative matrix for many of his theories on historical materialism and class relations, and make up the subject of one of his most compelling narratives, the process of "primitive accumulation" in the transition from feudalism to an early capitalist economy in England. See Bruce Holsinger and Ethan Knapp, ed., "Marxist Premodern," *JMEMS* 34.3 (Fall 2004), for the enduring power of the medieval in Marxist theory.

6. Hannah Arendt, *The Human Condition* (1958), 7.

into an expanded bourgeoisie, who nevertheless perpetuate their subordination within this system by purchasing and consuming the commodities they toil to earn.[7] Revolution, the inevitable by-product of the theory of historical materialism and its agent of political change, seems to have been bought out by the satisfaction of ever-expanding appetites. The very act of consumption has become transformed into a kind of productive labor, a total engagement with the conditions and limits of existence, a bodily practice that seems to justify itself.[8]

Eating, however, has not always been taken for granted. It is one of our first traumatic interactions with the world. We are dependent upon foreign material in order to survive, incorporating what lies outside into ourselves. This can be the occasion for an ambiguous and disturbing sort of celebration, according to Mikhail Bakhtin:

> The body transgresses here its own limits: it swallows, devours, rends the world apart, is enriched and grows at the world's expense.... Man's encounter with the world in the act of eating is joyful, triumphant; he triumphs over the world, devours it without being devoured himself. The limits between man and the world are erased, to man's advantage.[9]

Bakhtin's carnivalesque bodies revel in their infantile incorporation of the outside, yet the frontier within is rather more uncertain. Jane Bennett observes: "Eating appears as a series of mutual transformations in which the border between inside and outside becomes blurry: my meal both is and is not mine."[10] Every meal is a transubstantiation of the exterior into the intimate stuff of our bodies, a magical metamorphosis of what is not-me into my very being. It is no wonder that children sometimes distrust their food, and that so much children's literature depicts monstrous acts of eating and states of hunger.[11] Adults too, in accelerating numbers over the course of history, seek

---

7. This cycle of work to consume differentiates middle-class consumers from those who hold true sovereignty in our society, those who, according to Georges Bataille, consume the products of other people's labor without the pain of laboring themselves (*The Accursed Share*, vol. 3, *Sovereignty* [1949], trans. Robert Hurley, 198).

8. See chapter 4 for an application of Marx's theory of "productive consumption" found most fully in the "Introduction to the Critique of Political Philosophy," an 1857 essay found in *Grundrisse*, trans. Martin Nicolaus.

9. Mikhail Bakhtin, *Rabelais and His World* (1965), trans. Helene Iswolsky, 281.

10. Jane Bennett, *Vibrant Matter: A Political Ecology of Things*, 49.

11. Not only fairy tale ogres and witches in edible candy houses but other forms of defamiliarization of food: for example, the predicament of Wilbur, the pig in E. B. White's *Charlotte's Web* (1952), aware of his fate to be slaughtered for food, or Maurice Sendak's *In The Night*

to control their circumstances and lives by exercising constraint on their food intake by dieting and even more extreme measures.[12] Food preferences and practices often mark cultural and social identity in ways that separate and join different groups of people, and the taste for a particular foodstuff bears the weight of sometimes hostile national, ethnic, and racial distinctions. Yet acts of ingestion and assimilation are fundamental to survival; the costs of living in a consumable world.

The need to eat is sometimes seen as a fallibility of the body, evidence of the fallen condition of humanity. During the Golden Age, according to Hesiod and Ovid, primitive humans lived in a world of effortless acquisition and satisfaction, and labor—imaged as violence against the earth—only becomes necessary as the ages devolved.[13] In a parallel story, the punishment of Adam and Eve upon their expulsion from the Garden of Eden is a perpetual binding of consumption and pain: "In the sweat of thy face shalt thou eat bread till thou return to the earth, out of which thou wast taken" (Genesis 3:19). In both accounts, the agony of labor is fundamentally connected to obtaining food. Our need for replenishment dooms us to a prolonged struggle with our environment and its denizens. This connection between toil and food is reaffirmed by Geoffrey Chaucer's hypocritical Pardoner (ca. 1390):

> Allas, the shorte throte, the tendre mouth,
> Maketh that est and west and north and south,
> In erthe, in eir, in water, men to swynke
> To get a glotoun deyntee mete and drynke!
> (VI.517–20)[14]

Gluttony, the sin of improper eating, perpetuates the curse of Adam, damning those unfortunate enough to a lifetime of "swynke," suffering to acquire rare and choice food for more privileged consumers. An enigmatic thirteenth-century lyric puts it another way: "Erþe toc of erþe erþe wyþ woh"

Kitchen (1970), where the hero, Mickey, falls into an enormous bowl of cake batter and flies an airplane made from bread dough.

12. See Caroline Walker Bynum, *Holy Feast and Holy Fast*, for accounts of saintly *inedia* and other methods of food control practiced by holy men and women in the Middle Ages, practices relatable though not equatable to contemporary trends of anorexia nervosa and bulimia in the developed world.

13. Hesiod, *Works and Days* (ca. 700 BCE), in *Hesiod*, trans. Glenn W. Most, 109–20; Ovid, *Metamorphoses* (8 CE), trans. Frank Justus Miller, 1.101–12.

14. Quotations from Geoffrey Chaucer are from *The Riverside Chaucer*, ed. Larry D. Benson.

[Earthly creatures wrongfully wrest earthly commodities from the earth].[15] Such tropes associate eating and consumption with self-recrimination and distrust, situating the body within borderlands of edibility. We are ourselves the food of worms and carrion beasts—as both epic *topoi* and popular meditations on death often remind their readers. Old English war poetry lingers over the "Beasts of Battle"—the wolf, the eagle, and the raven—who gloat and rejoice at the prospect of conflict, raring to gorge upon fallen human bodies.[16] The Anglo-Saxon "Soul and Body" poem in the Exeter Book (ca. 950–1000) expresses this inevitable fate of the body as "Bið þonne wyrmes giefl, / æt on eorþan" (119–20) [It will be a platter for the worms, a meal in the dirt].[17] The uncertain nature of the world, and its biological imperative, ensures that any of its creatures that may eat today might be eaten tomorrow.

Yet eating is never just dangerous or negative, for it is has been considered one of life's joys, an expression of triumph over the painful circumstances of human existence. The true measure of the good life experienced by Chaucer's Franklin is that "it snewed in his hous of mete and drynke," the cheerful plenty of his board expressed as a meteorological marvel.[18] The Franklin does not, however, just enjoy this plenteous display: his social aspirations and pretensions derive from his many bird coops and fishponds, as well as the lustrous setting of his table (I.349–54). This plenum embodies aristocratic largesse, especially as he offers board and hospitality better than the best of them. Though he will never become noble himself, he understands better than anyone the *fons et origo* of noble identity. In the Anglo-Saxon lyric *The Ruin*, the broken buildings still echo with feasting: "Meoduheall monig mondreama full" (23) [many a mead-hall, filled with the joys of humanity]; the resounding nature of the former good life enhoused there only emphasized by its absence now.[19] "The feast is a conquest over nature," posits Derek Brewer, and it celebrates social identity, as well as victorious circumstances.[20] Sufficiency and abundance in food production make human culture possible—the word "culture" itself originates in the process of cultivating the earth, as if the ethos of human accomplishment is the product of agricultural labor.[21] Politics and economics are founded upon

---

15. Carleton Brown, *English Lyrics of the Thirteenth Century*, no. 73.
16. See *Beowulf*, 3024–27; *Elene*, 28–29 and 110–13; *Exodus*, 162–69; *Judith* 205–12; and *The Battle of Maldon*, 106–7.
17. Bernard J. Muir, ed., *The Exeter Anthology of Old English Poetry*, 178.
18. Chaucer, *General Prologue* to *The Canterbury Tales* (ca. 1387–99), I.345.
19. Muir, ed., *Exeter Anthology*, 360.
20. Derek Brewer, "Feasts in England and English Literature in the Fourteenth Century," in *Feste und Feiern im*, ed. Detlef Altenburg, Jörg Jarnut, and Hans-Hugo Steinhoff, 26.
21. *OED*, "culture" n. 1.

acquisition and distribution of food among members of society, and neither exists in any sophisticated form until there is enough to go around.[22]

The empowering observation of *Political Appetites* can be expressed in a maxim: *Food choice is always a political act.* By the word "political," I intend to convey a broad array of human activities in this world: indeed politics could be defined as any action made by humans that influences other humans, acting as if all are members of a "polis," a conglomeration of other agents bound together by mutual interests. Seen with the structures of human relationships in mind, anything that affects or is affected by these structures can be considered political—even eating coconuts alone on a desert island does not happen without some degree of human intervention. According to this definition, literature as an expression or a critique of a given social order's ideology is eminently political even (or especially) when it purports to eschew political reference. Most literary productions—especially the medieval romance—fall into Sarah Kay's definition of "political fictions": they are "bounded by assumptions about the nature of the personal and the social, the licit and the illicit, the ethical and the unethical, the representable and the unrepresentable," and these assumed subjects inform how these productions engage with the world of its making.[23]

Food choice, not only within this realm of politically active literature but also in the terms of real action in the world,[24] signifies and projects a series of complex statements about self-identity—both one's physical and social circumstances, as well as one's aspirations for advancement.[25] By eating, humans acknowledge that they have a body, and these bodies are the most immediate site of not only an intimate material connection with the world but also of pervasive political inscription, marking them with race, gender, or class. The act of satisfying our bodily needs for sustenance also imbricates us into prevailing political structures. Consumption, whether of food or any other commodity, completes the cycle of production and makes the creation of new

---

22. See Thorstein Veblen, "Theory of the Leisure Class" (1899), in *A Veblen Treasury*, ed. Rick Tillman, 5–7.

23. Sarah Kay, *The Chansons de Geste in the Age of Romance: Political Fictions*, 5.

24. Indeed, they are the same thing, as Robert M. Stein observes, "Representational practices, too, are real actors in the social world" (*Reality Fictions: Romance, History, and Governmental Authority, 1025–1180*, 210).

25. For the signifying power of food, see Roland Barthes, "Toward a Psychosociology of Contemporary Food Consumption," in *Food and Drink in History*, ed. Robert Forster and Orest Ranum, trans. Elborg Forster and Patricia M. Ranum, 168; and Mary Douglas, "Deciphering a Meal," in *Implicit Meanings: Essays in Anthropology* (1975), 2nd ed., 249. These observations are extended and amplified by Pierre Bourdieu in *Distinction: A Social Critique of the Judgement of Taste* (1979), trans. Richard Nice.

products necessary, as argued by Marx.²⁶ Through acts of consumption, one tacitly perpetuates extant systems of commodity production (as well as participating in the ideological formations that protect and explain them), and even if a person "poaches" these products (as Michel de Certeau suggests is possible), one still needs the existence of society's products in order to deliberately misuse them.²⁷ In the act of choosing food, the original commodity produced by human society and its dominant product for much of its history—however it is enjoyed—we acknowledge our place within the forces of production and the structures of cultural capital.

Yet we also dream up a narrative of repletion, a romance wherein we are the heroic consumer who confronts this edible realm alone, pursuing the culinary object of desire. The hero of this mini-legend, acquiring the chosen food, further nuances his or her self-image through specifying the manner by which hunger will be gratified. Methods, manners, and mess partners all contribute to determine one's ingesting persona. The act of eating culminates in a catharsis of fullness that renders the distressing feeling of want forgiven, if only for a moment, and leaves behind a trace that guides the newly hungry toward a renewed quest for satisfaction. In a cycle of endless recurrence, the part of the consuming hero is played and replayed as long as life endures.

As long as life endures, food will be there to influence and shape the world around it. So argues Jean Anthelme Brillat-Savarin, French magistrate and food connoisseur, who in 1826 finally published the work of his life, *Le Physiologie du Goût, ou Méditations de Gastronomie Transcendante*, a sprawling *Tristapædia* of all things associated with food and the love of eating. He examines the uses and experiences of eating, drinking, and cooking, charting their meaning beyond the dining room and kitchen. Digesting the latest scientific and medical discoveries of his time, Brillat-Savarin wittily unites the pleasures of the table with the operations of society, codifying in the process the new field of gastronomy. He defiantly pronounces the scope of his invented field of inquiry: "La gastronomie régit la vie tout entière" [It rules over our whole life], becoming the most important and capacious of the sciences.²⁸ Despite his late date, Brillat-Savarin is in many ways the guiding *daimon* of this book, a kindred spirit who observes the world-fashioning power of food and explores the implications of that power wherever it directs him. In the explication of this unique discipline, he discovers the political force of food choice, observing the ways that gastronomy encompasses the entire earth as well as every-

---

26. Marx, *Grundrisse*, 91.
27. Michel de Certeau, *The Practice of Everyday Life*, vol. 1, trans. Steven Rendall, xii.
28. Jean Anthelme Brillat-Savarin, *Physiologie du Goût, ou Méditations de Gastronomie Transcendante*, 58. Translation: *The Physiology of Taste*, trans. M. F. K. Fisher, 61.

thing that it contains. Brillat-Savarin celebrates what the Pardoner condemns: our domain is only improved in his eyes through its culinary productivity. The table itself is a locus of political and economic power, which can be a lofty place where decisions that affect millions can be made over roasted turkeys stuffed with truffles, where profits are generated and circulated by way of human tastes for food. Just as often it is where the nuclear family convenes to secure its affective structures and power dynamics, as well as reaffirm its location in the order of society. The choice of menu ripples outward, for better or for worse, influencing the local and faraway alike, enriching some, impoverishing others, and subjugating the very earth to provide these cultivated palates with their inmost gratification.

2. THE MATTER OF CUISINE

Generic forms in literature are themselves consumable items, savory formations that are conceived and devoured in political conditions. Among them, the medieval romance is especially delectable—a hodgepodge of disparate influences, tongues, ideas, and inspirations, combining mythology with history, vernacular with Latinity, warfare with love, gritty politics with high fantasy. *Political Appetites* crosses between the wonders of the table and the fantastic realms of story, tracking the intersection of food and the romance literature of medieval England, from its earliest iterations in hagiographic verse to their descendants of the fifteenth century. This intersection reveals the physical, embodied terms of romantic fascinations with political economy. These captivations are also explored by Vance Smith, who observes that "the discursive frame of the fourteenth-century English romance takes on an economic cast, that is concerned in inextricable ways with matters that are relegated to the household."[29] Smith's paradigm reveals that the romance genre does not just adumbrate exotic locales and extravagant situations for purposes of entertainment only, but it also comprehends and defines what belongs properly to the home and to the entire social order, especially since the household was considered the fundamental unit of the medieval economy, and therefore the foundation of the political realm itself (in fact, it is often its initiating metaphor). These material, homey resources not only project a ground for literary tradition and production but also lend corporeality to its characters and signifiers. These are combined with the particularities and peculiarities of medieval English culture and economics that give these

---

29. D. Vance Smith, *Arts of Possession: The Middle English Household Imaginary*, 6.

texts their own savor, which cannot be imitated or reproduced. The English romance can be identified by its *terroir*—literally, the "taste of the soil"—a term that originates in the appreciation of wine, and which expresses an ineffable quality that makes one local product unique among others like it.[30] In applying the term to poetic texts, *terroir* proposes a revised image of English romances, which have been traditionally (and unjustly) disparaged as limited and clumsy translations of French originals, but which should be considered essential expressions of the tastes and needs of English literary culture: "English romances are *differently* sensitive," notes Susan Crane upon the distinctions between insular and continental examples, and this difference means that we should not expect these English romances to do exactly the same work in exactly the same manner as their French *confreres*.[31] Given a unique flavor by its linguistic, literary, cultural, and social conditions and contexts, the English romance has an aesthetic and political integrity of its own that renders it a worthy object of serious critical study.

Thorny and intractable to circumscription, amorphous almost by definition, romance has largely defied critical attempts to delineate its nature, functions, or uses.[32] W. R. J. Barron perhaps expressed its strangely elusive nature best, "Romance, though we scarcely recognize it, is so much with us, penetrating so many aspects of our lives, that the objective attention needed to define it confuses and embarrasses us."[33] This formal inscrutability has led to wildly differing assessments of the genre. W. P. Ker recognizes a lack of "romantic" freshness to these productions, which deteriorate, as he describes, as they pass "through the mills of a thousand active literary men, who know their business, and have an eye to their profits."[34] Linking it to popular literature, Lee C. Ramsey sees the chivalric romance as shamelessly pandering to its audience's preconceived desires for escapist entertainment.[35] Eric Auerbach dismisses the social reflections of the romance entirely, arguing that the stories have no "basis in any political reality."[36] This stance is mediated by Dieter

---

30. *Terroir* is becoming more frequently used today in burgeoning locavore subcultures, which favor agricultural products produced near to the market and the eater.

31. See Susan Crane, *Insular Romance: Politics, Faith, and Culture in Anglo-Norman and Middle English Literature*, 208 (emphasis in the original); and Smith, *Arts of Possession*, 6.

32. Excellent, thorough overviews of the romance genre include: Laura Loomis Hibbard, *Mediæval Romance in England* (1924); the essays by Rosalind Field and Helen Cooper in *The Cambridge History of Medieval English Literature*, ed. David Wallace; Roberta Krueger, ed., *Cambridge Companion to Medieval*; and Corinne Saunders, ed., *A Companion to Romance*.

33. W. R. J. Barron, *English Medieval Romance*, 1.

34. W. P. Ker, *Epic and Romance: Essays on Medieval Literature*, 324.

35. Lee C. Ramsey, *Chivalric Romances: Popular Literature in Medieval England*, 6.

36. Erich Auerbach, "The Knight Sets Forth," in *Mimesis: The Representation of Reality in Western Literature*, trans. Willard R. Trask, 133.

Mehl, who notes the romances "did not aim at a faithful representation of present-day reality, but . . . at the illustration of moral truths."[37] Yet reflexes of Auerbach's political agnosticism can be found in later criticism, such as in John Finlayson's statement that "the character of the romance hero is largely an idealization which bears little relation to social reality and certainly did not spring from it."[38]

Other studies challenge these claims of unimaginative homogeneity and political irrelevance. R. W. Southern relates the transition in medieval French literature from epic to romance to the cultural shift toward individual spirituality in the twelfth century.[39] Robert W. Hanning further explores the development of the individual as the proper subject of the romance genre.[40] Eugène Vinaver argues for the skillful formal experimentality of romance, locating the emergence of *conjointure*—the iconoclastic interlaced patterning of narrative—as its defining achievement.[41] Stephen Knight reads works of the romance genre against the grain by connecting to them ideas of class ideology, stating that "they are [the] best testimony to the hopes and fears of the medieval English ruling class, and a part of the cultural pressure on those who permitted them to rule."[42] Arguing, however, against the tried-and-true assumptions of romantic individualism that limit the social applications of the genre, Stein convincingly locates a profound kinship between romance and historical writing: "They grow out of the same cultural need and intend to do the same cultural work" by articulating the secular, political world in its own terms.[43]

Whatever their assessment, medieval romances have preoccupied literary scholars across the twentieth century. Even George Kane, in his ruthless appraisal of the weaknesses of the Middle English romance, acknowledges the

---

37. Dieter Mehl, *The Middle English Romances of the Thirteenth and Fourteenth Centuries*, 4–5.

38. John Finlayson, "Definitions of Middle English Romance," *Chaucer Review* 15 (1980): 54.

39. R. W. Southern, *The Making of the Middle Ages*. As Kay and Stein have shown, the Old French *chansons de geste* cannot be considered entirely a precursor to the romance genre, as many of these epic texts were actually produced in the twelfth and thirteenth centuries, at the exact same time as the so-called "innovation" of romance in France (See Kay's *The Chansons de Geste in the Age of Romance*, 4–5, and Stein's *Reality Fictions*, esp. 167–68).

40. Robert W. Hanning, *The Individual in Twelfth-Century Romance*.

41. Eugène Vinaver, *The Rise of Romance*, 34–37.

42. Stephen Knight, "The Social Function of the Middle English Romances," in *Medieval Literature: Criticism, Ideology, and History*, ed. David Aers, 119.

43. Stein, *Reality Fictions*, 2. He states later that "romance is an attempt to seize directly the significance that in history appears only as a disappearance, the meaning at the heart of events that seems always about to announce itself but remains ever out of reach, and to seize it directly as a matter of historical understanding" (106).

"common and unchanging humanity" of the genre, which renders romances important records in the history of narrative.[44] In recent decades, key critical interventions have elevated the status and value of romances, rendering them central documents to the understanding of the Middle Ages. The work of Susan Crane has authorized renewed interest and generous critical rereadings of this perplexing form.[45] In the wake of Geraldine Heng's work, it is common for scholars to read in romance "structures of desire" that triangulate geographical understanding with the canny creation and enforcement of political mythologies.[46] Vance Smith projects romance desire past the *limen* of the household, licensing the genre's exploration of uncanny domains of narrative abundance and surfeit by its return to the well-known confines of economic sufficiency, a moderation that characterizes domestic propriety in ancient and medieval ethical theory.[47] Helen Cooper links romantic motifs to cultural memes—familiar devices that are replicated across time in a wide variety of historical contexts—to create an image of medieval romance as a genre that is alive and well, for example in the twentieth-century works of J. R. R. Tolkien or the latest science fiction television series.[48] Perhaps adapting Ker's metaphor, Nicola McDonald identifies medieval English romance as a vibrant form of "pulp fiction" that self-consciously employs sensationalism to explore its own political and social contexts.[49] In these studies, the work of romance is similar: exterior spaces and strange identities—weird realms populated by fantastic creatures—coalesce a cultural understanding of the intimate and familiar. Romances reimagine the fantasies of a social order, or even a nation in formation, in order to discover what is necessary to build and maintain a shared sociopolitical identity.

Unable to be limited to any particular form,[50] romance is alternately termed a genre or a mode,[51] or else it is described by its contents or effects. It is most

---

44. George Kane, *Middle English Literature: A Critical Study of the Romances, the Religious Lyrics, [and] Piers Plowman*, 103.

45. Crane, *Insular Romance*.

46. Geraldine Heng, *Empire of Magic: Medieval Romance and the Politics of Cultural Fantasy*, 3.

47. Smith, *Arts of Possession*.

48. Helen Cooper, *The English Romance in Time: Transforming Motifs from Geoffrey of Monmouth to the Death of Shakespeare*, 3–4.

49. Nicola McDonald, "A Polemical Introduction," in *Pulp Fictions of Medieval England: Essays in Popular Romance*, 1–21.

50. Romances in English, medieval and beyond, exist in almost every form conceivable: octosyllabic couplets, alliterative meters, stanzas, blank verse, prose, and drama.

51. The term *mode* is sometimes preferred by critics, since romance often eludes the formal or subject containment of literary genres. The use of this term descends from Northrop Frye, who defines it as "conventional power of action assumed about the chief characters in fictional

compellingly defined as the transgression of internal boundaries. Originally a word used to demarcate a crossing from one linguistic state to another—from Latin to French (*romanz*)—the term expanded to refer to the kinds of stories written in the vernacular, which could be anything from a hagiography (for example, Cynewulf's *Elene* [late eighth or ninth century] or Hartmann von Aue's *Gregorius* [ca. 1190]), to idiomatic adaptations of the European classical inheritance (such as Benoît de Sainte-Maure's *Roman de Troie* [ca. 1155–60]), to works of sustained allegory (like the *Roman de la Rose* of Guillaume de Lorris and Jean de Meun [finished ca. 1275]), to chronicle histories (like Wace's *Roman de Rou* [ca. 1170]), before becoming consolidated in the stories of knightly adventure around the time of Chrétien de Troyes (ca. 1170–90). Romance finds inspiration in other genres around it, existing on the borders not only of the tongue but also of the media that express that tongue. It is as much a bookish genre as it is oral. Its contents are transgressive: stories of insurmountable warriors brought low by passionate love; tales of travel to exotic lands and dangerous worlds; narratives of the overthrow of the mundane by miracle, monster, and magic. The exoticism of romances, however, is tempered by their insistent replication of contemporary political and economic hierarchies—whether in support of these conditions in the lives of its audiences, or to expose ironically their injustice.

Romance is a genre that is exhilaratingly open and receptive to change and violation, to repetition and variation, to continuation and amendment, to shifting form,[52] to the retelling of fantastic narratives regardless of their origin. The overflowing fullness of romance provides a reader both with a Jaussian "horizon of expectations"—a vast array of possibilities that can exist within generic confines—and also what Frederic Jameson terms "social contracts between a writer and a specific public, whose function is to specify the proper use of a particular cultural artifact."[53] The medieval romance was used by a diverse audience, from the base to the heights, aristocrat and bourgeoisie, both recited and read alone, and all these publics were astounded. The reader

---

literature, or the corresponding attitude assumed by the poet toward his audience in thematic literature. Such modes tend to succeed one another in a historical sequence" (*Anatomy of Criticism: Four Essays*, 366). The teleological, determining, prescriptive narrative of literary change implied by Frye's definition is problematic, since it assumes, like Marx's modes of production, that one form necessarily gives way to the next in sequence.

52. A classic example of this formal amorphousness can be found in the Auchinleck Manuscript's version of *Guy of Warwick* (complied ca. 1330), which changes from couplets to stanzas, after some 7,000 lines, midway through the poem.

53. Hans Robert Jauss, *Toward an Aesthetic of Reception*, trans. Timothy Bahti, 79. Frederic Jameson, "Magical Narratives," in *The Political Unconscious: Narrative as a Socially Symbolic Act*, 106.

of romance learns to expect the improbable, and the author promises always to surprise—yet always with the use-value of the genre in mind. Romance fantasies are grounded in everyday needs to not only promulgate and consolidate political realities but also to provide a stage for their investigation and often their critique. Romance is an inclusive and aggregative genre, rife with the enjoyment of its own processes of consumption. It assimilates but never is filled; it is excessive but never abashed by its surplus, spinning a story from the myriad materials and resources it has incorporated.[54]

The medieval English romance is a hungry genre, grasping and restless. This appetite for disparate materials has led some to dismiss its Gothic stew as tasteless and overprepared, but its extravagances are an essential part of the recipe. Food is just one of these disparate materials, though one that has been understudied. *Political Appetites* proposes that the romance genre derives part of its purpose and pleasure from these representations of the material processes of food. The edible world is a vital referent for these narratives, an authorizing metaphor as well as a reflection of the social realm around them. As the four chapters that make up this book will demonstrate, scenes of cooking and consumption dramatize political and economic tensions in aristocratic culture, anxieties that expose the ideological roots of these elaborate literary productions of medieval England.

3. FOOD AS GATEWAY

Surprising things occur at the dinner tables of medieval literature, from the extraordinary compact of Chaucer's pilgrims to tell stories along their route to Canterbury, to *Richard Coer de Lyon*'s eponymous hero earning his cognomen by consuming a slain lion's heart whole, dipped in salt straight from its dish, to Balyn killing the invisible knight Garlon at his meal in Sir Thomas Malory's *Morte D'Arthur* (a turn of events that eventually brings the entire castle down around his ears).[55] Medieval plots are often moved forward in amazing ways while characters are eating. Banquets are a threshold to wonder, even if that

---

54. An excellent example of an exotic adventure in a contemporary political milieu is Chrétien de Troyes's *Le Chevalier au Lion* (ca. 1177–81), when Yvain liberates a realm ruled by a pair of demon brothers, who have enslaved noblewomen to perform sweatshop-like sewing piecework, discovering an opportunity for heroism amidst the specters of protoindustrial economies (*The Complete Romances of Chrétien de Troyes*, ed. and trans. David Staines, 318–25).

55. Chaucer, *General Prologue*, I.747–821; *Richard Coer de Lyon: Der mittelenglische Versroman über Richard Löwenherz*, ed. Karl Brunner, 1105–9; Sir Thomas Malory, *Morte D'Arthur* (in *The Works of Malory*, ed. Eugène Vinaver, 53).

wonder is just the narration of another marvelous story, delivered by a teller fueled by the food and hospitality of the house, as is suggested in the exordium to *Havelok the Dane* (ca. 1295):

> Havelok was a ful god gome—
> He was ful god in everi trome;
> He was the wicteste man at nede
> That thurte riden on ani stede.
> That ye mowen now yhere,
> And the tale you mowen ylere,
> At the biginnig of ure tale,
> Fil me a cuppe of ful god ale;
> And wile drinken, her I spelle,
> That Crist us shilde alle fro helle.
> (7–16)[56]

This invocation of a storyteller in need of a sustaining beverage is a nostalgic setting of the scene of minstrel performance. By the time *Havelok* finds its way into its lone extant manuscript (Oxford, Bodleian Library MS Laud Misc. 108, in the early fourteenth century), in a domain of mercantile purchasers of legendary material, the wandering minstrel was largely gone.[57] His or her place was instead taken by private performances of aurality in *praelect* (as suggested by Joyce Coleman)—intimate circles of readers who take in text together, perhaps as after-dinner entertainment.[58] But the image of the itinerant storyteller persists in the genre, as Rosalind Field observes, "The romantic image of the minstrel is internalized into the romance genre to provide the audience with a sense of the past and of community."[59] Wonder—by way of written narrative performed within the *domus*—was now the province of the professional writer and the enthusiastic amateur, though the newfangled situation nevertheless yearned for its mythologized ancestry. And so *Havelok* harks back to an imagined circum-

---

56. *Havelok*, ed. G. V. Smithers.

57. For the current state of research concerning this very important manuscript, see the essays in Kimberly K. Bell and Julie Nelson Couch's collection *The Texts and Contexts of Oxford, Bodleian Library, MS Laud Misc. 108: The Shaping of English Vernacular Narrative*.

58. Joyce Coleman, *Public Reading and the Reading Public in Late Medieval England and France*, and idem., "Aurality," in Paul Strohm, ed., *Middle English: Oxford Twenty-First Century Approaches to Literature*, 68–85.

59. Rosalind Field, "Romance in England, 1066–1400," in *Cambridge History of Medieval English Literature*, ed. David Wallace, 168. See also Ananya J. Kabir, "Forging an Oral Style? *Havelok* and the Fiction of Orality," *Studies in Philology* 98 (2001): 18–48.

stance of textual exchange, of singers who make their living by their stories, a dusty traveler celebrating the fabled origins of the English nation.

Sometimes a diner experiences an actual wonder where an adventurous tale would suffice, as in the preeminent English romance *Sir Gawain and the Green Knight* (ca. 1390), when the fabulous Green Knight intrudes upon Arthur's New Year's Day feast to challenge the complacent Round Table. The young king rashly will not eat until he hears or sees some sort of marvel:

> . . . he wolde neuer ete
> Vpon such a dere day, er hym deuised were
> Of sum auenturus þyng, an vncouþe tale
> Of sum mayn meruayle þat he myȝt trawe,
> Of alderes, of armes, of oþer auenturus.
> (91–95)⁶⁰

> . . . He would never eat
> Upon such a precious day, before it were devised to him
> Of some extraordinary event, a strange tale
> About some great marvel that he might believe,
> Of princes, or feats of arms, of other chancy things.

Arthur's demand to be astonished before he will eat crosses a taste for culinary innovation with an appetite for the spectacles of romance narrative.⁶¹ As Sharon Wells notes, however, this display of regal petulance threatens the success of the entire dinner, his breach of proper decorum evidence of his "childgered" (86) state.⁶² Certainly, when the feast is served, there is plenty to admire. It is generous and bountiful, as befits a king, with "Dayntés dryuen þerwyth of ful dere metes / Foysoun of þe fresche, and on so fele disches" (121–22) [Dainty things of very precious meats driven therewith / An abundance of fresh meat, and on so many dishes]. There is such plenty that every two guests have twelve dishes between them (128). As the course emerges from the kitchen and the

---

60. *Sir Gawain and the Green Knight*, in *The Poems of the Pearl Manuscript*, ed. Malcolm Andrew and Ronald Waldron.

61. This theme of waiting for wonder in order to eat is borrowed from Old French Arthurian romances, such as Raoul de Houdenc's satirical *La Vengeance Raguidel* (ca. 1220–30), and is discussed by Beate Schmolke-Hasselmann, *The Evolution of Arthurian Romance: The Verse Tradition from Chrétien to Froissart*, trans. Margaret and Roger Middleton, 88–89, as well as by Sarah Gordon, *Culinary Comedy in Medieval French Literature*, 58–59.

62. Sharon Wells, "Manners Maketh Man: Living, Dining, and Becoming a Man in the Later Middle Ages," in *Rites of Passage: Cultures of Transition in the Fourteenth Century*, ed. Nicola F. McDonald and W. M. Ormrod, 77.

platters are served, a terrible noise is heard at the hall door. In comes the menacing and supernatural Green Knight, whose weird greenness extends even to his horse and mighty axe.

The Green Knight's fantastic entrance and appearance recalls another sort of wonder, the *entremet* or *soteltie*, a culinary interlude between courses of a banquet, often consisting of imaginative food spectacles or miniature *tableaux vivants*.[63] Any lordly diner could expect to be stunned by a well-made *entremet*, especially on such an important feast day. The cookery book known as the *Viandier* (ca. mid-thirteenth century) describes a dish that mimics the hulking figure of the Green Knight:

> Coqz heaumez. Mettez cochons rostir, et poulaille comme coqz et vielles poulles, et quant le cochon sera rosty d'une part et la poulaille d'autre convient farsir la poullaille—sans escorcher, qui veult; et la convient [dorer] de paste batue aux oeuf; et quant ell'est doree la convient mettre a chevauchons sur le cochon, et fault ung heaume de papier collé et une lance fichié a la poittrine de la dicte poullaille, et les fault couvrir de fueil d'or ou d'argent pour les seigneurs, ou de feul d'estain blanc, vermeil ou vert.

> Helmeted cocks. Roast piglets and such poultry as cocks and old hens; when both the piglet and the poultry are roasted, the poultry should be stuffed—without skinning it, if you wish; it should be [glazed] with an egg batter. And when it is glazed it should be seated astride the piglet; and it needs a helmet of glued paper and a lance couched at the breast of the bird and these should be covered with gold- or silver-leaf for lords, or with white, red or green tin-leaf.[64]

Arriving as he does with the wondrously ample and diverse first course, the fulfillment of Arthur's immature desire for astonishment and titillation, the mysterious Green Knight could be considered just one of a host of miraculous things served up for the complete dining experience: roasted peacocks and swans served in their plumage, pâtés decorated with the coats of arms of

---

63. Wells also connects the Green Knight's entrance to an *entremet*, noting that his appearance means the feast is proceeding as expected ("Manners Maketh Man," 78–79). *Entremets* literally means "between-meat" or "between-courses." See Terence Scully's description of the Castle of Love staged by the Savoyard chef Maître Chiquart ("The Mediaeval French Entremet," *Petits Propos Culinaires* 17 [1984]: 52–53) and the history of the "genre" in his *The Art of Cookery in the Middle Ages*, 104–10.

64. *The Viandier of Taillevent*, ed. and trans. Terence Scully, 250 and 300. The *Viandier* is attributed to the French chef Taillevent (ca. 1315–95), yet it first appears in manuscripts in the middle of the thirteenth century, making it impossible that Taillevent actually wrote it.

important guests, or roasted fish swimming in gelatinous sauce.[65] Mounted on its suckling pig steed, equipped with paper arms and armor, the whole thing perhaps colored a lively green, the *coq heaumez* is an example of material culture that mirrors the Green Knight, a magnificent *entremet* come to life to demand the amazement and attention of the guests, to glut their culinary yen for new and unusual experiences. The practice of gastronomic wonder found ways to parallel the marvels of romance.[66] The culinary logic of the scene is fleshed out by invoking the relationship between strange guest and unusual fare. Just as the *soteltie* was designed to shock the jaded appetite, so the Green Knight challenges the self-satisfied court of King Arthur, replete with the amazing, elaborate cuisine of the late Middle Ages.

4. MEDIEVAL AESTHETICS, MEDIEVAL APPETITES

Medieval cuisine has long been subject to misunderstanding, the object of pernicious myths of spoilage and grotesque excess. Meals of Croesan magnificence are solemnly invoked as an example of the gastronomic decadence of our early ancestors, often following the incredulous tone of Richard Warner's *Antiquitates culinariæ; or curious tracts relating to the culinary affairs of the old English* (1791), which cites the 1467 installation feast of George Neville as the Archbishop of York as an a particularly excessive affair. Warner breathlessly catalogues the supplies procured for the weeklong event as a shopping list of his own: 18,000 birds of various sorts, including such perennial favorites as curlews, cranes, egrets, peacocks, bitterns, herons, and pheasants; thousands of cows, wild bulls, sheep, deer, calves, and pigs; many thousands of premade pasties, tarts, jellies, and custards; and, for the fish days that would doubtlessly intervene among the days of the feast, 608 pikes and breams (surely there were more fish needed than that) and even eleven porpoises and seals.[67] Yet not just the ample service but also the food itself is critiqued and misunder-

---

65. This is the "pyk in galauntyne" of Chaucer's lyric "To Rosamounde" (*Riverside Chaucer*, 649). For a similar recipe, see Odile Redon, Françoise Sabban, and Silviano Seventi, *The Medieval Kitchen: Recipes from France and Italy*, trans. Edward Schneider, 190–91.

66. The *Gawain* poet was possibly associated with the court of Richard II, who was known, among other things, for his gourmandize (See John M. Bowers, *The Politics of Pearl: Court Poetry in the Age of Richard II*). One manuscript of the cookery book *The Forme of Cury* announces its origins in the kitchens of Richard II (in Constance B. Hieatt and Sharon Butler, ed., *Curye on Inglysch*, 20).

67. Richard Warner, *Antiquitates culinariæ; or curious tracts relating to the culinary affairs of the old English*, 93–94. According to medieval physiology, creatures that spent most of their time in the water, such as whales, barnacle geese, and beavers (or at least their tails), were con-

stood. Following Alfred Franklin's 1889 characterization of medieval dishes as "abominables ragoûts,"[68] W. E. Mead portrayed the cuisine of the Middle Ages as heavily processed and mashed to a pulp, probably to suit the also prevalent myth that medieval people had very bad teeth:

> Out of the mortar came the impalpable messes so characteristic of the medieval table. Nearly every dish, whatever its name, was soft and mushy, with its principal ingredients disguised by the addition of wine or spices or vegetables. The skill of the cook was attested by the fact that his strange compounds were actually eaten. It was apparently not worth the pains of a cook of any reputation to prepare food simply, and hence practically everything had to be mashed or cut into small pieces and mixed with something else, preferably of so strong a flavour as to disguise the taste of most of the other ingredients. Nearly every dish was a riddle.[69]

While it is true that the stews and sauces and other prepared dishes of the Middle Ages were often ground in a mortar to combine the ingredients, or strained through a cloth to achieve the desired consistency, it does not follow that everything these diners ate was goop.[70] Variety was the most highly sought virtue in medieval cuisine, not only of flavor and texture but also of appearance, and elaboration—even colors were manipulated and altered in extravagant ways.[71] Cuisine suited not only medieval tastes and medical theories but also medieval banqueting practices, and the cooks in the kitchen had to be sure that their guests could consume their products with the technol-

---

sidered to be fish (see Bridget Ann Henisch, *Fast and Feast: Food in Medieval Society*, 47–49; Melitta Weiss Adamson, *Food in Medieval Times*, 44).

68. Alfred Franklin, *La Vie Privée d'Autrefois*, 3.44. Warner seemed to have a clearer sense of the aesthetic appeal of medieval fare, even if he found it just as cryptic and potentially distasteful: "Many of the receipts contained in the 'Forme of cury,' are indeed as unintelligible to a modern, as the hieroglyphics of an Egyptian pillar; but such as we do understand, are not calculated to prejudice us much in favor of the culinary art of the fourteenth century. The combination of such a variety of different articles in the formation of one dish, would produce an effect very unpleasant to a palate of this day; and the quantity of hot spices, that were mixed in almost all of them, would now be relished only by those accustomed to the high-season dishes of the East- and West-Indies" (*Antiquitates culinariæ*, xxxii–xxxiii, long esses have been silently changed to their modern equivalents for ease of reading).

69. W. E. Mead, *The English Medieval Feast*, 57.

70. See Scully, *Art of Cookery*, 34–35 on the variety of medieval cooking techniques, and 40–58 on the theories behind the practices. For the medical and humoral rationales behind recipes and preparation techniques, see ibid. 42–45, and Ken Albala, *Eating Right in the Renaissance*.

71. For perspectives on the color of medieval food, see Adamson, *Food in Medieval Times*, 68–69; Redon et al., *The Medieval Kitchen*, 26; and Scully, *Art of Cookery*, 114–16.

ogy they had at hand. Even spoons were not common—several guests usually had to share one—and so dishes needed to be enjoyed by hand or with pieces of bread. It is a mistake, furthermore, to read too much into the dishes suggested by extant medieval cookbooks. These were not exactly used in the same way that they are today, but rather as *aides-mémoire* to guide a cook through an unfamiliar or infrequently made dish.[72] The chefs of the day did not need to be reminded how to roast an animal or grill a fish—simpler dishes which probably formed the bulk of medieval banqueting fare, from which it can be inferred that medieval teeth as well as their fare have been unjustly maligned.

Medieval *haute cuisine* was intentionally designed to appeal to all the senses of its projected diners. If the dishes seem overspiced to our tastes, we should remember that we exist on the other side of the culinary horizon, after the innovations of the French cooking of the seventeenth and eighteenth centuries, which often takes for granted that food is better when simply prepared.[73] Readers of medieval recipes are often misled by the vagaries inherent to the form, which usually do not specify precise amounts of an ingredient added to a particular dish. An English recipe for "stewed strawberries" may provide a typical example of the style and approach of medieval cookery books:

> Take Strawberyes, & waysshe hem in tyme of ȝere in gode red wine; þan strayne þorwe a cloþe, & do hem in a potte with gode Almaunde mylke, a-lay it with Amyndoun oþer with þe flower of Rys, & make it chargeaunt and lat it boyle, and do þer-in Roysonys of coraunce, Safroun, Pepir, Sugre grete plente, pouder Gyngere, Canel, Galyngale; poynte it with Vynegre, & a lytil whyte grece put þer-to; coloure it with Alkenade, & droppe it a-bowte, plante it with þe graynys of Pome-garnad, & þan serue it forth.[74]

There is no indication of the amount to be used of the precious spices, the saffron, black pepper, ginger, cinnamon (canel), and galingale (a root much

---

72. Barbara Santich, "The Evolution of Culinary Techniques in the Medieval Era," in *Food in the Middle Ages*, ed. Melitta Weiss Adamson, 61–3.

73. Most influential in this progression was the cookbook of François Pierre de la Varenne (1615–78), who advocated the use of fresh ingredients and reductions that emphasized the natural flavoring of foodstuffs (See *Le Cuisinier François* [1651], ed. Jean-Louis Flandrin, Philip Hyman, and Mary Hyman, translated in *La Varenne's Cookery: The French Cook, the French Pastry Chef, the French Confectioner*, trans. Terence Scully). The diminishing importance of spices, however, was well underway in the cooking of Western Europe, hurried along by the discovery of direct sea-routes to the Far East, which placed Europeans into contact with the disappointingly quotidian methods of growing and harvesting these once exotic commodities (see Paul Freedman, *Out of the East: Spices and the Medieval Imagination*, 220–22).

74. As found in London British Museum Harleian MS 279, f. 22v. Edited text taken from *Two Fifteenth-Century Cookery Books*, ed. Thomas Austin, 29.

like ginger), that grace this unusual dish, other than noting that sugar must be added in "grete plente" (sugar, as an exotic, imported commodity, was often categorized as a spice). Yet the results are quite refreshing and, far from overwhelming it, tickle the palate with a complex, subtle interweaving of flavors and textures. From this sort of imprecision, some scholars deduce these rare, expensive ingredients were added to a cloying degree, arguing that such overwhelming flavoring would have been required to mask the taste of spoiled meat.[75] Contemporary scholarship generally no longer believes this myth to be true, reasoning that meat often was butchered just before it would be needed, and practices of salting, drying, and curing were widespread. Most compelling of all is the simple economic argument: spices were simply too precious and expensive to waste on spoiled meat.[76]

Medieval dishes were often finely spiced, however, and the best of the era's cooking shows a high degree of elaboration and imagination in the presentation and service of these dishes. In *Sir Gawain and the Green Knight*, the feast served to the hero upon his arrival at Hautdesert is so extraordinary that, despite the fact that it is fast day (when only fish dishes could be eaten), this restriction does not detract from the meal's quality.[77] The description of Arthur's New Year's banquet at the start of the *Alliterative Morte Arthure* (ca. 1400) gives an attractive picture of another exorbitant meal:

There come in at þe fyrste course, befor þe Kyng seluen,
Bareheuedys þat ware bryghte, burnyste with syluer,

---

75. Where this myth started is unknown, but possibly arises from confusion in terms in early modern cookbooks, such as that by de la Varenne, which specifies the need for "frais" meat. The opposite of "fresh" in this case is not "spoiled," but rather "salted." The myth of spoiled food is so prevalent in modern culture that many authoritative histories of food still repeat it. For a repetition of this misgiving, see Hansjörg Küster, "Spices and Flavourings," in *The Cambridge World History of Food*, ed. Kenneth F. Kiple and Kriemhild Conée Ornelas, 1.435–37.

76. Timothy Morton hedges in his conclusion that "it is unclear whether disguise was ever a primary motive in the medieval use of spice" (*The Poetics of Spice: Romantic Consumerism and the Exotic*, 17.) Jack Turner puts the case even more sharply: "Why waste good, expensive spices on poor, cheap meats?" (*Spice: The History of a Temptation*, 108). See also Christopher Dyer for evidence that contradicts the widely held notion that medieval husbandry practiced a mass slaughter of their livestock every winter, so that eaters only would have had salted, dried, and otherwise preserved meat available during the winter months ("English Diet in the Later Middle Ages," in *Social Relations and Ideas: Essays in Honour of R. H. Hilton*, ed. T. H. Ashton et al., 193).

77. *Sir Gawain and the Green Knight*, 888–900. For inventive ways that cooks and diners found around the restricted diets of frequent fast days, by preparing eggs, bacon, ham, and other animal-based dishes with processed fish, see Barbara Ketcham Wheaton, *Savoring the Past: The French Kitchen and Table from 1300 to 1789*, 12.

> All with taghte men and town in togers full ryche,
> Of saunk reall in suyte, sexty at ones;
> Flesch flurist of fermyson, with frumentée noble,
> Thereto wylde to wale, and wynlyche bryddes,
> Pacockes and plouers in platers of golde,
> Pygges of porc despyne that pasturede neuer;
> Sythen herons in hedoyne hyled full faire,
> Grett swannes full swythe in silueryn chargeours,
> Tartes of turky—taste wham þem lykys—
> Gumbaldes grathely, full gracious to taste;
> Seyne bowes of wylde bores with þe brawn lechyde,
> Bernakes and botures in baterde dysches,
> Þareby braunchers in brede—bettyr was neuer—
> With brestez of barowes that bryghte ware to schewe;
> Seyn come þer sewes sere, with solace þerafter—
> Ownd of azure all ouer and ardaunt þem semyde—
> Of ilke a leche þe lowe launschide full hye,
> Þat all ledes myghte lyke þat lukyde þem apon;
> Þen cranes and curlues craftyly rosted,
> Connygez in cretoyne, colourede full faire,
> Fesauntez enflurischit in flammande siluer,
> With dariells endordid and daynteez ynewe.
> (176–99)[78]

> There came in at the first course, before the King himself,
> Boar's heads that were bright, burnished with silver,
> All with trained and urbane men in cloaks full rich,
> In a company of the high-born, sixty at once;
> Flesh fattened with the season with frumenty noble,
> Thereto game to choose and joyous birds,
> Peacocks and plovers on platters of gold,
> Piglets of *porc d'espyne* that never had eaten,
> Afterwards herons in hedoine, glazed full fair,
> Great swans right away in silver chargers,
> Tarts of Turkey—taste when one likes—
> Excellent morsels of meat, quite gracious to taste,
> Then the shoulders of wild boars with the brawn sliced,

---

78. *The Alliterative Morte Arthure*, ed. Valerie Krishna. "Hedoine" (line 184) is an unknown variety of sauce.

Barnacle geese and bitterns in battered dishes,
thereby breaded young fowl—there was never better—
With the breasts of boars that were bright to show;
Then came sundry sauces, with solace thereafter—
Waving with azure and flaming they seemed—
At every slice the flame launched very high,
So that all the people might like to look upon them;
Then cranes and curlews craftily roasted,
Coneys in cretoyne sauce, colored very fairly,
Pheasants enflourished in flaming silver,
With pastries colored gold and plenty of dainty things.

The dazzling magnificence of Arthur's table literally astonishes the narrator, freezing him in place to amplify and enumerate the elements of the first course. Each line piles dish upon dish of sumptuous food even as it logophilically embellishes the alliterative diction of romance. We see, and are astounded, too, by the gastronomic panorama, from the heads of boars (*boreheuedys*, often served painted bright colors, with mouths sputtering flame), to the whimsical "hedgehogs" (*pygges of porc despyne*),[79] to the sauces that appear a burning blue, to the pheasants flourished with silver flames. Arthur's invitation to his visitors is more than just good form, and his self-deprecating comment to his Roman visitors about the homegrown nature of his banquet: "Enforce ʒow þe more / To feede ʒow with syche feble [fare] as ʒe before fynde" (225–26) conceals the political message communicated by the extravagant meal: the legitimacy of his rule can be understood through the splendor of his feast. Arthur is a true sovereign because he eats like one.

Such depictions of medieval cuisine are designed to convey a sense of good living, the best that their world can provide, exciting their readers' tastes for food as well as for literary wonder. Both indulge in the conspicuous consumption that is an exercise in economic power, a competition to show off one's wealth and *savoir-faire* among one's peers.[80] Spices and other exotic ingredients demonstrate a host's supremacy not only over the local environment but also domination over larger realms, and a lord proved himself capable of moving heaven and earth to bring these far-flung and almost mystical

---

79. The knights of the Round Table are probably not eating porcupines (a word derived from the French *porc d'espine*), but rather the charming illusion food known as *yrchouns* (hedgehogs): balls of pork decorated with slivered almonds to imitate the animal's quills. For a recipe, see Hieatt and Butler, ed., *Form of Cury*, 139, and a modernized version is available in Hieatt and Butler's *Pleyn Delit: Medieval Cookery for Modern Cooks*, recipe no. 29. These are both delicious and enjoyable to make and serve to guests, a true gastronomic pleasure.

80. For conspicuous consumption, see Veblen, 42–43.

ingredients home.⁸¹ Spices tasted like power to the medieval palate, and they were the province of the powerful.

5. POLITICAL APPETITES AS CRITIQUE

Recognizing the human appetite for power as well as sustenance opens up avenues for the critique of politics through the edible. The overwhelming hunger for recognition from their subordinates creates a curious dependence of master upon servant, a need to constantly perpetuate the rituals of political and economic submission, replaying the moment of victory *ad infinitum*.⁸² This dependency is analogous to any other appetite, for without the demonstration of abasement, the lord will be starved of acknowledgment from his social inferiors.

Food can therefore become a locus of the critique of authority, the voracious appetite of the master for power metaphorized by a seemingly limitless need for bodily sustenance. In the late fourteenth-century version of the romance of *Richard Coer de Lyon,* the eponymous king and hero discovers in himself a powerful urge for the flesh of Saracen captives after a trick played upon him by his cook. After learning of the prank, he merely laughs as he says:

> Schole we neuere dye for defawte,
> Whyl we may in any assawte
> Slee Sarezynys, þe flesch mowe take,
> Seþen, and roste hem, and doo hem bake,
> Gnawen here fflesch to þe bones.
> Now j haue it prouyd ones,
> Ffor hungyr ar j be woo,
> J and my ffolk schole eete moo!
> (3219–26)

His mission to win the Holy Land from Saladin poises him perfectly to satisfy such a hideous hunger. Richard gleefully anticipates the solution, terrible as it may seem but diabolically practical, to the perennial problem of foreign wars:

---

81. Freedman discusses the near-mythological status of spices and the fantastic stories about their cultivation (*Out of the East,* 130–36). Popular travelogues often repeated fascinating untruths about the cultivation of spices in Asia, such as the widely copied and translated *Mandeville's Travels* (ca. 1356–66).

82. For the Lord/Bondsman dialectic, see G. W. F. Hegel, *The Phenomenology of Spirit,* trans. A. V. Miller, §§191–95. See Andrew Cole's "What Hegel's Master/Slave Dialectic Really Means" (*JMEMS* 34 [2004]: 577–610) for a discussion of the medieval influences on and implications of this foundational argument.

the delicacy of supply lines and the travails of keeping a massive army fed during the campaign. This is a matter already paid some attention in the poem, when its author catalogues the king's expenditures to victual his approaching Crusade (1755–64), yet at this moment, horror stems out of an awful pragmatism that nonetheless expresses a fantastic yearning. The imperialist Western European ambitions of the Crusades are evinced by the king's anthropophagic desires, his craving for political power glutted directly by human carnage.[83]

Though not as gorily spectacular in its execution, the late Middle Scots romance known as *The Knightly Tale of Golagros and Gawane* (printed 1508) also blends food with political criticism. It is a canny revisiting of the politics of King Arthur's reign, which recognizes the ambitions of the fabled lord as imperial and appropriative—a fact often occluded or misperceived by English versions of the legend. The ambitions of this fascinating story revolve around the presence of food. A dazzling poetic *tour-de-force* that features stanzaic verses built upon both rhyme and vigorous alliteration, *Golagros and Gawane* is presented as a narrative in diptych, folding together two separate stories in which King Arthur is fed not only bodily but also in his political authority. In the first part, King Arthur asks Sir Kay to inquire within a strange castle whether his perambulating court can be feasted there. When Sir Kay enters the (unnamed) knight's castle, he finds it richly appointed but preternaturally deserted except for its kitchen, where:

Ane duergh braydit about besily and bane
Small birdis on broche be ane bright fyre.
Schir Kay ruschit to the roist and reft fra the swane,
Lightly claucht throu lust the lym fra the lyre;
To feid hym of that fine fude the freik wes full fane.
(79–83)[84]

A dwarf turned about busily and eagerly
Small birds on a spit by a bright fire.
Sir Kay rushed to the roast and snatched from the swain,
Lightly grabbed through his desire the flesh from the cheek;
To feed himself of that fine food the man was very desirous.

---

83. Fantastic tales of cannibalistic Crusaders were not just limited to the sensationalistic accounts of romance: Guibert of Nogent recounted the horrible deeds of the Tafurs, impoverished and fanatical hangers-on to the First Crusade, who were reputed to have eaten corpses outside of Antioch in 1097 to avoid starvation (*The Deeds of God Through the Franks*, trans. Robert Levine, 146). See also Heather Blurton, *Cannibalism in High Medieval English Literature*, 117–19.

84. *The Knightly Tale of Golagros and Gawane*, ed. Ralph Hanna.

Sir Kay becomes suddenly overwhelmed by hunger at the sight of the tiny roasting birds, and rather than ask for permission, he steals the meat off the spit and starts to eat. Never the most courteous or graceful of Arthur's knights, Sir Kay jeopardizes his diplomatic mission to obtain food for Arthur's army through his great hunger for this tiny morsel.[85] The castle's lord suddenly appears, accusing Kay of "ladis vnlufsum and ladlike" (95) [deeds uncourteous and churlish], and then pummeling his unwelcome guest. The discrepancy between the enormity of Sir Kay's blunderous, willful actions and the size of the meal he is eager to steal is highlighted here, indicating that Kay betrays both his own honor and his king's over almost nothing, and then further and even more rudely devalues the angry presence of the castle's lord by dismissing his complaint with a culinary insult: "Thi schore compt I noght ane caik" (104) [Your threat I account not at a cake]. Hunger for Sir Kay is about power and submission rather than a square meal: he snatches up the birds rudely because he believes the advantage is his. In Kay's mind, he should be able to take what he wants because he represents the land's liege lord. Fortunately, the diplomatic Gawane resolves the breach in manners, obtaining not only food from the strange knight but also a promise of loyalty.

The issue of edibility continues into the second panel of the diptych. When the travelers discover the beautiful and independent kingdom of Golagros (while hunting doe deer [226–27], an act of foraging by which Arthur both feeds his court and satisfies his sense of aristocratic honor), Arthur demands to gain the unknown lord's fealty or take the kingdom by force. The ensuing fight with Golagros's army goes badly for Arthur, culminating in Gawane's courteous decision to submit to his foe's superior nobility after a prolonged and irresolvable single combat. Gawane's second display of noble grace reconciles Golagros to Arthur and preserves the independence of the former's realm. Yet Gawane enters to castle to bear witness to an awkward sort of feast between the court of Golgaros and Arthur's captured knights:

> Quhen þat Gawane the gay, grete of degre,
> Wes cummyn to þe castel cumly and cleir,
> Gromys of þat garisoune maid gamen and gle,
> And ledis lofit thair lord, lufly of lyere,
> Beirdis beildit in blise, brightest of ble.

---

85. Although the poem does not specify the type of small bird roasting on the dwarf's spit, medieval diners cherished a variety of small songbirds as delicacies. Ralph Hanna notes that the *Golagros and Gawane* episode is borrowed from the First Continuation of the *Conte du Graal*, where the unnamed lord beats Sir Kay with a fist still holding a roasted peacock, a much bigger bird (xxxiv).

The tothir knightis maid care of Arthuris here.
Al thus with murnyng and myrth thai maid melle,
Ay quhil þe segis war set to the suppere.
(1145–52)

When that Gawain the gay, great of degree,
Was come into that castle comely and clear,
Knights of that garrison made game and glee,
And ladies praised their lord, lovely of cheek,
Ladies confirmed in bliss, brightest of hue.
The other knights of Arthur's army made sorrow.
All thus with mourning and mirth made medley,
Ever while the men were set to their supper.

Even in defeat and humiliation, the knights of the Round Table are regaled by Golagros's men and ladies, though they refuse to participate in the gladsome celebrations. The nobility of Golagros is confirmed by his hospitality to these hostile warriors, his right to rule cemented by his sovereign expenditure to see that his captives are treated according to their station and included in his court's feasting. Arthur, on the other hand, looks more like a peevish child during the course of *Golagros and Gawane*, jealously seeking acclaim as sovereign and liege lord in every land he crosses.[86]

It does not require much stewing to reveal the essence of the politicized culinary implications of *Sir Gawain and the Green Knight*, the *Alliterative Morte Arthure*, *Richard Coer de Lyon*, and the *Knightly Tale of Golagros and Gawane*. These important poems are ripe for readings that demonstrate their preoccupations with food and politics.[87] Here, in the introduction, each case is but a taste—an appetizer—of my method throughout this book, outlined in the next section. *Political Appetites* surveys the kinds of cultural investigations made possible by the powerful and provocative imagery of the edible, seeking

---

86. See Schmolke-Hasselmann on the theme of Arthurian critique found in the later Old French verse romances, which often stage bad behavior on the part of the king or his favored knights (*Evolution of Arthurian Romance*, 61–67).

87. Such work is already well underway in the case of *Richard Coer de Lyon*, and numerous articles and book chapters have dealt with questions of power, postcolonialism, and the imperialist project in the poem's depiction of Richard's cannibalism. See for example Alan J. Ambrisco, "Cannibalism and Cultural Encounters in *Richard Coeur de Lyon*," *JMEMS* 29 (1999): 499–528, and Geraldine Heng, "The Romance of England: *Richard Coer de Lyon*, Saracens, Jews, and the Politics of Race and Nation," in *The Postcolonial Middle Ages*, ed. Jeffrey Jerome Cohen, 135–72. The only article devoted to food in the *Alliterative Morte Arthur* is Henry L. Harder's "Feasting in the *Alliterative Morte Arthure*," *Studies in Medieval Culture* 14 (1980): 49–62.

to push the outer edges of what food criticism can accomplish in medieval literature. I want to move beyond questions of what or how people ate in the Middle Ages (inquiries better left to food historians[88]) and rather examine how food impacts cultural and generic phenomena alike. In other words, this book seeks to explore how medieval writers of romance make use of culinary materials in order to think through the political implications of their poetry.

6. MENU OF THE DAY

Political Appetites ranges across the literary history of the English Middle Ages, beginning in the Anglo-Saxon era's curiously confident initiations of the hagiographic romance in *Andreas* (ca. ninth century?), then taking a seeming detour into Old French in the *Roman de Silence* (ca. 1275), a strangely contemporary romance that claims to have been written by an English author, and concluding with two Middle English romances: one of the earliest examples of the genre, *Havelok the Dane*, perhaps the preeminent expression of a nascent English nation, and *Sir Gowther* (ca. 1400), a much more jaundiced exploration of the aristocratic values that found the genre. The purpose of this book is not to convey a meticulously complete picture of food imagery in the medieval English romance, nor to catalogue the scenes in which characters eat or cook, although there is much value to be found in such a study.[89] Instead *Political Appetites* isolates a particular food image that animates an individual example of romance, seeking to illuminate how that resonance pervades its raison d'être, working both at the level of plot and structure as well as in the realm of poetic language. I show through the chapters that follow that foodways are fundamental to the political imaginary of these sometimes misunderstood and understudied works.

From its possible origins in the late ninth century to the heights and elaborations of the genre in the fifteenth, the breadth of this book engages romance as a diachronic phenomenon, one in constant and great flux throughout its

---

88. Modern studies of medieval food history include: C. Anne Wilson, *Food and Drink in Britain: From the Stone Age to Recent Times;* Madeleine Pelner Cosman, *Fabulous Feasts: Medieval Cookery and Ceremony;* Debby Banham, *Food and Drink in Anglo-Saxon England;* and Ann Hagen, *Anglo-Saxon Food and Drink: Production, Processing, Distribution and Consumption.* Allen J. Frantzen's *Food, Eating, and Identity in Early Medieval England,* while not a food history *per se,* is an examination of food and its related objects as a cultural nexus of meaning, primarily by way of archaeology and material culture.

89. Such a catalogue can be found in Sarah Gordon's *Culinary Comedy in Medieval French Literature,* which documents the appearance of food used to invoke humor and level social critique in many extant genres in Old French literature, such as romance, fabliau, and beast fable.

spectacular history, as Cooper shows in her magisterial survey of its *longue durée*. Intensely local, but composed with an epochal perspective, *Political Appetites* reveals that as culinary and literary tastes and technologies change over the Middle Ages, food and eating consistently captivate and preoccupy the authors and audiences of these works. Political details may shift and vary, but the signifying, authorizing power of cuisine endures. This is because food reminds us of the circumstances of our basic condition in the material world: our dependence on labor, our concern with status and recognition, our relation to government, our yearning for a coherent narrative of historical progress. These are eminently political questions, posed by "political animals" (*zöon politikon,* as Aristotle famously defined humanity)[90] and vexing many generations of theorists and practitioners. The ensuing chapters will explore how one author (usually anonymous)[91] attempted to think through them using food not only as a fundamental image but as a vital connection to the material world.

I begin with the scandal of anthropophagy, a menace to temporal as well as bodily integrity. The eating of human flesh ruptures the reckoning of history in the hagiographic romance of *Andreas*. Food criticism establishes this story as an ironic and playfully multivocal narrative, contrary to traditional readings, which tend to emphasize only the doctrinaire aspects of the text. I refuse to allegorize Mermedonian cannibalism—instead, considering it a material practice with real-world political resonances despite its outlandish horror. The food imagery of *Andreas* allows a reading that is teasingly critical of Christian assumptions about the text: namely that its hero is justified in his violent suppression of Mermedonian culture, and that the converted cannibal nation is better off for it. The *Andreas* poet relates the horrific culinary procedures of the Mermedonians as fascinating foreign customs, yet also acknowledges an uncanny similarity between his Christian realm and the unholy object of his quest. Through their own incorporative appetites, apostles praying for salvation become man-eaters who prey on other man-eaters. The making of missionary history, as told through the fantastic armature of romance, is foundationally a gastronomic process—engulfing, digestive.

In the second chapter, I turn from a text often read unironically to one that is virtually dripping with it. If the cannibalistic cookery of *Andreas* exposes the dark underbelly of ecclesiastical imperialism, the *Roman de Silence* equates

---

90. Aristotle, *Politics,* Book 1.2, 1253a. Translation: *Aristotle's Politics,* trans. Carnes Lord, 4.
91. As are the authors of three of my romances here. Additionally, "Heldris de Cornüalle" may well be a *nom de plume*. All four authors (and their story's narrators) are referred to as "he" throughout this book for the sake of convenience, though they are not gender-identified.

food preparation to the evolution of medieval culture itself. *Silence* explores a different kind of assimilation in a world fractured by category crises: gender-bending, upward social mobility, and nonchivalric aristocrats. Its innovative mélange, well-studied in recent years, frames an unusual story about a cross-dressed noblewoman, in which culinary registers ground sophisticated feudal politics and gender codes. Cooking is a mediating process that alters natural products in ways both necessary and pleasurable to acculturated humanity, kneading a Nature not always tractable to human needs and wants. In this intellectually ambitious and avant-garde story, the narrator becomes enmeshed in his own ingenuity: if the allegorical figure of Nature is a baker that molds bodies like cakes, then her "naturalness" is called into question by the very figure that represents it.

The idea of right rule suggested in *Silence*'s critique of the reign of its King Ebain corresponds to a similar provocation to narrative in the romance of *Havelok the Dane*, a story of one of the hungriest heroes in medieval literature. And so it is not surprising to find food doing the work of political theory in this account of Havelok's life and ascendancy. In charting his path from exile to the reclamation of his throne, the romance tracks his efforts to sustain himself. In feast or famine, in sustenance or starvation, Havelok is no different from any of his subjects: bound to labor, land, and political economy. His struggle to regain his birthright—while toiling in a kitchen—is as much a fight to transcend this vulnerable, appetitive humanity as it is a contest to be recognized as king. Food concentrates questions about the sovereignty and sufficiency of a legitimate government: Havelok needs food to preserve his life as he strives to regain his inheritance, but oddly, once he does, banqueting must be suppressed. It is unseemly for a sovereign to flaunt his food in this poem, or to concede a dependence on it. A ruler's cuisine is a dicey political signifier—an abundance enabled by the labor and deprivation that differentiate the highest lord from the lowest thrall. The suppression of conspicuous consumption, and of food itself, at the end of the poem paradoxically provokes attention to this nutritional inequity.

From tables replete with fine dishes, lordly abundances fall into horrific excesses of gluttony, disgust, and disease in the viciously satiric *Sir Gowther*, which tracks the corruption of noble values by unwholesome appetites. In this romance, the protagonist, a murderous half-demon duke, must transform his savage nature by eating only what he can seize from the mouths of dogs—a bizarre inversion of the advice of medieval courtesy books, and, by extension, a perversion of the foundational idealism and chivalric etiquette of the romance genre. The public nature of Gowther's penance, performed in the convivial atmosphere of an emperor's banquet-hall, suggests that his lesson is an instruction in social grace. But social grace does not cure the psychopath of his bloodlust; *Sir Gowther* reveals instead the terrible truth of aristocratic living and the genre that celebrates it—in this romance, violence is just as natural as eating. And so violence, directed appropriately at the enemies of Christian Europe and tempered by courteous display, redeems not only the appetite of this savage hero but his body as well, rendering him into a healing saint as well as a virtuous ruler.

As all of these poems suggest, food plays a fundamental role in the plots, pleasures, and purposes of medieval English romance. Food imagery implies a sacrament but also takes the measure of an often brutal material world. *Political Appetites,* in its widest scope, shows how the political imaginary of medieval heroic narratives emanates from the symbolic, material, and phenomenological presence of food. Food imagery draws the exotic into the quotidian and materializes the mythology of social power. Key to the examination of serious political and economic problems, scenes of eating and cooking expose the social artifices and the artistic skill of romances through which medieval cultures read their illuminations and shadows. Together these four chapters constitute their own sort of survey of the potential for political intervention to be found in realms of the esculent. Both exploration and critique are mustered in the emphasis on eating in these poems, and the political world becomes sharply defined through their attention to objects experienced every day. The table, as well as what is served upon it, draws humanity together through shared appetites, but it also distinguishes them by means of an inflexibly drawn guest list. The medieval English romances I study here straddle this dual task of the convivial world: they crystallize the political engagements of their wondrous narratives at the same time they fracture and fragment these endeavors with often tart, satiric possibilities. *Political Appetites* reads the romance as the most important document conveying the complexity of medieval social awareness, which by generating and promulgating cultural mythologies, simultaneously calls their fundamental rationales into question. One realizes exactly what one is eating once the teeth sink into the dish's ornately prepared flesh: there is no hiding the substance of what is being consumed. This is why the French word *savoir* connotes both knowing and tasting; the experience that comes with physical consumption is presumed to produce an awareness of things as they really are. The consumers of medieval English romance savored their narrative feasts in exactly the same apocalyptic manner—the terms of human domination of an edible world sweet in the mouth but also they felt the belly burn with the understanding of the excesses and abuses of this very same consumptive reign.

CHAPTER 1

Andreas

Cannibals at the Edge of History

> Geseoh nu, þu earma, et nu þas sidan þe her gehrysted is ond acer me on þa oðre.
>
> Look now, you wretch—now eat this side that's roasted here, and turn me onto the other!
>
> —Saint Lawrence, *Old English Martyrology*

1. LAMBS AND WOLVES

ANDREAS ASKS an impertinent question: how can a servant of God, charged to "eat such things as are set before you" (Luke 10:8), convert a land of cannibals?[1] What food or identity can these two peoples ever share? The prospect of man-eating feasts tantalizes author and audience alike with a deranged commensality. This is a shared banquet that never should be: the pilgrim who makes himself a stranger and survives on foreign food meets the nation that has no food of its own and so must eat strangers. Such playful perversity resounds through this daring poem, which proposes a startling relationship between Christian and cannibal.[2] In *Andreas*, anthropophagy is reciprocal: the can-

---

1. *Andreas* appears in the Vercelli Book, a late tenth-century compilation. The poem's date of composition is uncertain. Allison Powell's meticulous study of lexicographical similarities in *Andreas, Beowulf* (ca. eighth century), and the signed poems of Cynewulf (ca. late eighth century), suggests that *Andreas* was composed latest of the three (*Verbal Parallels in Andreas and Its Relationship to Beowulf and Cynewulf*, PhD diss., Cambridge University, 2002).

2. The word "cannibal" is technically anachronistic to medieval texts, as it originates in English in 1553, derived from a slanderous appellation of the Carib Indians encountered by Columbus (*OED*). A more correct term for the time would be "anthropophagite." Though the two words are used more or less synonymously throughout this book, there is a distinction usually understood between them: "anthropophagism" is the act of eating human flesh, while "cannibalism" often implies a moral judgment or a political condemnation of a people so labelled.

nibals of Mermedonia are preyed upon by apostles who pray for them, hungry for their conversion. The grotesque paradox of Andreas's mission conjures fantasies and fears that emerge when the familiar confronts the foreign, when the present relives the past. *Andreas* exposes the chronological distortion vital to the apostolic project of converting foreign peoples: it is a culinary battle on the "sæl-wange" (1493) [plains of time], to command the direction of cultural progress, to eat or be eaten.[3]

Saints' lives are timely collisions, torturous and triumphant narratives wherein secular powers ravage saintly sufferers. They capture the moment of conversion, lingering on the border of past and present. Saint Lawrence's grim yet gleeful injunction contains a powerful irony: the roasting saint grotesquely turns the other cheek, daring his tormenters to glut themselves on his beatitude. Torture becomes cooking, a productive shift into metaphor that tempts its reader/consumer with an abominable repast. The blunt force of Lawrence's last words seems almost to command *us* to eat him, as if appreciating his sacrifice means participating in his horrific death across the gap of time—negotiating the razor's edge of historical change, where pagan past becomes Christian present.

Andreas takes up Lawrence's challenge; it is a poem from a self-conscious avant-garde that confronts and consumes its past selves. Its mélange blends the poet's cultural and literary moment with apostolic time and the dimly lit cannibal past, convergences that purposefully suggest these pasts are not so distant and inaccessible. *Andreas* reveals that a culture is always engaged in a conflict among its various histories. Its thrilling tale from "on fyrndagum" (1) [in the days of yore] dramatizes the throes of Anglo-Saxon culture attempting to define itself in a time of crisis.[4] Yet the poem stages this historical amalgamation as a dietary problem, brought to a crisis point by the improbable survival of the Mermedonians' elaborate anthropophagic customs, which are destined to be straightened out by Andreas's equally brutal, convivial miracle by the end of the poem.

Andreas is itself difficult to define, alternately pious and playful, bloodthirsty and beatific. The poet delights in tonal and generic experimentation,

---

3. Citations of *Andreas* are from *Andreas and the Fates of the Apostles*, ed. Kenneth R. Brooks, in consultation with a facsimile of the original (Celia Sisam, ed. *Early English Manuscripts in Facsimile*, vol. 19, *The Vercelli Book*). Line citations are from Brooks. Translations mine.

4. Critics have speculated about the presence of historical referents in *Andreas*, using them to better date the poem. Heather Blurton suggests that *Andreas* exhibits tenth-century anxieties about Viking invasion and settlement (*Cannibalism in High Medieval English Literature*, 31–32). For Robert Boenig, *Andreas* reflects ninth-century theological debates, particularly the controversy regarding the nature of the Eucharist (*Saint and Hero: Andreas and Medieval Doctrine*, 55–77).

continually reassessing and recombining diverse sources to explore the interconnectedness of food practice, cultural identity, and political power.⁵ It is a prime example of a text from an era often deemed to lie before "signification became complex, irony corrosive, politics stressful, and transgressive thinking possible," that nevertheless evinces all four of these qualities.⁶ *Andreas* is a hagiographic romance, an apostolic epic—its saint is at once a warrior-hero on a quest for national victory, a peace-bearing missionary, and a vulnerable human being. For all their torture and persecution, hagiographies are often passionless *passiones* whose saints do not seem to feel their agonies. Andreas approaches his mission with all the brute strength and charisma of a Beowulf, yet he suffers nonetheless. Mermedonia as well exists in a romantic landscape, reachable only after an eventful journey, its denizens an exorbitant race of humans both monstrous and familiar. *Andreas* exults in the standard *topoi* of heroic romance: intriguing villains, supernatural forces, a setting long ago, and a persistent fascination with sensationalism, magic, and the fantastic. Even the role of Jesus is romanticized, giving him a character to play in an amicable relationship with his disciple. All of this nestles in an integument of ironic storytelling and forceful humor.

The appearance, perhaps as early as the late ninth century, of this hagiographic romance troubles the standard line of criticism that dates European romance from the Old French *romans d'antiquite* (ca. 1155–60). The *Andreas* poet is not alone in Anglo-Saxon literature (he has Cynewulf's *Elene* and the anonymous *Guthlac A* [ca. ninth century] as generic compatriots) in drawing upon a rich classical and Mediterranean romance tradition. This extends from Homer's *Odyssey* (ca. eighth century BCE) to the *Argonautica* of Apollonius of Rhodes (ca. third century BCE), from the Greek prose romances such as the *Ephesian Tale* (ca. third century BCE) or *Callirhoe* (ca. first century BCE), to Ovid's *Metamorphoses,* the biblical Acts of the Apostles (ca. 80–90 CE), Apu-

---

5. *Andreas* adapts its legend of St. Andrew from a wide array of sources, including the New Testament and the Greek prose romance *Praxeis Andreoui kai Mathias eis ten Polin ton Anthropophagon* (*The Acts of Andrew and Matthias in the Country of the Cannibals,* hereafter *Acts of Andrew*) (ca. fifth century). Later analogues include a Latin version, the *Recensio Casanatensis* (ca. twelfth century), a closely related Anglo-Saxon homily found incomplete in *Blickling Homilies* 19 (ca. 971), and a full version, "The Legend of St. Andrew," in Cambridge Corpus Christi College MS 198 (ca. eleventh century). For an argument that the *Andreas* poet was influenced as well by style of the Christian Latin poet Arator (fl. sixth century CE), especially his epic *De Actibus Apostolorum,* see Alexandra Hennessey Olsen, "The Aesthetics of *Andreas*: The Contexts of Oral Tradition and Patristic Latin Poetry," in *De Gustibus: Essays for Alain Renoir,* ed. John Miles Foley Jr., 391–99.

6. The phrase is used by Sarah Kay, describing the temporal bind early medieval genres often find themselves in when viewed by modern critical perspectives (*The Chansons de Geste in the Age of Romance,* 4.)

leius's *The Golden Ass* (ca. late second century), and the anonymous *Apollonius of Tyre* (ca. fifth or sixth century, adapted into Anglo-Saxon prose [in probably the eleventh century]). Despite its early date, the richness of *Andreas* anticipates the generic multiplicities, ornate language, and sensational exploits of Geoffrey of Monmouth's *Historia Regis Britanniae* (ca. 1136), especially its Arthur narrative; Benoît de Saint-Maure's *Roman de Troie*; the chivalric romances of Chrétien de Troyes; and the *lais* of Marie de France (ca. 1190s). *Andreas* reveals the *longue durée* of the romance genre, participating in its marvelous traditions of border crossing and amalgamation with curious self-confidence.

Andreas is a generic hybrid that has always rested uneasily in the Anglo-Saxon canon. Despite its audacious, transgressive narrative—or maybe even because of it—the poem was condemned for much of the twentieth century as a "rather inferior imitation of *Beowulf*,"[7] its author deemed a "poetic dunderhead."[8] Thomas D. Hill's 1969 examination of the patristic sources of *Andreas* set the tone for exegetical scholarship that revalued the poem, but mostly for its figural designs and scriptural resonances.[9] Although the theological inheritance of literary culture is important to consider, these studies can render a text's complex historical consciousness and compelling poetics into a flat unidirectional voice.[10] In the past few decades, however, scholarship has begun to explore the formal, stylistic, and ideological peculiarities of *Andreas*. John P. Hermann's *Allegories of War: Language and Violence in Old English Poetry* (1989) is a vital intervention in Anglo-Saxon studies. Hermann draws a line in the exegetical sand, demonstrating that *Andreas* is not easily reducible into religious allegory. For Hermann, allegorizing the poem's fierce

---

7. Claes Schaar, *Critical Studies in the Cynewulf Group*, 243.

8. Eric Gerald Stanley, "Beowulf," in *Continuations and Beginnings: Studies in Old English Literature*, ed. Stanley, 114. In the same volume, Rosemary Woolf deems the *Andreas* poet "lightweight, mechanical, even occasionally ludicrous" and inferior to the *Beowulf* poet ("Saints' Lives," 53). Carol Hughes Funk provides an exhaustive critical bibliography of such comparisons in *The History of Andreas and Beowulf Comparative Scholarship* (PhD diss., University of Denver, 1997).

9. Thomas D. Hill, "Figural Narrative in *Andreas*: The Conversion of the Mermedonians," *NM* 70 (1969): 261–73. See also Penn R. Szittya, "The Living Stone and the Patriarchs: Typological Imagery in *Andreas*, Lines 706–810," *JEGP* 77 (1973): 167–74; Constance B. Hieatt, "The Harrowing of Mermedonia" *NM* 77 (1976): 49–62; James W. Earl, "The Typological Structure of *Andreas*," in *Old English Literature in Context*, ed. John D. Niles, 66–89; and Lisa J. Kizer, "*Andreas* and the *Lifes Weg*," *NM* 85 (1984): 65–75.

10. Daniel G. Calder makes the simple observation: "Identification of a typological system, however necessary, however applicable should not be equated with analysis; discovery is not the same as understanding" ("Figurative Language and Its Contexts in *Andreas*: A Study of Medieval Expressionism," in *Modes of Interpretation in Old English Literature: Essays in Honour of Stanley B. Greenfield*, ed. Phyllis Rugg Brown, Georgia Ronan Crampton, and Fred C. Robinson, 119.

ethnic and racial animosities ignores its political motives and the possibility of its propagandizing impact upon contemporary readers.[11] Though lauding patristic approaches in general, Jonathan Wilcox explores rollicking incongruities nevertheless apparent between the poem's doctrine and the poet's humor, in order to "revivify a surface . . . too quickly sublated by typological criticism."[12] Hugh Magennis makes the first study of food imagery in *Andreas*, examining the theological aspects of the poem's dichotomy of "good" and "evil" eating.[13]

More recent work has further interrogated older critical paradigms, exposing new layers of inquiry inherent to the poem. In *Saint and Hero*, still the only book-length investigation of *Andreas*, Robert Boenig mobilizes the hoary methods of exegetical criticism and source study and innovates upon them by historicizing their subject, using meticulous theological context to determine New Historicist concerns with the poem's "political unconscious." In Boenig's hands, by way of Paschasius Radbert, as well as Frederic Jameson and Michel Foucault, *Andreas* becomes a receptacle of historical meaning, tracing out a frame of reference that allows him to discern both an author and his politics.[14] Tracing the anti-Semitic rhetoric of the Vercelli Book, Andrew Scheil locates a powerful scapegoating effect in *Andreas*, which mobilizes tropes of eating and mental derangement to equate the cannibalistic Mermedonians with the Christ-denying Jews of the poem's historical imagination, positing either as a people to be suppressed in the Christian sublationist now.[15] Heather Blurton extends the historical and political valences of the poem, recognizing that both are generated by its attention to cannibalism. The result is a deliberate blurring of distinction: "Where Mermedonian cannibalism should, in the context of the Anglo-Saxon literary tradition, be a mark of monstrous alterity, the poem turns it back upon Andreas, making it just another point of similarity,"

---

11. John P. Hermann, *Allegories of War: Language and Violence in Old English Poetry*, 120.

12. Jonathan Wilcox, "Eating People Is Wrong: Funny Style in *Andreas* and Its Analogues," in *Anglo-Saxon Styles*, ed. Catherine E. Karkov and George Hardin Brown, 204.

13. Hugh Magennis, *Anglo-Saxon Appetites: Food and Drink and Their Consumption in Old English and Related Literatures*, 152.

14. Robert Boenig, *Saint and Hero*, 11. Later he concludes that for the medieval period "doctrine was politics" and that "like any book, *Andreas* is a social act as well as a text" (105 and 109).

15. Andrew Scheil, *The Footsteps of Israel: Understanding Jews in Anglo-Saxon England*, see 231, 253–58. Janet Thormann, in an article published the same year as Scheil's book, also engages the "Jewish Other" in Anglo-Saxon poetry, concluding that the projection was useful in "furthering a national cultural [Christian] identity among the Anglo-Saxons ("The Jewish Other in Old English Narrative Poetry." *Partial Answers: A Journal of Literature and the History of Ideas* 2 [2004]: 16).

a creation of a "cannibal narrative" that resists easy allegorization of the poem and muddles its message of virtuous interventionism.[16]

This groundbreaking scholarship has inspired me as I examine the poem's resistance to its own dominant interpretation as Christian triumphalism. *Andreas* deploys the spectacular trappings of romance to critically engage the politics of time inherent in the construction of historical narrative. The poem exposes history-making as a perverse gastronomic process that incorporates foreign material (and foreign timekeeping), and digests it to create an image of the past. It represents encounters between *modern* and *primitive* cultures as struggles to determine whose history will tell the tale of the meeting. The avant-garde, anthropological energies of *Andreas* resonate remarkably with the twentieth-century scholarship of Johannes Fabian, which also approaches historiography as a politics of time. Fabian posits that gathering "knowledge of the Other" is always a "temporal, historical, a political act."[17] He is alarmed by what he identifies as an ideological disjunction between anthropologists' experiences in the field and their subsequent reports of those experiences. Such after-the-fact accounts, he argues, tend to deny "coevality"—intimate, spontaneous moments of "shared time" between observer and observed, when presumptions of difference melt away. By doing so, anthropologists isolate their subjects of study from modernity, partitioning them into alternate chronologies—"allochronic time," or the "time of the other." The denial of "coevality" is a reflexive disavowal, a measure of self-protection: the passage of time turns the intense pleasure of "shared time" into a "problem with time."[18] The rich volatility of Fabian's "coevality"—a term that consumes itself, that signifies an extraordinary union across time as well as its inevitable disruption—is just the flux of bliss and torture, appetite and abstinence, that electrifies *Andreas*. Coevality is its problem, its desire, and its narratological principle.

The denial of coevality leads to periodization in order to account for differences in time. Periodization is a dangerous prospect, fraught with political peril, no less in the Middle Ages than in the modern era. The hazards of reckoning time—distinguishing the past from the present leading into the future—were well known to medieval historians and philosophers. Bede's *Ecclesiastical History of the English People* (ca. 731) chronicles the tempestuous cycles of

---

16. Blurton, *Cannibalism in High Medieval English Literature*, 32. An example of the allegorization of cannibalism is made by John Thomas Casteen, who interprets Mermedonian predilections, by way of the Bible, as a punishment for sin ("Mermedonian Cannibalism and Figural Narration," *NM* 75 [1974]: 76). For the idea of *Andreas* as espousing virtuous interventionism, see Marie Nelson, "The Old English *Andreas* as an Account of Benign Aggression." *Medieval Perspectives* 2 (1987): 81–89.

17. Johannes Fabian, *Time and the Other*, 1.

18. Ibid., 31–37.

pagan backsliding and reconversion that characterized the Christianization of the English kingdoms. Throughout the *History,* Bede represents conversion as a fundamentally temporal conquest, as the English nations move into the "now" of Christian revelation, the Anno Domini. The count of time becomes a political gesture. Kathleen Davis remarks that the *History* proposes "a political theology of time, not because certain kings are approved by God . . . but because the calculation as well as the experience of time inherently relies upon political systems."[19] The *Andreas* poet shares Bede's conviction that reckoning time is a political operation that fractures the identity of a present self and its past other.

The mythology of cannibalism represses history: impossibly distant, fantastically barbaric others reinforce a culture's sanitized self-image of progress and enlightenment. Yet these man-eaters become a nostalgic necessity for the definition of current politics: a terrible tradition that makes all other traditions, no matter how brutal or exclusionary, both distinct and desirable to their society. It is a past phenomenon that renders the present legible. Common to most cultures worldwide, cannibalism lurks at the psychic roots of society—the foundational sin, committed at the dawn of time, waiting to erupt when least expected. From Hesiod's mythological account of Zeus's rebellion against his father Cronos, who eats his own children (ca. 650 BCE) to Sigmund Freud's 1913 hypothesis of a primordial act of cannibal patricide that sparks civilization and its neuroses, anthropophagic stories mark epochal shifts.[20] In locating this horrifying initiatory impulse in hagiographic, historical time, *Andreas* offers its own wry version of these origin stories: the Mermedonians' attempt to eat one of their own children catalyzes their conversion, as if by the sheer extravagance of cannibal-on-cannibal violence. A taste for self-annihilation launches them into their own future (1108–28).

An insistence upon anthropophagy's continuing practice *elsewhere* separates a civilization from its deranged past, yet never banishes that prehistory. William Arens's study, *The Man-Eating Myth: Anthropology and Anthropophagy,* demonstrates that cannibalism is a vehicle for pushing away the specter of the past: "Cannibalism becomes a feature of the faraway or foregone, which is much the same thing. In the way that the dimensions of time and space are interpreted, 'they,' in the form of distant cannibals, are reflections of us as we once were."[21] As Arens reveals, this dubious displacement recurs in

---

19. Kathleen Davis, *Periodization and Sovereignty: How Ideas of Feudalism and Secularization Govern the Politics of Time,* 105.

20. Hesiod, *Theogony,* in *Hesiod,* 453–506; Freud, *Totem and Taboo,* trans. James Strachey, 164–72.

21. William Arens, *The Man-Eating Myth: Anthropology and Anthropophagy,* 19. His study discredits much of the classic evidence for cannibalism—"first-hand" accounts of man-eating by European sailors, missionaries, and explorers—and posits the deep ideological affinity of

the mythologies of diverse cultures across thousands of years. Indeed, cannibalism haunts the present persistently in Anglo-Saxon literature. Four of the five texts in the early eleventh-century Nowell Codex, for example, feature some form of (at least latent) anthropophagy that threatens the identities of humans in the now—including *Beowulf*'s Grendel, the semi-human "Caines cynne" [kin of Cain], who emerges from a mythic past to devour Danish warriors, and Judith, who outrages Mosaic food-law by placing the bloody head of Holofernes into her kosher food sack.[22] The Donestre, of the *Wonders of the East,* are the Mermedonians' closest analogues in the Anglo-Saxon canon. Both groups of island-dwellers are self-conscious and self-reflective, tormented by the very appetites they eagerly overindulge. The Donestre lure visitors into their clutches by using their own homesickness against them— telepathically speaking their languages and addressing them as family members, and then attacking them in a sudden burst of savagery. Yet they weep over the heads of their victims (the only part left uneaten): the familiarity that baits their trap is too powerful for their own sensibilities, and they long for homes and intimacies that they can speak but never know.

In either account, the cannibals seem aware of the difficulties and dangers in negotiating the borders of self and other, past and present, foreign and familiar. Cannibals eat humans by definition, yet this commingling appears to disturb them: these anthropophagic accounts often describe efforts to forget or to undo shared humanity. The weeping Donestre simply eat their victims as quickly as possible, as if to get it over with. The "gealg-mod" (32) [sad-minded] Mermedonians of *Andreas,* on the other hand, make an art form of dehumanizing their food. They impose their own form of ritual time upon their captives in a grotesque parody of Christian eschatology, "resurrecting" them as livestock in an intricate, precisely timed thirty-day process, a calendar of slaughter and feast that juxtaposes time schemes even as it separates body from soul.

The cannibals of *Andreas,* however, are terribly real in the story, though hardly joyful about their diet. Yet the poem mobilizes its representation of these people in terms of cultural critique, with an awareness of the political nature of such observation. *Andreas* operates with the understanding that hunger for human flesh elides the lust for imperialist incorporation, substituting horror for horror in a manner that resonates with contemporary perspectives. Crystal Bartolovich links the growth of the cannibal fantasy to the early

---

early anthropological projects and the colonization of foreign peoples. Arens's anthropologists "discover" cannibalism because they assume it is there and organize their findings accordingly.

22. *Beowulf,* 107. Citations are from *Klaeber's Beowulf and the Fight at Finnsburh,* 4th ed., ed. R. D. Fulk, Robert E. Bjork, and John D. Niles.

modern European development of protocapitalist economies: "Cannibal appetite is essential to capitalist/colonial forces which reinforce proto-*Heißhunger* as a general acquisitive energy even as they undertake a repression of its 'savage' (that is, unlimited) form [in cannibalism]."[23] "*Heißhunger*" (often translated as "voracious appetite") is the appetitive state of the capitalist extractor of surplus-value from human labor-power, who devours human potential and only hungers for more capitalization from his investment.[24] This condition of perpetual voracity forms the "supplementary logic" of capitalism, a restless and violent yearning shared by many political bodies, including the early Christian church's desire for expanding borders, a need imagined in *Andreas*'s romantic fantasies.[25] Cannibalism, as a practice to be repressed by the poem's action, is a distorted twin of the apostolic yen for foreign converts in foreign lands, drawing together Mermedonians and Christians while insisting upon their absolute difference.[26]

The apostle's mission is a strikingly similar balancing act between union and disjunction. Conversion incorporates new believers into the Christian body—the apostle must spiritually "digest" his neophytes. The apostolic imperative to travel into distant countries and evangelize the word of God demands that he exist in continuous flux between identity and alterity, in a process of dialectical exchange with the strangers he meets. According to the commands of Jesus, the apostles must embrace a life of imminent changes:

> Go: Behold I send you as lambs among wolves. / Carry neither purse, nor scrip, nor shoes; and salute no man by the way. Into whatsoever house you enter, first say: Peace be to this house. / And if the son of peace be there, your peace shall rest upon him; but if not, it shall return to you. And in the same house, remain, eating and drinking such things as they have: for the labourer is worthy of his hire. . . . / And into what city soever you enter, and they receive you, eat such things as are set before you. (Luke 10:3–8)

---

23. Crystal Bartolovich, "Consumerism, or the Cultural Logic of Late Cannibalism," in *Cannibalism and the Colonial World*, ed. Francis Barker, Peter Hulme, and Margaret Iversen, 225.

24. *Heißhunger* derives from Marx, *Capital*, 1.344–5. There Marx notes that "Capital did not invent surplus labour," arguing that is has been a part of economic expropriation throughout human history, whenever economic drives exceed the satisfaction of local needs. For capitalism consuming human labor-power, defined as "the mental and physical capabilities of a human being," see 1.270–73.

25. Supplementary logic is the raison d'être of the *Fates of the Apostles*, the Cynewulf poem that immediately follows *Andreas* in the Vercelli Book.

26. Blurton also underlines this push-and-pull of identification in *Andreas*, by nothing that the Mermedonians and the apostles are described in very similar ways, using similar heroic epithets (*Cannibalism in High Medieval English Literature*, 28).

These are hazardous and haphazard quests, unplanned and unequipped. The apostles are as vulnerable as "lambs among wolves," and martyrdom is always imminent. This is no fatal directive, however, but rather practical advice on living apostolically. Jesus' instructions to "salute no man" and to leave belongings behind are designed to transform the traveling apostle into a spiritual exile, utterly dependent upon the unsolicited kindness of strangers. Yet if the "sons of peace" can be found, they will always offer goodwill in edible form. This guaranteed sustenance is the substance of salvation: Jesus invests the communal meal with the power to create bonds between nations and peoples. The apostle is the point of culinary connection—he digests the food of strangers, metabolizing himself into foreignness as the foreigner is transformed by his message. Jesus hints that the apostles may have to disregard customary dietary proscriptions to affect this vital exchange; their meal may be forbidden or disgusting, but they must eat it anyway. According to the supplementary logic of the apostolic mission, they must savor their own dietary defilement to fatten the body of the faithful.

Andreas satirizes the effectiveness of these conversionary methods with preposterous literalism. The poem likens the Mermedonians' desire to eat Christian strangers to the apostolic imperative to seek out and incorporate the furthest reaches of the pagan world. Shannon N. Godlove notes this connection in the poem's use of "shifting metaphors of incorporation . . . focusing on images of physical and spiritual assimilation of human beings."[27] Just as the apostles need strangers in order to make converts, the Mermedonians need *elþeodige* [strangers] in order to feed their entire nation. The two sides have developed their own, strangely parallel attitudes toward the foreigner—two sides destined to clash in this romantic scenario. Although their desires for consumption are mirror images, the poem's hints at apostolic eating are meant to cast the Mermedonians into a more grotesque light: consuming Mermedonian food is impossible—it would not foster shared humanity; it would only turn Andreas into a monster. The "freoðoleas" (29) [peaceless] cannibals are ghastly inversions of the gracious hosts Jesus envisions. In *Andreas,* food and time are the means by which Christian power is exerted upon the foreign convert. In Mermedonia, the apostle is in danger of being devoured by the past. He faces the culinary outrages of a foreign hostility that is illegible, unmanageable, and beyond his ken.

---

27. Shannon N. Godlove, "Bodies as Borders: Cannibalism and Conversion in the Old English *Andreas,*" *Studies in Philology* 106 (2009): 138.

2. THE ANTHROPOPHAGIC IMAGINARY

Andreas thrills to the sensational, romantic narrative possibilities of cannibalism, which transform hagiography into a tale of exotic adventures. At the same time, the poem values Mermedonian culture for its own sake; descriptive detail renders the cannibals tantalizingly plausible, as if the poem were a travelogue or even a field report.[28]

The anthropological imperatives of the travelogue, a popular medieval genre from the earliest times, often engage in wondering observation of the dietary practices of the foreign people in question. The account of Ohthere and Wulfstan, interpolated into several manuscripts of the Alfredian translation of Paulus Orosius's *Historiarum Adversum Paganos* (ca. 880), breathlessly recounts the fish and fowl gathered by the far northern tribes the two travelers visited, before describing their hunting of "horschwælum" or walruses.[29] Later travelogues follow similar patterns, including the ever-present cannibals of the *Wonders of the East* and the usually more quotidian fare of exotic peoples found in the massively popular *Le Divisament dou Monde* of Marco Polo (ca. 1300, also known as *Il Milione*) or *Mandeville's Travels* (ca. 1357).[30] If Andreas's mission is a form of apostolic anthropology, then the Mermedonians' man-eating rituals are cultural food practices, the material signifiers of a foreign people. The poem and its hero share anthropological aspirations. Andreas's mission is a fact-finding as well as a conversionary one, a duality that he acknowledges. To change the Mermedonians' lives, he states that he must know something about them, and frets that he does not: "ne þær æniges wat / hæleða gehygdo" (199–200) [I do not know / the thoughts of any of those men].

Even discovering where these mysterious cannibals live is a challenge. Their island is a geographical paradox. It is impossibly far away—Andreas despairs of arriving there in the allotted three days (190–92)—yet somehow its borders encroach. Mermedonia is at once an "igland" [island, but also "land beyond the water"] and a "mearc-land" (19) [borderland] that presses threat-

---

28. David Hamilton does not give the *Andreas* poet much credit for complexity in the representation of the Mermedonians, although he claims such richness is not the poet's purpose: "The Mermedonians are little more than a vehicle for the idea of spiritual hunger; their deprivation is unnaturally strained and can be understood only by recourse to an imposed, allegorical meaning" ("The Diet and Digestion of Allegory in *Andreas*," *Anglo-Saxon England* 1 (1972): 151). Although this article is the first to really engage the food in *Andreas,* Hamilton remains focused on its allegorical purposes.

29. Paulus Orosius, *King Alfred's Orosius,* ed. Henry Sweet, 17.

30. Marco Polo, *The Travels,* trans. Ronald Latham; John Mandeville, *The Travels of Sir John Mandeville,* trans. C. W. R. D. Moseley.

eningly upon one's own country. A "mearc" (cognate to the modern English "march" and "mark") is the delineation of a border, and also a symbol on a page. Like all written signs, borders are arbitrary and unstable: drawing a border invites its transgression. The word contains the simultaneous menace and promise of proximity, of invasions to be feared and invasions to be planned, a consistent preoccupation for an Anglo-Saxon audience. Fabienne L. Michelet remarks that "one of the recurrent features of the Anglo-Saxons' sense of space is their constant fear of invasion," an anxiety that their defining borders are too porous and unstable.[31] Marches both consolidate and endanger a nation's identity.

The Mermedonian borderlands are prison walls as well as expanding frontiers. The cannibals are trapped within the bounds of their own barbarity: they are "morðre bewunden, / feondes facne" (19–20) [wound up in murder, in the deceit of the enemy]. Their land is enclosed in a fiendish hostility. Yet Mermedonia is also a "folc-stede gumena / hæleða eðel" (20–21) [dwelling-place of men / homeland of heroes], descriptions that quickly reinstate the humanity jeopardized by their murderousness. The man-eaters are "guman" and "hæleðas," disturbingly identifiable as civilized people. The kenning "folc-stede" even suggests a legal entitlement to their land, a claim that the Mermedonians defend vigorously as its rightful owners: "ellðeodigra eðles ne mihte, / blædes brucan" (16–17) [strangers cannot enjoy the fruits of their native land]. The complex verb *brucan* here ranges in meaning from eating to the use and enjoyment of things, signifying the pleasure and privilege of lordly ownership, of using and discarding objects as one pleases.[32] Yet the Mermedonians do not "enjoy" or "eat" the *bladu* (fruits) they so jealously guard:

> Næs þær hlafes wist
> werum on þam wonge,   ne wæteres drync
> to bruconne,   ah hie blod ond fel,
> fira flæsc-homan,   feorran-cumenra,
> ðegon geond þa þeode.   Swelc wæs þeaw hira
> þæt hie æghwylcne   ellðeodigra
> dydan him to mose   mete-þearfendum,
> þara þe þæt ealand   utan sohte.
> (21–28)

---

31. Fabienne L. Michelet, *Creation, Migration, and Conquest: Imaginary Geography and Sense of Space in Old English Literature*, 23–24.

32. "Brucan," in *Bosworth-Toller*.

> There was neither bite of bread
> nor drink of water for Mermedonian men to enjoy.
> Instead they consumed blood and skin,
> the flesh-homes of foreign-coming men.
> throughout the nation. Such was their custom—
> that they made all strangers seeking their island
> from outside into meat for the meat-lacking.

It seems the Mermedonians harvest the "flesh-homes of foreign-coming men" because they lack other natural resources. The verb "ðegon" [consumed], in its oblique relation to *þegn* [a servant], also signifies a measure of helplessness, of terrible dependency in their eating. Visitors are not welcome, but they seem necessary, and the Mermedonians cannot "own" the foreigners they eat in the way they might possess their own crops or livestock. The poem's denouncement of the Mermedonians' devilish customs is textured by the earnestness of its anthropological approach, its desire to document bygone times or faraway places. The diplomatic tone of the phrase "swelc wæs þeaw hira" (25, 177) [such was their custom] introduces an attitude of cultural relativism that humanizes the cannibals, construing their abominable diet as a deliberate choice.[33]

The Mermedonians have teeth: even as they are absorbed into the Christian whole, they leave a trace (or taste) of their previous abominations to haunt the collective past of the civilized world. They are limited by their anthropophagy, yet liberated by its possibilities, elaborating and refining it to suit their cultural tastes. Their cannibalism is more than an abstract concept; more than a sinful negation of Christian values. Rather, as Edward B. Irving Jr. observes, their man-eating practices invoke both Germanic customs of culinary generosity as well as the perpetual body of Christian theophagy.[34] Cannibalism is a parodic food practice that situates *Andreas* in geography and history. It opens fissures between the ideological purpose and the pleasures of the text, calling into question the possibility of neat resolution through scriptural exegesis. The materiality of man-eating in the poem generates a conviviality that cannot be explained or contained by the terms of Christian allegory.

Mermedonia is rendered lifelike by an imagery of nefarious gastronomy. Unlike the Donestre or Grendel, who eat in a gluttonous hurry, the Merm-

---

33. This phrase is apparently borrowed from *Beowulf*—it appears nowhere else in the extant corpus—where it is used to explain why the Danes turn to idol-worship to seek redress from the depredations of Grendel (175–88).

34. Edward B. Irving Jr., "A Reading of *Andreas*: The Poem as Poem," *Anglo-Saxon England* 12 (1983): 219.

edonians fix their meals with extreme care, and *Andreas* exults in the details of these terrifying cooking practices. These "grædige guð-rincas" (155) [greedy war-fighters] are unlikely epicures, masters of the culinary arts. These are their "token" practices, the signs of their cultural distinctiveness:

> Swylc wæs þæs folces   freoðoleas tacen,
> unlædra eafoð,   þæt hie eagena gesihð,
> hettend heoro-grimme,   heafod-gimmas
> agetton gealg-mode   gara ordum.
> Syððan him geblendan   bitere tosomne,
> dryas þurh dwol-cræft,   drync unheorne,
> se onwende gewit,   wera ingeþanc,
> heortan on hreðre,   hyge wæs oncyrred,
> þæt hie ne murndan   æfter man-dreame,
> hæleþ heoro-grædige,   ac hie hig ond gærs
> for mete-leaste   meðe gedrehte.
> (29–39)

> Such was the peaceless token of these people,
> the violence of the wretched, that the enemy,
> sword-grim and sad-minded, destroyed the sight of the eyes,
> the head-gems, with the point of spears.
> Afterwards their druids bitterly mixed together
> a frightful drink through error-craft for their victim—
> their wit was perverted, the conscience of men,
> their mind was altered, the heart in breast—
> so that their victims mourned no longer
> for the joys of men so that they, ravenously hungry,
> exhausted, tormented by famine, would eat hay and grass instead.

The poet eagerly recounts these intricate torments in a tone that joins sensationalism and scientific rigor. He lingers over the preliminary eye-gouging: as the windows of the soul, eyes—flourishingly denoted "head-gems" and "heafdes segl" (50) [sails of the head]—must be the first to go.[35] The Mermedonians repurpose the tools of war—spear-points and swords—to this task, to suit a different sort of butchery. But their victims' main course is a magical drink that banishes the imbiber's humanity, a triumph of culinary "frightful-

---

35. I retain the manuscript's "segl" [sails, flags, banners], typically emended to "sigel" [suns].

ness," a peaceless pièce de résistance. The wicked potency of the "drync unheorne" perverts wit, conscience, mind, and heart at once, and by way of Exeter Book Riddle 27 (the mead-riddle), whose speaker steals its quaffers' human capacities, it also anticipates the terrible "meodu-scerwen" and "beor-þegu" [mead-service and beer-taking] that awaits the Mermedonians at the climax of the poem. The captives digest this potion in prison stalls loaded with grass and hay, their only food for their allotted thirty days of captivity. They are terrifyingly altered into, as Brian Shaw notes, "grotesque parodies of humanity, having the form but not the true essence," forced to act as animals, without eyes to return their captors' gaze, unable to speak or feel their own rationality.[36] By feeding their victims animal fodder, the Mermedonians effect a physical transformation to match the mental one, modifying their humoral makeup by changing their diet.[37] The apostle Matheus, who Andreas is sent to rescue, laments that in the Mermedonian prison he must "daeda fremman swa þa dumban neat" (66–67) [perform my deeds as cattle deprived of speech]. This is more than a figurative complaint; Matheus accurately predicts the physical metamorphosis that the cannibals require.

By referring to Mermedonian food practices as a "tacen," a signifier of their convivial way of life, the *Andreas* poet anticipates the aims of structuralist anthropology, likening social practices to systems of signification. To borrow a term from Mary Douglas, the poet experiments with a "grammar" of food that can transmit cultural and political messages in the details of a meal.[38] Cannibalism is the most obvious form of political appetite. In this man-eating repast, the appetitive energies of human social orders are manifested and rendered patently literal. Humans that usually battle for distinction and precedence here eat their weaker victims wholesale rather than just dominate them. The sovereign who normally grows fat off the labor-power of others, here actually engorges himself on human bodies. Yet this is no feeding frenzy: the Mermedonians eat their horrifying meals with decorum, participating in an organized though perverse event, in line with their meticulously ordered laws and customs. Michelet notes that these practices reassure the Mermedonians' "deep-seated fear . . . of losing the limits of one's personal identity," that is, actually becoming what one eats (to paraphrase Brillat-Sava-

---

36. Brian Shaw, "Translation and Transformation in *Andreas*," in *Prosody and Poetics in the Early Middle Ages: Essays in Honour of C. B. Hieatt.* ed. M. J. Toswell, 167.

37. See Albala, *Eating Right in the Renaissance,* for the ancient medicinal idea that bodily humors can be altered by diet: "You become what you eat. Just as you can acquire a taste for something, an aliment can be so thoroughly absorbed into the system that it alters the human fabric" (51).

38. Mary Douglas, "Deciphering a Meal," in *Implicit Meanings,* 231–51.

rin's most famous aphorism).[39] Their grammar of food joins cooking, writing, and the "fyrstgemearc" (931) [count of time] to forecast the awful transformation of their victims:

Hæfdon hie on rune   ond on rimcraefte
awriten, wælgrædige,   wera endestæf,
hwænne hie to mose   meteþearfendum
on þaere werþeode   weorðan sceoldon.
(134–37)

They, slaughter-greedy, had inscribed in both secret
letters and computation, the men's death-stick,
when their victims ought to be made into food
for the meat-lacking in that nation of men.

While perhaps not the literary equals of Matheus, who "ongan . . . god-spell ærest / wordum writan wundor-cræfte" (12–13) [first wordfully wrote with wondrous skill the Gospel], the Mermedonians are undeniably persuasive writers.[40] Their "death-stick" marks the progress of dehumanization. The runes slowly, inexorably erase the human lives they represent. This is a nightmare of signification, a cannibal language that tears itself apart. The death-stick, physically bound to each captive, also binds its victims to Mermedonian time and its thirty-day course of death. These unfortunates are doomed to be metabolized, not resurrected—to be torn to pieces by "blodigum ceaflum" (159) [bloody jaws] and consumed to die in an alien body, in an alien moment.

Food in *Andreas* is a politics of time. In chronicling human life in Mermedonia, the poem explores the political consequences of food choice that constitute social and metaphysical identity in a nation of consumers, and that place them into a trajectory of satiety and want. Selecting sustenance sets fundamental economies into motion and establishes a basic political ideal that violates the sacred culinary duty of host to guest. Even as the *Andreas* poet delights us with exotic customs and outrageous violence (both of cannibals and apostles), he aims to instruct. With all the gusto of St. Lawrence, the poet

---

39. Fabienne L. Michelet, "Eating Bodies in the Old English *Andreas*," in *Fleshly Things and Spiritual Matters: Studies on the Medieval Body in Honour of Margaret Bridges*," ed. Nicole Nyffenegger and Katrin Rupp, 189; Brillat-Savarin, *Le Physiologie de Goût*, 37.

40. See Christopher Fee for the use of productive and destructive forms of writing within *Andreas*. He links the Mermedonian "runes" ultimately to their practice of torture, a bodily inscription of another kind ("Productive Destruction: Torture, Text, and the Body in the Old English *Andreas*." *Essays in Medieval Studies* 11 [1994]: 59–60).

challenges the reader to digest the connection between eating and power in a convivial social order. Food imagery has narrative force in *Andreas*, just as food practice has political effect in society. The poem's "grammar" of food adumbrates the complexities of Christian and Mermedonian values, laws, and foreign policy. The apostles are tasked with modeling Christian behavior in foreign lands; they have a grave responsibility to be sinless, immaculate, orthodox. Yet Jesus unconcernedly—even teasingly—commands them to eat the food of strangers, to break the dietary rules, to risk defilement. This tension threatens to fracture the apostolic paradigm, as the impossible task of converting the Mermedonians makes clear. Andreas both demands and resists conviviality in his encounters with the Mermedonians. They, too, perceive a threat to their national identity in their bloody "incorporation" of foreigners. Their "error-craft" is contrived to set them apart from other cultures, even as self and other inhabit the same body.

Cannibals and apostles alike are plotted by the poem's volatile politics of time, hurled into epochal conflict, contending for spiritual and temporal dominance on a narrative battleground. There is a truce, however, if only a temporary one. During the poem's long oceanic interlude—when Andreas and a disguised Jesus travel to Mermedonia—narrative sword-play and culinary discord settle into an intimate after-dinner conversation that has the power to pass the impossible time and distance to Mermedonia.

3. PRESENTING PAST *SELVES*

The ocean in *Andreas* is a frenzy of figurative language, churning with its own ravenous appetites.[41] This world of "wæter-egsa" (375) [water-terror] and "gar-secg" (238) [spear-waves] teems with hungry creatures eager to feast upon human flesh. The "horn-fisc" (370) [horned fish] and "græga mæw / wælgifre" (371–72) [grey and slaughter-greedy gull] are watery versions of the "Beasts of Battle" that scavenge war scenes across Anglo-Saxon poetry, as also observed by Alexandra Hennessey Olsen.[42] The huge waves are "sæ-beorgas" (308) [sea-mountains] and powerful "eagor-streamas" (492) [water-currents] dredge the ocean floor, as if scouring up the secrets of the past. This tempest, however,

---

41. See Karin Olsen for a forceful invocation of the rapturous, "almost skaldic" power of the *Andreas* poet during the ocean scene ("The Dichotomy of Land and Sea in the Old English *Andreas*," *English Studies* 79 [1998]: 394).

42. See the introduction, n. 24, for the presence of the Beasts of Battle tradition in Anglo-Saxon poetry. Alexandra Hennessey Olsen remarks that the third beast is the "whale" in the kenning "hwælmere" found in line 370a ("Aesthetics of *Andreas*," 408–9).

belies arrestingly tranquil depths. Its wild poetic "flod-wylm" (516) [flood-welling] creates an unlikely narrative harmony: past, present, and future circulate in currents of dialogue. Oceanic turbulence displaces political unrest. The ship and the poem itself are becalmed suddenly in "coevality." Jesus himself (in maritime drag) presides over this interlude of shared time, a deft "steora" (495) [steersman] who breaks bread with his passengers as he glides the "famigheals" [foamy-necked] boat in graceful flight, "fugole gelicost" [very much like a bird] (497), across the roiling sea. His drolly self-referential discussion with Andreas is at once a catechism and a conversation—a reaffirmation of God's power over time, yet also a mutually enjoyable spinning of yarns. Here, sharing food is not the means of forcible conversion or assimilation. Instead, breaking bread bonds very different beings—divine and human—in amicable partnership.

This unlikely peace upon the seas inheres in the language of their unique conversation, which diverges from patterns of Anglo-Saxon dialogue. The *Andreas* poet's penchant for conversation is not unusual; Anglo-Saxon narrative poetry is rife with spoken exchange.[43] Yet these parleys are often furiously adversarial, sometimes a dramatic replacement for physical battle. The bristly preposition "wið" [against, opposite to] attaches obstinately to verbs of speaking, rendering any conversation into confrontation. This can be the case in *Andreas* as well (299–300; 1358–59). During the ocean voyage, however, this grammar of conflict has a unifying power. Jesus' repeated "wið-þingode" [addressed, made a speech] indicates a coming together of minds, in spite of the prepositional opposition. Jesus "wið-þingode" whenever he offers a boon to Andreas, whether passage on the ship, food, or his goodwill (263, 306, 632). The harmonizing power of the storm can overcome combative tendencies in the most elemental units of the poem's language.

Such rhapsodic juxtapositions animate the whole range of the sea-scene's narrative features, from syntax to metafiction. Upon the rough seas, poems jostle one another companionably across time. The *Andreas* poet explores the past of his own discourse, speaking directly to his predecessors in the Old English canon. *Beowulf*, in particular, appears in a series of witty and deliberate allusions that constitute an engaging conversation about the cultural values of both poems. The ship in *Andreas* sails straight out of the language

---

43. For example, the plot of *Guthlac A* is a series of flyting exchanges between a horde of devils and the warrior-saint. Guthlac promises them that he will only contest their aggression with a "leofran lace" (307) [a dearer sort of play], indicating he has punningly and self-referentially renounced violence (a *guð-lac*) in favor of verbal resistance (*Guthlac A*, in Muir, ed., *Exeter Anthology*, 111–39).

of *Beowulf,* laden as "splendidly" as King Scyld Scefing's funerary vessel and extolled by the same awe-struck narratorial voice:

> Æfre ic ne hyrde
> þon cymlicor   ceol gehladenne
> heah-gestreonum.   Hæleð in sæton,
> þeodnas þrymfulle,   þegnas wlitige.
> (*Andreas,* 360–63)

> I have never heard
> of a ship laden the more splendidly
> with such high-treasures. The heroes sat therein,
> glorious princes and proud thanes.

> Ne hyrde ic cymlicor   ceol gegyrwan
> hildewaepnum   ond headowaedum,
> billum ond byrnum.
> (*Beowulf,* 38–40)

> I've never heard of a ship equipped more splendidly
> with war-weapons and battle-shirts,
> with swords and with sarks.

These descriptions share the phrase "cymlicor ceol" and are nearly identical structurally, from their narrators' wondering protestations to their catalogues of treasures. Yet this is a delicately calibrated reference, not a formulaic repetition.[44] The *Andreas* poet engages *Beowulf* cannily in *Beowulf*'s voice. In this capacious, polyvocal language, materialistic pagan splendor meets virtuous poverty on the level of the word. Both vessels are heaped with "high treasures," but of very different sorts: the funeral barque brims with precious armor and weapons, while the treasures of *Andreas* are worthy men of abstinence and holy destitution. The shift from secular to spiritual value is, in part, a Christianizing revision. But the *Andreas* poet aspires to something more: to channel the aesthetic power of *Beowulf,* to foment spiritual life from the *materia* of death. As Scyld's bier drifts away into the obscurity of the heathen afterlife,

---

44. Rosemary Woolf contends that "the author of *Andreas* . . . flaunts his many borrowings from *Beowulf.* Lines or even pairs of lines are repeated for the sake of allusion rather than for their propriety in the new context" ("Saints' Lives," in *Continuations and Beginnings,* ed. Stanley, 51).

to be salvaged by an unknown race (50–52), the apostle voyages into clearer focus, out of the pagan darkness of Achaia, toward the assurance that his own martyrdom will be of value in the world.

In another instance, *Andreas* captures the abundance of its predecessor to evoke further the great value of holy impoverishment. The "lands and locked rings" (2995) with which Hygelac dazzlingly rewards Wulf and Eofor for their war-deeds become the resplendent generosity of the holy steersman who offers Andreas passage, though the apostle has neither "lands nor locked rings" (303). *Andreas* "converts" *Beowulf*'s worldliness, but it also digests *Beowulf*'s riches with relish—a metafictional meal to match the apostle's shipboard collation.[45]

Amid the mighty waters between Achaia and Mermedonia, in language that is itself a borderland between eras and texts, Andreas has the extraordinary experience of teaching while being taught by Jesus. The steersman asks for tales of Jesus' miracles, and the apostle obliges, relating many wondrous events he witnessed himself. As Andreas tells stories of his savior to his savior, the reader is treated to narrative magic—the miracles happen again. Tales of Jesus calming the waters (438–60), healing the sick (577–81), and feeding the hungry (589–94) have the power to nullify immediate dangers. The "lagu lacende" (437) [tossing waters] of the storm subside in response to the storytelling. The exchange between disciple and Jesus is at once a lesson for Andreas in God's power to alter time and space, a textbook case of conversion, and a coeval encounter.[46] In the charmed "now" of the sea-voyage, their palimpsestic dialogue enriches the present by rewriting wonders over their own histories. Miracles, like martyrdoms, gain power in retelling. They reverberate by repetition, transcending narrative and temporal constraints. The past shapes the urgencies of the present, just as the present reveals the contours of the past.

On the ocean, the politics of time become a nourishing and convivial commerce. The apostolic imperative operates perfectly here. The incorporation of the "foreign" steersman is neither violently appropriative nor a hor-

---

45. David Hamilton extols the borrowings of the *Andreas* poet, calling them collocations, and noting that the poem "takes significant liberties with an old story; the poet, however, matches adventuresomeness on some fronts with restraint in other matters" ("*Andreas* and *Beowulf*: Placing the Hero," in *Anglo-Saxon Poetry: Essays in Appreciation for John C. McGalliard*, ed. Lewis E. Nicholson and Dolores Warwick Frese, 96).

46. Angela Abdou describes the ocean-voyage as a micro-conversion that parallels the larger Mermedonian conversion narrative ("Speech and Power in Old English Conversion Narratives," *Florilegium* 17 [2000]: 198–99). Amity Reading argues that *Andreas*'s "fantasy of conversion ... is not the conversion of the 'other,' but rather the true conversion of the self" ("Baptism, Conversion, and Selfhood in the Old English *Andreas*," *Studies in Philology* 112 [2015]: 5).

rifying violation—for once, it is just dinner. Andreas needs a meal and the gracious steersman provides it, offering "mete" (366) [food] that comforts the disciples during the storm. This "son of peace" immediately makes good on his own promise. Amid ravenous cannibals and spiritual hungers, this is the only time anyone actually eats in *Andreas,* and it is a peaceful and edifying occasion. The steersman's kind gesture prompts Andreas to bless his benefactor, promising him "heofonlicne hlaf" (389) [heavenly bread] in the hereafter. This is a neat bit of convivial and theological clowning—Jesus is offered his own body in an ironic Eucharist—that highlights the political implications of the event. The circulation of food from lord to people binds together a Christian brotherhood in the joy of repletion, and creates a chain of satiety that will endure even in the afterlife. Food is a requirement of political bodies: satisfying bodily needs cements ideological bonds. With their bellies filled, Andreas's dispirited followers find the strength to profess their renewed allegiance to their leader (405–14).

In the course of his miraculous dialogue with Jesus, Andreas even talks himself out of doubt and disbelief. His bizarre tale of Jesus' animated statue, a mighty being that raises patriarchs from the dead to convert unbelievers, is also a confession of his own flagging self-confidence. If statues and reanimated corpses—impervious to fatigue, injury, doubt, and sin—can be Christian soldiers, then why does the Lord need frail, fallible human apostles? Both Andreas and Matheus are weak, liable to question their mission when it gets uncomfortable, prone to physical limitations and lapses in faith (63–87; 1401–2). Keenly aware that he could be served up for dinner in Mermedonia, Andreas fantasizes about an incomestible super-apostle. Surely a proselytizing army of angel statues could do the job more efficiently, without the human tendency to be martyred. Yet, as it happens, the statue fails to convert anyone, and it is this very invulnerability that spells its failure. Though impressively miraculous, the statue cannot share a meal with a foreigner; it cannot sacrifice its life for its faith. The frailty and fallibility that Andreas fears will compromise his mission to Mermedonia are the very qualities that the statue lacks. The fragile body of the apostle who "frið lædan" (174) [conducts his peace] into danger is the secret weapon of conversion.[47]

A kindly Jesus prompts Andreas to recite this phantasmagoric miracle in order to encourage the apostle to lay to rest the specter of his self-doubt. Yet the legend of the statue has a dark double meaning that preaches disjunction and animosity even as it reaffirms the value of human relationships. The story

---

47. Hamilton notes the repeated motif of Andreas bearing his body or peace into battle ironically recasts similar language from *Beowulf,* where the warrior-hero instead bears weapons ("Diet and Digestion of Allegory," 148).

is haunted by ethnic hatred that catapults *Andreas* back into its own contentious present, while intimating that these conflicts have always been present. It is the apostle's response to the friendly steersman's jarringly hopeful curiosity about the anti-Semitic nature of Jesus' miracles; he asks if they are designed specifically to punish Jewish "deop gedwola" (611) [deep heresy]. This is a traumatic tonal shift: the tale is a harsh injunction to its audience (both Andreas's disciples and the reader) to oppose and oppress the Jews. The statue, which adorns a Jewish temple, ventriloquizes Christian doctrine and then places the same message in the mouths of the reanimated patriarchs, twice appropriating Jewish history and culture to the Christian triumphal march. Hermann notes the circularity of this scene: "The narrative invents the miracles which sustain and authenticate it."[48] Venerated Hebrew architecture and ancestors alike are made to proclaim their own supersession by new historical forces. Even the dead foresee the course of events and subsume themselves into its triumph.[49]

The statue story is a grim teleology of oppression that sends shockwaves through time: a past miracle crystallizes contemporary Christian hostility toward the Jews and anticipates the genocide of the Mermedonians. The statue creates a "mearclond" in which its patriarchs must cross in order to "edniwinga andweard cuman" (783) [come forth into the present renewed], trapped between faiths, and between life and death. Likewise, Andreas's retelling sparks a temporal and narrative rift, unmooring the poem from the blissful ocean of "shared time." The statue story's bitter oppositions replace the generative union of texts and times. It carries the apostles from Jesus' magical geography, where literary canons and gaps in faith are navigated deftly as they fly across a vast ocean with incredible speed, to the Mermedonian "mearclond," daunting in its oppressive nearness to and unassailable distance from all they hold dear.

The tempestuous voyage is an eye in the ideological storm of *Andreas*, a fleeting moment of peace and spiritual insight for its troubled hero. Yet Jesus' very accessibility on the ship, as a friendly, unintimidating interlocutor and guide, proposes that this is a fantastic voyage—a utopia impossible to replicate in the terrestrial world of the poem. Sharing food or time with the Mermedonians will be much more difficult with only Andreas present to facilitate the sharing. Worse, Jesus' anti-Semitic vituperations hint that there may be peoples who exist beyond the pale of the apostolic imperative, who may be

---

48. Hermann, *Allegories of War*, 128.
49. Denis Ferhatović relates the angel statue's animation to a form of divinely ordained *spolium*: "An angel-likeness wrenched from its immediate architectural context, calls up the Old Testament heroes who themselves will be the spoils after Christ's Harrowing of Hell" ("Spolia-Inflected Poetics of the Old English *Andreas*," *Studies in Philology* 110 [2013]: 211).

indigestible into the Christian brotherhood. Like the Jews of the statue legend, the Mermedonians may have sinned beyond measure. Perhaps it is this sinful nature that renders dialogue with either nation ineffective.

When Andreas leaves the ship, his own dialogue breaks down. Upon their arrival, Jesus, now in the shape of a child, chastises Andreas sternly for the same doubts that, as the steersman, he gently and patiently tries to assuage. While on the ship, Andreas is thrilled to relate the Christian Word in dialogue, to treat his "convert" as his equal, even his "hyse leofesta" (595) [dearest lad]. On land, he yearns for conquest as well as conversion, glorying in his bloody extirpation of the Mermedonians, perhaps even seeing in it a prefiguration of Christianity's ultimate victory over its Jewish past. Yet his frenetic urge for triumph at any cost will drive him away without satisfying his new converts' need. Eager for his next mission, Andreas will leave the Mermedonians on the verge of relapse and renunciation.

4. A TERRIBLE SYMPOSIUM

The apostle wrestles with coevality as Fabian's anthropologists do. The ocean interlude teaches Andreas the importance of sharing time; it also points to the difficulties of doing so. Foreign peoples may hold fast to their own timekeeping in the face of a Christian present, denying its dominance, like the Hebrew high priests who face down the miraculous statue. The most obstinate nonconformers may even attempt to impose their own chronologies upon Christians by force, as Mermedonians do when they torture Andreas. The apostle effects their conversion at last—everyone is at least nominally Christian in the end. Yet Andreas denies coevality even after he forces the various time-schemes of the poem into alignment, spending the rest of the mission rebuffing the connection he went to such ferocious lengths to create. Andreas does not connect with the anthropophagic Mermedonians by sharing words or food with them—thereby dodging the impertinent question of what would be served on the table. Instead, the poem veers into the more familiar territory of hagiographic romance—torture, devils, miracles, and death—to achieve its narrative climax.

The final movement of *Andreas* travesties the apostolic imperative, ironizing the instructions of Jesus that it deliberately invokes. The Mermedonians are anything but the "sons of peace": their interaction with the apostle is war from the moment he arrives. Andreas, rendered invisible by God, is a holy tornado, breaking open the prison, killing the guards, and freeing hundreds of captives. No food passes between them, and even the terms of exchange are deranged: the Mermedonians, not Andreas, attempt to "eat what is set before them." Starving without their human livestock, they consume their dead guards and then try to devour one of their own children. Amid this hungry chaos, Andreas must experiment with new and increasingly brutal methods of conversion, by suffering the cannibals' wrath and by inflicting his own upon them. The Mermedonians subject him to three days of torture, and these horrors nearly break his faith in the Lord's plan: "Is me feorh-gedal / leofre mycle þonne þeos lif-cearo" (1477–78) ["Life's severance is much / more desirable to me than this living sorrow"], he complains to the Almighty.

Yet tactics and tastes change in Andreas's favor on the fourth day, when God heals his wounds and makes trees and flowers bloom everywhere his blood has been spilled. This Eden springs to life in the dead of winter—a gloriously unseasonal victory for Christian chronology over the pagan "count of time" (1448–49). Mermedonia, it seems, is truly a land of latent plenty, with abundant natural resources to feed godly appetites. Andreas himself benefits from a wealth of ancient stones littering Mermedonia: from his dungeon window, the battered apostle finally effects his escape and his revenge with the aid of sentient stone columns just outside, "wundrum fæste / under sæl-wange . . . eald enta geweorc" (1492–95) [wondrously rooted beneath / the plains of time . . . the old work of giants].[50] He commands the stones to break open and pour forth "wæter wid-rynig to wera cwealme" (1507) [wide-streaming waters as a slaughtering of men], drowning the Mermedonians in a deadly flood. Like Andreas's story of the animated stone statue, this miracle is intended to shock the reader into a reverence of divine power and to compel conversion every time it is repeated. The very stones submit themselves to the triumphal forces of God when hostile humans will not—a contrast implicitly created by the presence of the obedient "marman-stan" (1498) [marble stone] as opposed to the land of "Marmedonia" as it is spelled three times in the poem (264, 844, 1676).

The responsiveness of the ancient stones suggests that time itself is tractable—that history serves the dominant side in the struggle for supremacy. The columns are the "eald enta geweorc" [old work of giants]; this phrase is a formulaic expression of awe with which numerous Anglo-Saxon poems evoke the uncanny appearance and improbable survival of ancient ruins, remnants of a sublimely remote past that cannot be assimilated fully through narrative or

---

50. I retain the manuscript's "sæl-wange" instead of the common emendation to "sælwage" [wall of the hall]. "Sælwage" is a highly improbable usage (it occurs nowhere else in the Anglo-Saxon canon), while "sæl-wongas" appears once in *Genesis A* and twice in the *Exeter Book Riddles*. The outdoor connotations of "sal-wange" are more consistent with the stone columns' "storm-battered" appearance (1494). Most importantly, the emendation ignores a provocative, unusual, richly suggestive kenning that rings true to the *Andreas* poet's unique voice.

nostalgia.⁵¹ In *Andreas*, however, the ruined columns (*stapulas, sweras*) grow in the "sæl-wange" or "plains of time," reactive to present stimuli as if they were alive. The living, regenerating condition of these Mermedonian stones complicates the melancholic picture of ruination presented by R. M. Liuzza: "Ruins represent the obliteration of memory, the end of the arc of civilization in a crumbling pile of forgotten rubble. They are a figure of the anxiety of history itself, of being forever perched on the mute lip of oblivion."⁵² In *Genesis A* or the *Wanderer*, broken stones only communicate a discontinuity between past and present, at this moment of *Andreas*, however, similar monuments of time respond to the "now" of divine revelation. They seem to exemplify what Renée R. Trilling invokes as "simultaneity rather than linearity; the past may be something separate and foreign, but it is something that constitutes a part of the present as well."⁵³ The pastness of these stones is undeniably present, and their presence pushes them toward a future of activity, of redefinition through their heeding of God's call. "Sael," meaning both "time" and "season," shares a stem with "sælþ" [prosperity], a resonance evoking the harvest of plenty to be gained by well-budgeted time. Andreas reaps the fruit of the "plains of time," interpellating the stones into a Christianizing narrative that marshals the "fyrndagas" [days of yore] to his cause. Here, the well-worn *topos* of "old work of giants" no longer signifies an unattainable, inscrutable past: the apostle recuperates the ruins by uniting them to their usefulness in the present moment.⁵⁴ In their dramatic answer to the apostle's call, the revivified pillars obediently pour forth a flood that disrupts and reestablishes temporal and cultural continuities.

Andreas's murderous miracle is unexpectedly irreverent in its shocking twist of metaphoric register, recalling St. Lawrence as well as outdoing him. The comic anarchy invoked by the apostle's adventures in Mermedonia reaches a crescendo in *Andreas* with the crashing arrival of the deadly flood:

> Stream ut aweoll,
> fleow ofer foldan.   Famige walcan
> mid ær-dæge   eorðan þehton

---

51. The concordance to the *Dictionary of the Old English Corpus* cites instances of "enta [ar]geweorc" in *Beowulf* (1679, 2717, and 2774) and in three later texts: *The Wanderer* (87), the *Ruin* (2), and *Maxims II* (2).

52. R. M. Liuzza, "The Tower of Babel: *The Wanderer* and the Ruins of History," *Studies in the Literary Imagination* 36 (2003): 14.

53. Renée R. Trilling, *The Aesthetics of Nostalgia: Historical Representation in Old English Verse*, 51.

54. Ferhatović, in comparing *Andreas*'s use of the ancient stones to medieval practices of "spoliation," discerns a relationship in these mineral images to the poem's own practices of literary plunder ("Spolia-Inflected Poetics," 215).

myclade mere-flod. Meodu-scerwen wearð
æfter symbel-dæge, slæpe tobrugdon
searu-hæbbende.
. . . .
   Fæge swulton,
geonge on geofene guð-ræs fornam
þurh sealtne swelg. Þæt wæs sorg-byrþen,
biter beor-þegu. Byrlas ne gældon,
ombeht-þegnas. Þær wæs ælcum genog
fram dæges orde drync sona gearu.
(1523–35)

   Rushing water gushed out,
flowed over the earth. Foamy billows covered the ground
by early day, as the watery-flood amassed.
A mead-service was made after the feast-day,
the armor-havers torn from their slumber
. . . .
Doomed they died, the young taken away by the ocean's sortie,
by the salty abyss. That was a sorrowful brewing,
a bitter beer-taking. The cup-bearers delayed not,
the attending servants. There was enough
drink immediately ready for all from the start of day.

It is a beer-party, not a shared meal, that finally converts the Mermedonians, combining catastrophe and the imagery of what Wilcox describes as "a really heavy drinking session."[55] Paul Battles takes this identification with conviviality even further, noting the kindred nature of this moment to other "Sleeping after the Feast" scenes in Old English literature to present a picture of an Anglo-Saxon thematic commonplace.[56] Yet such a commonplace is invoked here to heighten the tension and shock of the scene: in *Andreas* it is a canny repetition that approaches the parodic.[57] These "foamy billows" are at once comically incongruous and terrifyingly destructive—we are meant to chuckle and also flinch at this "mead-service" gone horribly wrong. Critics have attempted to resolve this perverse bifurcation of imagery and action into typo-

---

  55. Wilcox, "Eating People Is Wrong," 215.
  56. Paul Battles, "Dying for a Drink: 'Sleeping After the Feast' Scenes in *Beowulf, Andreas*, and the Old English Poetic Tradition," *Modern Philology* 112 (2015): 435–57.
  57. Brooks disapproves of this imagistic excess here: "This metaphor is elaborated to point of absurdity in 1533ff." (*Andreas and the Fates of the Apostles*, 114).

logical parallels: between the flood and baptism or a vengeful God's "bitter drink."[58] Andreas tailors his miracle to be a perverse act of lordly largesse. The Mermedonians are miserable and peaceless precisely because they do not possess liquor to lubricate conviviality. The good life—the "sele-dreamas" (1656) [joys of the hall]—is fueled by drink, and it is the lord's task to keep his thanes' glasses full. In Anglo-Saxon literature, imbibing alcohol signifies victory and prosperity as well as the warm comforts of the warrior-band. Here, where the "sad-minded" Mermedonians can imbibe only human blood, liquor is deadly: the people drown in a cataclysm of drink that leaves their barren lands even more desolate than before. The flood descends in a dirty, beery, brown-yellow "fealone stream" (1538) [fallow stream]—as if the Mermedonians' agricultural unproductivity has come back to haunt them.

The poem's imagery turns upon this catastrophic "meodu-scerwen," a *hapax legomenon* of tantalizing possibilities. The *Bosworth-Toller Dictionary* speculates that "scerwen" could mean "scattering," "sharing," or "giving" ("serving" is the usual English translation); yet the word also resonates with a verb that is almost its opposite: "bescerwen" [to deprive]. The righteous apostle's "scerwen" of mead offers salvation while it guarantees death to the Mermedonians; its cloying sweetness is at once a "biter beor-þegu" [bitter beer-taking]. The *Andreas* poet may have chosen this multivalent term for its capaciousness. It encompasses the complexities of the poem's troubled perspective on conversion, which conflates religious unification and cultural dispossession, commensality and cannibalism, spiritual enlightenment and persecution.

With typical allusive alacrity, the *Andreas* poet intensifies these narrative and linguistic multiplicities by inviting *Beowulf* to the feasting. *Beowulf* contains the only other instance of "scerwen" in Anglo-Saxon literature; as in *Andreas*, the context is a perverse outpouring of drink.[59] As the Danes quiver outside of Heorot, listening to the terrible din of Beowulf's fight with Grendel, they quaff an "ealuscerwen" (769) [(terrible) serving of ale]. The same liquor that braces their bravery in the hall unites them now in convivial terror. They are immersed in the sobering fear that Beowulf will fail, as well as in shame at

---

58. "Bitter drink" is found in *Isaiah* 24:9. The baptismal link is made by Hill ("Figural Narrative in *Andreas*," 265–68) and Sister Marie Michelle Walsh ("The Baptismal Flood in the Old English *Andreas*: Liturgical and Typological Depths," *Traditio* 33 [1977]: 137–58). Albert Stanburrough Cook makes the connection between the flood and Isaiah's metaphor for God's wrath ("Bitter Beer-Drinking," *MLN* 40 [1925]: 286–87).

59. As several critics have concluded, as does Robert M. Lumiansky, "The Contexts of Old English '*ealuscerwen*' and '*meoduscerwen*,'" *JEGP* 48 (1949): 116–26. See Harvey DeRoo for a particularly thorough affirmation of this ("Two Old English Fatal Feast Metaphors: *Ealuscerwen* and *Meoduscerwen*." *English Studies in Canada* 5 (1979): 249–61. In either article, the context of *Beowulf* seems rather more interesting than that of *Andreas*, which appears simpler to interpret.

their own inaction. The Mermedonians, also, communally suffer a bitter reckoning in the honeyed irony of the "meodu-scerwen." They can only be a normative social body as they drown in the sweetest and most social of drinks.

The flood that overwhelms the Mermedonians has the effect of normalizing them religiously (as Christians) and also gustatorially (as mead-drinkers). As Magennis notes, drinking typifies literary Anglo-Saxon hall-feasting, even to the exclusion of cooking or eating.[60] The miraculous and devastating intervention of the flood will teach the Mermedonians who to worship and how to drink. The Christian believer can take grim satisfaction in the gushing waters' melodramatic delivery of justice, which redresses not only Mermedonian cannibalism but also Andreas's torture. Yet the reader is flooded with sheer sensational pleasure as well: the poet means for us to savor his material, comestible approach to the rarified conceptual heights of doctrine and divinity, of politics and time.

Analogues to *Andreas* do not share its refined palate. They linger over the deadly saltiness of the water, that is so "exceedingly brackish" that it "consumed human flesh," searing the meat from the Mermedonians' bones in a wickedly fitting end.[61] In *Andreas*, on the other hand, it is the flood's conflicting flavors that generate its manifold horrors. The alternations from cloyingly sweet to salty to bitter create an image of multifarious, gustatory lack—we savor a complex palate of everything that the Mermedonians do not have yet are in the process of losing.

The flood is a total cultural annihilation—"death-sticks" and "peaceless signs," "frightful drinks" and "error-craft" are erased, and with them would seem to go the poem's anthropological preoccupations. Instead, the *Andreas* poet turns an ethnographic lens upon his own culture's drinking rituals, in counterbalance to the details of Mermedonian cannibalism. As the Mermedonian "mead-service" rages, an Anglo-Saxon "feast-day" proceeds apace in all its lively elements, from "brewing," to "cup-bearing" by "attending servants," and finally to lordly "beer-taking," with "drink immediately ready for all." This etiquette of Anglo-Saxon conviviality invokes the food practices of the present to subsume the cannibalistic past, right down to the cup-bearing lackeys of the well-appointed mead-hall. The flood renders these boozy conventions magnificent and awful: God himself ratifies the drinking practices of Anglo-

---

60. Magennis, *Anglo-Saxon Appetites*, 11. He cites several feast scenes in *Beowulf* where revelers drink but do not eat. In *Judith*, Holofernes pours massive quantities of drink upon his thanes at the feast, but offers them no food.

61. J. K. Elliott, ed., *The Apocryphal New Testament: A Collection of Apocryphal Christian Literature in an English Translation*, 297. This detail is echoed in the Latin *Recensio Casanatensis* and in the Old English "Legend of St. Andrew."

Saxon heroic literature, and punishes the noncompliant Mermedonians for their lack of spirit.

5. FEEDING MERMEDONIA

Something about the end of *Andreas* does not taste right. There is a climactic feast in Mermedonia, but it leaves everyone hungry. The earth itself yawns open to "forswealg" (1590) [swallow] the floodwaters, along with fourteen of the most vicious Mermedonians, the "þæs weorodes . . . ða wyrrestan" (1592) [the worst of that nation]. This seismic act of consumption forecloses the possibility of further eating. The geologic convulsion catalyzes a narrative one: the vibrant juxtaposition of food practices that drives the poem's jostling plots vanishes entirely. Food is the stuff of peace and peacelessness between the peoples of *Andreas*: coeval camaraderie, conversionary machinations, oceanic tête-a-têtes, unholy carnage, and holy vengeance are all contingent upon the menu at hand. When there is no food—to eat, to cook, to share, or to withhold—these partnerships and power hierarchies break down. Without exchanges of food, Christian brotherhood is unsubstantiated, and even victor and vanquished are hard to determine.

The flood appears to wash animosity away quite neatly. The Mermedonians, docile and suddenly willing to convert, are struck suddenly by the "gumcystum" (1606) [manly virtues] of their sainted prisoner. As the floodwaters recede from his feet, the liberated apostle steps forth to return the favor, resurrecting all but the worst fourteen. An entire nation is reborn in its new faith. This revivifying resolution seems a resounding victory for the apostle, a transformation of the anthropophagic past that extends even to the future. In bringing the Mermedonians back to life, Andreas triumphs over Satan himself, as Jesus will do at the end of days. Yet this resplendent finale does not stick to the ribs; it may be doctrinally satisfying, but the Mermedonians never receive a new diet to go with their new religion.

Their frantic hunger, that drives them to become literal "sylf-ætan" (175)—to eat their own children and dead (1088–92), to abandon all the sacred details of their food rituals—becomes a conspicuous nonissue when they are converted. They never break the bread of Christian brotherhood; they never receive a first Communion. They *are* baptized, quite thoroughly, and on the very spot where "se flod onsprang" (1635) [the flood burst forth]—this is perhaps the favorite irreverent joke of the *Andreas* poet, who gleefully connects the language of baptism and the "flodes fær" (1629) [flood's fear] four times in fourteen lines (630–43). Mermedonia becomes a "winburg" (1637) [wine-town] of distinctly "mod-geomre" (1706) [mournful-hearted] and "meteþearfendum" (27) [meat-lacking] conviviality. Without some new savor to replace their former predilections, what hope do these people have for salvation? How can the Mermedonians remain in the Christian present?

These questions have more urgency for the reader than for Andreas. The apostle, who spoke so feelingly of Jesus' food miracles as the bedrock of Christian community, has other plans—grimly eager for the "sawul-gedal" and "beadu-cwealm" (1701–2) [soul-parting and battle-death] that await him in Achaia. Not only is Andreas reluctant to obey the Lord's command to voyage to Mermedonia, he begs to leave as well and has to be nudged by God to "getimbre" (1671) [betimber] the converts in their new faith. He plants a church on the ruins of Mermedonian temples, yet never plants a seed. He "gedwolan fylde" (1688) [fells their errors]—targeting the "error-craft" by which they prepared meals—yet never teaches them to hunt, fish, or farm. Andreas appoints a Mermedonian bishop because he is "wordes gleawne" (1648) [wise of words], yet the bishop, like the apostle himself, never articulates a new "feorh-raed" (1654) [plan of life] to his congregation. Andreas has the gift of Pentecost—a means of universal communication, a way to meet the Mermedonians on their own terms. He uses this precious ability, however, only to spy on them (1129–48), or to squabble with the occasional devil (1184–94). He is careful not to speak to the Mermedonians after their conversion, a conspicuous omission in a poem where dialogue is synonymous with joy and the equivalent of dramatic action. Now, when it seems like he might be able to spark a new conversation, to enjoy the connection that he has had to enforce, Andreas holds himself aloof from his formerly "wæl-grædig" (134) [slaughter-greedy] flock and the lingering pollution of their former sins.

With nothing to eat, the relationships that Christianity is supposed to foster and make delightful falter and fail. The Mermedonians have lost all the creature comforts of their own "fyrst-gemearces" (148) [count of time], and Andreas is unwilling to lead them in a new reckoning. He does not or cannot complete their conversion, and the reader is left to wonder how the ex-cannibals will sustain their "niowan gefean" (1670) [new joys]. The Mermedonians are unsettled and unsated in their newly "beorhtan byrig" (1649) [bright city]. Their individual bodies, and cultural body, are left in a state of becoming, still hungry for the fulfillment of conversion (and maybe still hungry for people). Their moods are peculiarly volatile for a nation supposed to be exulting in bliss. They do exult, "cleopodon on corðre" (1716) [crying out in chorus], yet they are just as likely to "gað geomriende, geohðo mænað / weras wif samod" (1665–66) [go about groaning. They show their sorrow, / Men and women alike]. As they "hweorfan hige-bliðe fram hell-trafum . . . / to fægeran gefean

(1691–93) [turn heart-glad from hell-houses to sweet joys], they send up a "wop" (1666) [wailing]; they are "murnende" [mournful] in "hyge," "mod," and "ferðlocan" (1664–71) [mind, spirit, soul-close].

The *Andreas* poet positively revels in this paradox of a people "witum aspedde" (1631) [made prosperous in punishment]. These exquisite ironies are louder than the apostle's speechless victory; the romantic indeterminacy of the poem's final scenes resists the doctrinal triumph that its hagiographic plot must impose. While we are encouraged to ruminate piously upon the victory of Andreas, to celebrate his "manly virtues," the poet means also to exhilarate and to challenge the reader with a cunning language of uncertainties that draws us into the Mermedonians' plight. We have our own ghoulish appetites that are frustrated when the sensational narrative flood abates, when church-building and bishop-hiring replace delicious cross-plots of talking statues, fantastic voyages, reanimated corpses—and all the culinary bizarrerie that interlaces them. *Andreas* appears to put aside romance to carry out its missionary responsibility of harrowing the Mermedonian "measuring field." Neither the Mermedonians nor the reader, however, can fully metabolize this civilizing transformation. We find ourselves sharing a moment of spiritual and narrative ambivalence with the erstwhile eaters of men, marooned between faiths and between genres. As the Mermedonians are without food, so the reader is left without cannibalistic thrills. This is no abandonment of romance, however—the poem's sympathetic portrayal of its man-eating victims constitutes its final, sensational twist. Romance is a genre of desire and dilation, of episodes that multiply and endings that are invitations to further storymaking. *Andreas* teases expectation to court speculation: the temptation to share in anthropophagic feasts becomes an invitation to discover new sources of sustenance and satisfaction.

This exuberant irresolution persists amid the final exultations like a conversation that the poet is reluctant to end. *Andreas* concludes in several registers at once: its prescient and perspicacious hagiographic romance explores ramifications of cultural encounter that have preoccupied theorists from the Middle Ages to the twentieth century. Like Bede, the *Andreas* poet recognizes that the history of Christianization is an expansive story of missteps and lateral motions; in other words, that it is essentially romantic. Bede acknowledges— despite his fervent wishes—that the English peoples' spiritual transfiguration is imperiled by the proximity of their deeply ingrained pagan past, which emerges whenever and wherever it can, even when time itself stands against it. Like Fabian, the *Andreas* poet characterizes the meeting of "civilization" and "savagery" as a pulse of attraction and repulsion, as a simultaneous desire for and denial of "coevality." The poem proposes that conversion must be a bipartisan politics of time—conversational, not coerced—but that this connection is impossible to maintain. Each side wishes to know the other, but only after enforcing their own terms of contact. The Mermedonians subject their foreign victims to a brutal process of domestication and harvest, just as Andreas drowns them in the flood. In either case, the coevality achieved is perverse and cannot last. The cannibals and the apostles will soon need another victim. Fabian's term connotes a connection that is powerful yet delicate, tempting yet discomfiting, longed-for yet unsustainable—like the fraught and fragile bond of Andreas and his cannibal converts. Even Christianity does not bring with it a utopic time of mutual brotherhood, of joyous expectation in the hereafter. This friction between Christian brotherhood and crusading imperialism is an inescapable part of coevality, a sore spot that cannot be healed. In order to combat the "freoðoleas tacen" (29) [peaceless sign] of the Mermedonians, Andreas wields his own defining symbol—the cross—in an equally belligerent manner.[62] Violence characterizes the encounter driven by ecclesiastical imperialism, leaving a mournful people in its wake. Christianity brings death to the exotic nation, and their newly built church commemorates the scene of trauma.

There is something missing from the Mermedonians' lives, something that a new religion cannot provide. A sense of historical continuity is lacking, a bridge from their anthropophagite past to their resurrected present. What traditions will the Mermedonians bring forward into their renewal to render themselves complete? Their final song of praise, sung as Andreas sails away, may hold a clue:

An is ece god eallra gesceafta!
Is his miht ond his æht ofer middan-geard
breme gebledsod, ond his blæd ofer eall
in heofon-þrymme halgum scineð,
wlitige on wuldre to widan ealdre,
ece mid englum. þæt is æðele cyning!
(1717–22)

Alone is Eternal God among of all creation!
His might and his possession is celebrated, blessed
across Middle-Earth, and his reward shines
over all holy things in heavenly majesty,

---

62. The idea of the Cross as a literal weapon of war is a central feature of *Elene*. The Emperor Constantine achieves victory in battle against immense odds due to this replica of the True Cross—brought to him in a prophetic dream—that he bears before his army (105–13).

beautiful in glory for the length of life,
eternal among angels—*That* is a worthy king!

Recalling Cædmon in Bede's tale of the generation of sacred English poetry, the Mermedonians' hymn combines Christian sentiment with vernacular verse patterns in much the same way that *Andreas* itself has done. This report of direct speech therefore does not stand out the way that the marginal glosses that record the language of "Cædmon's Hymn" in several manuscripts of the *Historia Ecclesiastica* do, but the performance is still there, preserved for future ages.[63] Like the illiterate cowherd's sacred song, this verse comes unlooked-for from the desperate and miserable, formerly anthropophagite Mermedonians, near miraculous in its apparent joy. Yet its final line suggests a very different sentiment. It alludes to a refrain in *Beowulf*—"Þæt wæs god cyning" (11, 863, et al.) [that was a good king] that often refers to Hrothgar with probable irony—the monster-plagued king's power to rule is certainly questionable. The Mermedonians seem to end the story by mocking the very religion they espouse and the apostle who represents it.

In this remarkable bit of metafiction, the *Andreas* poet's method of composition is adopted by the Mermedonians as they search for some sort of cultural continuity between their old and new lives. The gap left in the cannibals' existence reminds the reader that *Andreas* itself is a cultural amalgam, a bricolage of disparate cultural sources. From *Beowulf* to the Bible, from Latin theology to Greek romance, the *Andreas* poet manipulates worlds of influence in order to construct his text. The Mermedonian *sylf-ætan* are left in a position analogous to the author's and also the reader's, yearning to consolidate and reconcile the contradictions in their identity. The sharply ironic channeling of *Beowulf*'s "worthy king" is the poet's extraordinary means of honoring the Mermedonians' hunger for the past, even as they must subsume—or consume—that past into their Christian future. Consuming the self is not only culturally generative but also capable of constructing dazzling poetry that searches out how to express the anxiety of existing upon a tapestry of history.

For Anglo-Saxon poets, this anxiety can be eased by imaginatively recombining an array of Germanic, classical, and Christian cultural materials into evocative wholes that communicate the terms of inheriting these diverse treasures responsibly. But to create these Gothic stews of texts and traditions, one must first be famished for cultural integration. The Mermedonians, at this

---

63. For "Caedmon's Hymn," see the Venerable Bede, *The Ecclesiastical History of the English People*, ed. Judith McClure and Roger Collins, trans. Bertram Colgrave, 4.xxiv.215–18. For the marginal glosses recording the English version of the hymn, see the Leningrad Bede (Saint Petersburg, National Library of Russia Lat. Q v I. 18).

final moment, become the *Andreas* poet's ideal readers: self-aware consumers unwilling to be satisfied with promises of joy, desiring sustenance *now*, and bringing their culture into the present in new forms.

The generative potential of a ruined Mermedonian culture is a glimmering light illuminating the otherwise gloomy pall that characterizes the conclusion of *Andreas*. The apostle leaves them to fend for themselves, to feed themselves through the dark season of their conversion. The poem itself seems uncertain of the benefits of imposing an ideology it so belligerently advocates. There is even a grim suggestion not only that Andreas's mission has failed, but even that this failure is what he has desired all along. Keeping the Mermedonians hungry—or keeping them cannibals—conveniently displaces the apostle's own violent appetites, a desire for romantic savagery akin to our own imperialistic thirst for cannibals at the margins of civilization. Perhaps Andreas is as "freoðoleas" as his erstwhile anthropophagite flock, his bloodthirsty tastes for conversion and conquest elided by their outrageous hunger. The poem operates at the intersection of food and politics, proposing a potential for a world drawn together by food, yet aware that it is more often torn asunder. The apostolic imperative—the recipe for cultural unification—proves to be divisive in *Andreas*. There is no feast to be had by the former rivals, no convivial connections. And there is no appeasement of Andreas's drive for incorporation. This gluttony for power stands in the way of cultural togetherness. Flowers and trees may bloom from the saint's spilled blood; yet it is still winter in Mermedonia, and there is nothing to eat.

The next chapter in this study proceeds from *Andreas*'s jaundiced perspective on human unification through food, and further examines the idea that food and cooking are themselves signs of a fundamental schism between modern humanity and the world it inhabits. This is a notion well known in medieval culture from accounts of the Ovidian and Hesiodic Golden Age, when mankind ate freely without harming or manipulating the earth—a time of innocent consumption destined not to last. Its deterioration animates the ironic convolutions of Heldris de Cornuälle's *Roman de Silence*, the story of a woman cross-dressed as a knight who must cook to capture a bestial Merlin. Cooked food in *Silence* becomes the symbol of the masculine, the aristocratic, and the human. The very idea of "Nature," typically marshaled to underwrite the superiority of these categories, is revealed to mean nothing without the intervention of "Noreture" (nurture or culture) to give it definition, even to make it expressible.

CHAPTER 2

The Roman de Silence

Crossing Categories

> On devient cuisinier, mais on naît rôtisseur
>
> We can learn to be a cook, but we must be born a roaster.
> —Brillat-Savarin, *The Physiology of Taste*

1. NATURE WITHOUT NOURETURE

"NATURE PASSE nourriture / et nourriture survainc nature" [Nature surpasses nurture / but nurture vanquishes nature],[1] declares a thirteenth-century proverb that reads like a severely condensed inspiration for Heldris de Cornuälle's *Roman de Silence* (ca. 1275).[2] Both explore the tension between birth and environment in the development of the individual self, as the two sides of this equation battle for supremacy over human destiny. What the old adage proposes in two chiastic, mutually negating clauses, Heldris explores for more than 6,700 lines that chronicle the adventures of Silence—a biological woman cross-dressed as a knight, who exceeds all others in chivalric virtue, yet is unjustly accused of raping a queen and punished by being forced to tame a feral Merlin. What is cleanly expressed in the proverb is untidy and frustrating in the romance, which alternately favors Nature and "Noureture" [nurture, culture] in arguments that are no sooner stated than reversed by a chatty, interfering, sententious narrator who enjoys contradicting his own precepts and interpretations. *Silence* offers no way out of the conflict of heredity versus

---

1. *Le Livre des Proverbes Francais*, ed. M. LeRoux de Lincy, 2.352.

2. Citations from the *Roman de Silence* are from *Silence: A Thirteenth-Century French Romance*, ed. and trans. Sarah Roche-Mahdi, in consultation with *Le Roman de Silence*, ed. Lewis Thorpe, and Felix Lecoy's emendations of Thorpe ("Le Roman de Silence," *Romania* 99 [1978]: 109–25).

education—any sort of resolution is lost in its recursions. After rehearsing the slippery dichotomy exhaustively, the romance appears to reject its own surprising revelations regarding the fluidity—and concomitant equality—of gender. The poem's final lines are a decidedly unsatisfying conclusion; a bombastic, misogynistic tirade ostensibly directed at the wicked queen Eufeme that seems an abandonment of the exemplary life story of Silence. The narrator acts as though the good deeds and virtuous conduct of Silence have never happened, focusing avidly instead upon the gruesome punishment of Queen Eufeme (she is "a chevals detraite" [6656] [dragged apart by horses]). Eufeme's faults and her own cross-dressing transgressions (she has a male lover disguised as a nun) become the faults of all women, including Silence, who by now is stripped of her masculine garb, her body purged of its maleness—once a powerful knight, now only a bride. Perhaps this is why the narrator ignores her here. He complains that the only way any woman can be "good" in society is to act contrary to her nature, to be led by Noureture away from her inherent *malvaise*—but also that the kind of "nurturing" or education women are most likely to receive will only vitiate them further. This paradoxical protestation—abruptly at odds with the narrator's admiration of the masculinized Silence throughout the poem—is an act of deliberate irresolution that proposes an unlikely solution. The narrator's final hope is that the category-crossing work of the poem will continue outside its bounds; that moral cross-dressing will unravel the binds of social and gender inequality.

Radically, *Silence* proposes that Nature—a term that was ideologically mobilized as a hierarchizing force in medieval culture, and one that stood for the androcentric and aristocratic status quo—signifies nothing without the intervention of Noureture. Nature is cloaked, as it were, by human practice and discourse. To say it another way, Nature is far from "natural"—it has no prediscursive meaning and is therefore beyond the experience of any subject in the postlapsarian world of language and politics. In *Silence*, Nature is not ontologically prior to human understanding, but rather bound up in the transitory, imperfect realm of human knowledge and its politically charged, epistemological distinctions. *Silence* suggests that binaries believed to be fundamental to human identity—male and female, aristocrat and *vilein*—are in fact historically contingent constructs. They may have seemingly stable and permanent ideological status, but their meaning has actually changed over time and will continue to change in the future. *Silence* makes this point subtly by tempering its cross-dressing, class-transgressing plot with the narrator's fatuous protestations of its outrages. He mock-struggles to contain and even to controvert the implications of his radical romance, even as these frustrations amplify the poem's violative design.

Beginning with the narrator's cantankerous lament of a modernity in which avarice and ingratitude have replaced storied largesse of the Arthurian past, the *Roman de Silence* unfolds a plot obsessed with mixed and compromised categories: of "masculine" women; of kings who fail to demonstrate wise polity; of human nature that is the unnatural socializing influence of nurture. This muddled picture of contemporary life gestures at the relative purity of categories in bygone times, and the narrator balefully notes their transformation and hybridization as time moves on. To mourn the loss of a more perfect world is not unusual in a medieval text,[3] yet *Silence* explores the terms of this lament in a unique idiom—an elaborate constellation of cooking imagery. The author continually invokes culinary processes to signify the adulterated, denatured state of the world and its inhabitants. Dame Nature cuts her flour with bran to make human substance, Silence creates an edible trap for a bestial Merlin, and Merlin himself prepares prophetic revelation as if it were the main course of a courtly banquet. In each of these cases, cooking exposes the alienation of humanity from nature, a fundamental schism created by the application of labor to nature.

In *Silence*, labor—as represented by cooking—acts to restore characters to their predetermined "natural" state, despite the effort they have taken to achieve a status they prefer to have. As Marx reveals, labor is defined by its intermediary status: it is "a process between man and nature, a process by which man, through his own actions, mediates, regulates, and controls the metabolism between himself and nature."[4] Productive activity, itself driven by cultural, appetitive urges, renders the natural world digestible to human needs and human bodies. And though the natural world is creative in ways analogous to human labor—take Marx's examples of the spider and the bee—labor is a political force that drives humanity to intentionally change their environment, with some improving end in mind, regardless of whose circumstances are actually improved by the labor.[5] Labor is therefore a cultured force that usually works on behalf of the ideological status quo; that is, it conscripts nature to underwrite the powers that be. As an application of human effort, labor in the poem seemingly should be an aspect of Noureture, but instead in *Silence*, the figure of Nature strives to right the categorical "wrongs" that threaten binary stability. By laboring as a cook, Silence humanizes Merlin's

---

3. The traditional figure of Nature as an allegorical construct emerges most often in a context of complaint, satiric or otherwise. See George Economou, *The Goddess Natura in Medieval Literature* on the pedigree of Dame Nature from late antiquity to the fourteenth century.

4. Marx, *Capital*, 1.283.

5. Marx, *Capital*, 1.284. "But what distinguishes the worst architect from the best of bees is that the architect builds the cell in his mind before he constructs it in wax."

bestiality, while he metaphorically "cooks" (*decoverra le pot* [6186] [uncovers the pot]) when he discovers her gender ruse. The status of labor as rectifier of categories in Heldris's romance reveals a world that is hopelessly mediated, crossed, and queered; where Nature cannot stand alone without the intervention of a laboring Noureture to assist her. Silence's nearly flawless assumption of masculinity reinforces the idea that Noureture threatens the values of the "natural" aristocratic milieu.

The exploration of a mediated world extends even to the generic identity of the *Roman de Silence*. Romance is a genre that has always been notable for its mixture of heterogeneous elements. Medieval authors unite the martial and marvelous stories of the epic and *chanson de geste* with the lyric's examination of inner tensions and romantic love. The union of disparate parts is often thought to have created a wholly new mode of literature in France.[6] In fact, mélange is what makes the story, as Heldris reminds his audience:

Si com l'estoire le nos livre,
Qu'en latin escrite lizons,
En romans si le vos disons.
Je ne di pas que n'i ajoigne
Avoic le voir sovent mençoigne
Por le conte miols acesmer:
Mais se jel puis a droit esmer
N'i metrai rien qui m'uevre enpire
Ne del voir nen iert mos a dire
Car la verté ne doi taisir.
(1660–69)

Just as the story provides it to us
that we read written in Latin
so in French [*romans*] we tell it to you
I'm not saying that there are not
often lies joined with the truth
in order to embellish the tale better—
but if I can estimate rightly
I will add nothing there that impairs my work
Nor truly is there any word left to say
Because the truth should not be silenced.

---

6. Although there were many Greek, Latin, and Anglo-Saxon romances written before the 1150s, in both prose and verse. See chapter 1.

The narrator's disclaimers about mediating Latin with French, truth with fiction, are not surprising—they are part of the genre's efforts to authorize itself as worth telling. It is, however, remarkable that the narrator waits more than 1,600 lines to make this gesture. This sentiment must be expressed in order to sanction the labor that intervenes between the matter of storytelling and the product of the author, or in Eugène Vinaver's terms, between the *conte*, or the tale itself, and its *conjointure*, the particular arrangement that marks the tale as one's own.[7] This example is just one instance of the politics of adulteration to be found on nearly every level of *Silence*, from structure and idea to imagery and character. Here I will discuss the implications of this adulteration—the political use of impurity that points toward an imperfect state of affairs. Mixture is precisely what makes romance possible: the genre is both a symptom and a celebration of cultural and literary amalgamation. The intermediary nature of food matches that of romance: both are phenomena that reveal the contingencies of a "world grown old."[8]

Just as the first chapter of this book reconsidered definitions of romance, extending the genre backward in time, so this part requires a rethinking about what makes a writer of English romance. The *Roman de Silence*, a story written in a dialect of Old French usually considered to be continental,[9] nonetheless raises questions about its author and audience that expand the linguistic and national programs of modern critics. As Schmolke-Hasselmann first argued, the medieval idea of "Frenchness" was a cosmopolitan and international phenomenon; French-speaking court elites and literary patrons moved back and forth across the English Channel, bringing with them their political sympathies and feudal entanglements, as well as their favored authors.[10] Just like with Middle English, the differences between the dialects of French, though sometimes held up to ridicule, were not entirely incomprehensible to various speakers of the language. That a poem was not written in Anglo-Norman (or whatever local dialect) was no impediment to its circulation, nor should it be considered a hard limit to its appeal to a broad range of readers in any Francophonic area. So if verse romances were produced and disseminated in both England and France, for audiences living in either country, we should not be surprised if a writer of one of these texts was produced in England as

---

7. Vinaver, *Rise of Romance*, 36–37. The word *conjointure* appears to be a coinage of Chrétien de Troyes.
8. See James M. Dean's *The World Grown Old in Later Medieval Literature* for a thorough study of the *topos* of the *senectus mundi*.
9. For the linguistic analysis of the poem, see introduction to Heldris de Cornuälle, *Le Roman de Silence*, ed. Lewis Thorpe, 35–59.
10. Schmolke-Hasselmann, *Evolution of Arthurian Romance*, 282–85.

well. This may have been the case for Heldris de Cornuälle, about whom we know nothing except the name, which indicates a possible origin in Cornwall.

The textual history of *Silence* is as muddled and mediated as the poem itself. Its sole surviving witness, the Laval-Middleton Manuscript, was produced in northeastern France, near Tournai in Picardy, in the late thirteenth century.[11] It was probably seized as war booty during the long years of conflict between France and England, where it eventually ended up in the possession of Lord Middleton, discovered in 1911 by W. H. Stevenson in a box labeled "Old Papers—no value."[12] *Silence* seems out of place with the dominant trends of French vernacular narrative. A poetic romance written at a time when the French were primarily composing romances in prose,[13] *Silence* feels much more at home among its manuscript companions, *chansons de geste* and early verse romances like Benoît de Saint-Maure's *Roman de Troie* and Gautier d'Arras' *Ille et Galeron* (ca. late twelfth century).[14] It is possible that this sense of anachronism may be the result of an actual English origin of the poem—at the very least it plays, perhaps humorously, to the idea that insular romance was "behind the times" to urbane French audiences. At any rate, like many of the Arthurian verse romances examined by Schmolke-Haselmann, *Silence* is a poem about England: its hero and her king are both English, its excursus celebrates an English polity, and its conclusion salvages this same English kingdom.[15] Therefore, I treat the *Roman de Silence* as designed for Francophonic English audiences for the purposes of this book.

Silence has garnered a great deal of critical and pedagogical interest recently, becoming a fixture in collegiate syllabi and attracting scholarly attention with its freewheeling narrative and powerful story that uses cross-dressing to interrogate gender categories. It is not the only cross-dressing narrative in

---

11. The Laval-Middleton Manuscript is catalogued as University of Nottingham MS Mi.LM.6.

12. This anecdote is repeated in Heldris de Cornuälle, *Le Roman de Silence*, trans. F. Regina Psaki, xii; and Heldris de Cornuälle, *Silence: A Thirteenth-Century French Romance*, ed. and trans. Sarah Roche-Mahdi, xi.

13. Craig A. Berry argues that classifying *Silence* as such a late "chivalric verse romance" is justified by its attention to problems of inheritance and succession ("What Silence Desires," in *Translating Desire in Medieval and Early Modern Literature*, ed. Craig A. Berry and Heather Richardson Hayton, 193). See E. Jane Burns for an intriguing suggestion that the origins of French prose romance were in the English court of Henry II (1154–89), perhaps initiated by noted clerk and author Walter Map ("Arthurian Romance in Prose," in *A New History of French Literature*, ed. Denis Holier, 66–70).

14. The complete contents of the Laval-Middleton Manuscript are listed in Heldris de Cornuälle, *Le Roman de Silence*, ed. Thorpe, 3–6. For a description of the manuscript, see ibid., 1–12, and Keith Busby, *Codex and Context: Reading Old French Verse Narrative in Manuscript*, 415–20.

15. Schmolke-Haselmann, *Evolution of Arthurian Romance*, 242–44.

European medieval literature (its confreres are as diverse as the chauntefable *Aucassin et Nicolette* [ca. 1300–1400] and Ulrich von Liechtenstein's *Frauendienst* [*The Service of Ladies*, ca. 1255]). Nowhere else, however, is the idea of gender as a stable category of identity so relentlessly challenged, questioned, and even theorized as a cultural construct centuries ahead of a postmodernity that takes such ideas for granted. The poem's attention to issues of gender is so potent, so resonant to contemporary critiques, that the majority of criticism written about *Silence* has focused upon gender, sex, and sexuality in one way or another, almost to the exclusion of many other issues raised in its lines.

Scholarship on *Silence* is a relatively recent phenomenon; articles appeared only around thirty years ago to break the silence surrounding this intriguing romance. Kathleen J. Brahney, in a paper delivered in 1983, initiates the modern cycle of scholarship by observing that Heldris suspends the prevailing antifeminism of his milieu to engage in a bit of fantasy, to see what a woman could become in his society.[16] Anita Benaim Lasry counters that the literary status of women, who are defined at times as *hommes manqués* [men who are lacking], is dependent upon them acting like men in order to be represented as heroic at all.[17] Simon Gaunt identifies the repressive conclusion of the poem as "characteristically masculine," noting that Heldris cannot help talking about what disturbs him about gender and sexuality, desiring what he fears most— a masculine woman.[18] Peggy McCracken diagnoses the anxiety of aristocratic society about gender ambiguity, showing that romances are invested in policing proper gender roles in its characters.[19] Sharon Kinoshita interprets *Silence* politically, arguing that the heroine's cross-dressing "renegotiates the over-lapping, potentially conflictual relations" between interested parties in feudal bonds, which reveals aristocratic bodies were valued less for their war-making than for their perpetuation of dynastic lineage.[20] Queering the gender constructions of *Silence*, Elizabeth Waters recognizes the role of shame in motivating the heroine's cross-dressing performance, a self-censuring that ensures that heteronormative categories are reinscribed within the romance.[21]

---

16. Kathleen J. Brahney, "When *Silence* was Golden: Female Personae in the *Roman de Silence*," in *The Spirit of the Court*, ed. Glyn S. Burgess and Robert A. Taylor, 52–61.

17. Anita Benaim Lasry, "The Ideal Heroine in Medieval Romances: A Quest for a Paradigm," *Kentucky Romance Quarterly* 32 (1985): 227–43.

18. Simon Gaunt, "The Significance of Silence," *Paragraph* 13 (1990): 213.

19. Peggy McCracken, "'The Boy who was a Girl': Reading Gender in the *Roman de Silence*," *Romanic Review* 84 (1994): 517–36.

20. Sharon Kinoshita, "Heldris de Cornuälle's *Roman de Silence* and the Feudal Politics of Lineage," *PMLA* 110 (1995): 398.

21. Elizabeth Waters, "The Third Path: Alternative Sex, Alternative Gender in *Le Roman de Silence*," *Arthuriana* 7 (1997): 35–46.

In the same issue of *Arthuriana* (Summer 1997), Caroline A. Jewers outlines how *Silence* redefines the critical term *aventure* [chance, event] to incorporate feminine agency into its parameters—however, this reinscription has the effect of creating a "*Bildungsroman* focused not on the education of a hero, but of a heroine who experiences different structures of power without permanently appropriating them, and in so doing learns to submit to them."[22] Robert L. A. Clark identifies "category crisis" as the driving energy in the romance, one that queers gender performance in order to make social class seem more natural as a determination of human identity.[23] Also citing the work of Marjorie Garber, Robert S. Sturges reads cross-dressing in *Silence* as the "archetypal sign of the transgression of all categories" of a story that illuminates the vexed social position of the *juventus*—militarized, aristocratic youth who were not to inherit their fathers' lands, and so had to wander Europe seeking other noblemen to serve.[24]

Without denying the importance of gender to the poem and its study, or denigrating the laudable efforts by scholars to unravel its complexities, I follow Sturges and Clark in seeing its cross-dressing as a symptom of a more pervasive issue. Yet where these scholars see the class as the major issue of *Silence*'s critique, I return to the words of Marjorie Garber on the fullest implications of cross-dressing's threat to categories:

> Transvestism was located at the juncture of "class" and "gender," and increasingly through its agency gender and class were revealed to be commutable, if not equivalent. To transgress against one set of boundaries was to call into question the inviolability of both, and of the set of social codes—already demonstrably under attack—by which such categories were policed and maintained. The transvestite in this scenario is both terrifying and seductive precisely because s/he incarnates and emblematizes the disruptive element that intervenes, signaling not just another category crisis, but—much more disquietingly—a crisis of "category" itself.[25]

The cross-dresser raises the possibility that no dyadic category has any meaning whatsoever—that they are not natural, but rather enforced by cultural

---

22. Caroline A. Jewers, "The Non-Existent Knight: Adventure in *Le Roman de Silence*," *Arthuriana* 7 (1997): 92.

23. Robert L. A. Clark, "Queering Gender and Naturalizing Class in the *Roman de Silence*," *Arthuriana* 12 (2002): 50–63.

24. Robert S. Sturges, "The Crossdresser and the *Juventus*: Category Crisis in *Silence*," *Arthuriana* 12 (2002): 37.

25. Marjorie Garber, *Vested Interests: Cross-Dressing and Cultural Anxiety*, 32.

habits. *Silence* toys with this challenge, fixated upon the problem of mixture and mediation more generally, upon adulteration that complicates and threatens binary relationships. Masculine and feminine are obvious, very attractive, examples of the twofold thinking which organizes existence, forming putatively stable categories that inevitably prove to be anything but solid and predictable upon deeper scrutiny. *Silence* and its cross-dressing narrative challenge the legitimacy of these dualistic categories, defying their stability and exposing their fluidity.

The grand innovation of *Silence*, however, comes with how its disruption of fundamental categories is marshalled. Heldris mobilizes a pervasive imagery of the edible in order to drive home his critique of the social imagination. This rich metaphorical and material connection can be made because food is a mediating phenomenon: it transcends distinctions between inside and outside, between self and other. Cooking is the practice of labor by which these unusual objects are made palatable for ingestion—it cajoles the wary eater to incorporate its products. Both food and cooking imbricate the individual into a political world of economic production, social consumption, and class-based stratification, putting the self into circulation among a world of commodities and behaviors. The literary power of consumption renders social critique and humor deliciously appealing, as has been shown by Sarah Gordon, bringing the very structures of power into question by interrogating its appetites.[26] Gordon's study shows that food is often funny in medieval French literature, but in the *Roman de Silence* this trenchant power allows its author to move past lampooning social mores and conventions, and engage in an intellectual broadside attacking the epistemological foundations of an entire social order in desperate need of regeneration.

2. BAKING WITH DAME NATURE

Cooking directly challenges the stability of categories as well, as it transforms raw food into something desirable to humans. A natural foodstuff is altered by the addition of heat, which transmutes the texture and consistency of meat and other foods so they become digestible. Its purity is mediated by the process, as well as by the addition of other ingredients—herbs, spices, or salt at the very least—that change its native flavor into something designed to appeal to the sensory pleasure of an eater. But even in the famous "culinary triangle" of Claude Lévi-Strauss, there is no point where culture does not intervene in

---

26. Gordon, *Culinary Comedy in Medieval French Literature*, 1–4.

the presentation of the natural.[27] Foods eaten raw or rotted—both "natural" states to be sure—are consumed with the benefit of cultural wisdom and customary practice: even a nut right off the tree must be cracked with some sort of tool. Cooking is the act that reveals culture's dominance over its environment, translating all things into products useful for nutrition as well as good to eat. We almost never apprehend the natural world without some process of cooking, at least as far as our bellies are concerned.

Cooking first appears in *Silence* in the context of labor of another sort—the birth of the hero(ine)—which gives way to an account of the work required to create human bodies. During the harrowing account of Eufemie's labor pains (1775–94), Heldris's narrator averts his gaze, and the tale shifts from the realistic to the metaphysical. Here he introduces the figure of Dame Nature and diverges to speculate on the generation of living creatures. Anticipating the objections of his audience, who might become irritated with what seems to be a digression, the narrator signals that we are nonetheless meant to pay close attention to the description that follows:

> Se jo le vus di et descuevre
> Quels l'uevre fu, ne vos anuit,
> Car vos devés bien ester aduit,
> Se vos voles savoir un conte,
> D'entendre et oïr cho que monte.
> (1800–1804)

> If I tell and describe to you
> this handiwork, don't be annoyed [or bored],
> for you should be well instructed,
> if you wish to savor a tale,
> in order to understand and hear what it's worth.

In this extraordinary passage, tightly woven with internal rhymes, that belies its status as an off-hand remark, the narrator seems brazenly to diverge from Heldris's tale, insisting that he is returning (*repairier*) to the true matter of the story, which will speculate upon the metaphysical process of creating living matter (both senses are described by the word *matyre*). Challenging his audience to follow along with what he feels is important to tell, the narrator commands us not to become *anuit* [bored or vexed], stating that this detour is fundamental to a listener's experience of *savoir*—both tasting and understand-

---

27. Claude Lévi-Strauss, "The Culinary Triangle," trans. Peter Brooks, *Partisan Review* 33 (1966): 586–96.

ing the story. We cannot fully enjoy the narrative without comprehending of the role of Nature in the action to come.

As has been demonstrated by critics of *Silence*, Heldris de Cornuälle's reimagination of Nature takes many liberties with her traditional personification, altering her iconography in order to better suit the purposes of his narrative.[28] An allegorical character with a literary pedigree stretching back to late antiquity in the work of Boethius and Macrobius, Nature is a laboring goddess, emblematized by Alain de Lille in *De planctu naturae* (ca. 1160–65) as a stamper of coins (he calls her the "monetariam," [the mistress of his [God's] mint]).[29] Jean de Meun, in his continuation of the *Roman de la Rose* (ca. 1275), elaborates Nature even further, drawing her more clearly as a blacksmith in whose workshop "Toujourz martele, tourjourz forge, / Toujourz ses pieces renouvele / Par generacion nouvele" [she continues always to hammer and forge and always to renew the individuals by means of new generation].[30] The laboring figure of Nature naturalizes the secondary, mediated relationship that humans have created with the natural world: she labors because men are required to. The earth and its most basic products—plants, animals, food—have been converted through husbandry and breeding into instruments of labor, mere tools that intervene between the laborer and his object.[31] Nature, as an idealized allegorical figure, renders this indirect connection into a normal state of affairs through displacement, perpetuating an isomorphism between the work of the blacksmith and sexual, as well as intellectual, labor. Through this equation Nature identifies that the work of reproduction lies "not with gestation," as observed by Suzanne Conklin Akbari, "but with the impression of form upon matter."[32] Even though she is represented as female, Jean de

---

28. Important studies of Nature in *Roman de Silence* include: Suzanne Conklin Akbari, "Nature's Forge Recast in the *Roman de Silence*," in *Literary Aspects of Courtly Culture*, ed. Donald Maddox and Sara Sturm-Maddox, 39–46, and Barbara Newman, "Did Goddesses Empower Women?" in *Gendering the Master Narrative*, ed. Mary C. Erler and Maryanne Kowaleski, 135–55.

29. Alain de Lille, *De planctu naturae*, in *The Anglo-Latin Satirical Poets and Epigrammatists of the Twelfth Century*, ed. Thomas Wright, *Rerum Britannicarum Medii Aevi Scriptores*, vol. 59, part 2, 469. Translation: James J. Sheridan, *The Plaint of Nature*, 146. Economou's *The Goddess Natura* remains the most complete study of the iconography and uses of the allegorical figure of Nature, despite the fact that it omits the *Roman de Silence* in its survey. See also E. R. Curtius's survey of Nature in *European Literature and the Latin Middle Ages*, trans. Willard R. Trask, 106–27.

30. Guillaume de Lorris and Jean de Meun, *Le Roman de la Rose*, ed. Ernest Langlois, SATF, 16010–12. Translation: Charles Dalhberg, *The Romance of the Rose*, 271.

31. See Marx, *Capital*, vol. 1. An instrument of labor is defined as "a thing, or a complex of things, which a worker interposes between himself and the object of his labour and which serves as its conductor, directing his physical activity onto that object" (285–86).

32. Akbari, "Nature's Forge Recast," 39.

Meun's Nature takes the male role in procreation, hammering out the forms of living creatures upon her anvil. This image is aligned with the popular Aristotelian theory of the generation of offspring, which describes male sperm as the active *forma* that imposes shape and character upon passive female *materia*. The figure of Nature as a blacksmith is more than just cross-dressed like Silence; she (unlike Silence) performs the masculine sexual role. Nature as a blacksmith is a titillating, phallocentric image of the theory of generation.

Though the Aristotelian "one-seed" theory of procreation was widespread in medieval scientific thought, Heldris's alterations of the figure of Nature in *Silence* suggest that there may have been other theories in circulation.[33] In converting her from a blacksmith to a baker, Heldris preserves the image of a laboring Nature, not only reimagining how Nature should be personified but also retheorizing how procreation works, as Akbari observes:

> This transformation of the figure of Nature reflects an unusual perspective on human reproduction and, more generally, on gender roles. Here, Nature's forge is transformed into an oven where, instead of forcibly shaping matter, she prepares a concoction which is moulded and baked.[34]

The generation of form is no longer metamorphic, but metabolic. The violent, dramatic imposition of active form upon passive matter is given up in favor of a subtle process of mixture based upon inexorable chemical reactions that mutually change disparate parts into a whole. Heldris transforms a theory that valorizes conception into another that celebrates gestation, elevating the status of the female in reproduction to at least the equal of the male.

This conceptual innovation through personification proceeds at first from an analogy, a simile that likens Nature to a baker and expands to form a coherent theory from a strain of imagery. In other words, Heldris's philosophical figure is one in progress, that develops conspicuously as the narrator goes on. Framing the simile with an emphasis upon the quality of its results (the *ouvre forcible* [1807] or its *majestyre* [1827]),[35] Heldris shifts for a moment to a fascination with the technical vocabulary of baking. He revels in the redundancy and repetition of the lexicon, naming the tools of baking Nature uses—

---

33. According to Joan Cadden, medieval natural philosophers and physicians used an eclectic blend of Aristotelian, Hippocratic, and Galenic materials to formulate their own theories of reproduction (See *The Meanings of Sex Difference in the Middle Ages*, 54–88). Aristotle's theory of reproduction is called "one-seed" because he theorizes that only men produce reproductive material. "Two-seed" theories recognize that women produce a "seed" of their own.

34. Akbari, "Nature's Forge Recast," 39–40.

35. Brahney notes that Nature linguistically mixes the masculine and feminine in this passage ("When *Silence* Was Golden," 57).

whether *crible*, *bulette*, or *tamise*. This catalogue reveals an important step in the production of human forms: the sifting of the flour to remove the bran and other impurities. He repeats himself further: a description of the sifting process or its results is given twice more (1828–39; 1845–60). The more cleanly sifted the flour, the whiter the bread and the more valuable the final product—in effect he refigures the economic side of generation; shifting the attention from numismatics (the output of Alain de Lille's *monetariam*) to a product to be purchased with that coin, the commodifiable *blanc pain et biel* (1810) [white and lovely bread]. Reducing the bread to a view of its exchange-value also reminds us that the desirability of white bread is culturally determined: it is hardly a natural distinction, nor one in concordance with the use-value of bread.[36]

As observed by Barbara Newman and Robert L. A. Clark, the pure white flour does not primarily signify sex or gender in Nature's creation; instead, it represents class identity.[37] The division of pure flour from the bran creates two separate bodies, the first an aristocratic *gastial* [refined cake], and the lower-classed *torte a porciels* [cake for the pigs]. However, the process of filtering is far from gender-neutral. The carefully sifted flour is described as *vallant* [good, worthy, brave, powerful, as well as its cognate "valiant"]; it is an adjective that marks the flour as excelling at both aristocracy and masculinity.[38] Nature has winnowed out the impurities in her flour, leaving nothing but what is noble and male in her desire to bake the perfect female body.

Heldris's allegory of Nature's workshop, however, is far from ideal. The process is imprecise, often creating an impure mixture of components. Despite her efforts to separate the parts, accidents do happen:

> Si oste del gros le délie.
> De cel délie si fait sans falle
> Les buens et del gros la frapalle.
> Mais se il avient que Nature
> Soit corocie, u que n'ait cure
> C'un poi del gros al délie viegne
> Et al mollier avoec se tiegne,

---

36. White bread was the most desirable type in the Middle Ages, its expense precluded all but the most wealthy from affording it.

37. Newman, "Did Goddesses Empower Women?" 143, and Clark, "Queering Gender and Naturalizing Class," 61.

38. Heldris uses the same adjective to modify the *home* (man, human being) that Nature wishes to create in her bakeshop (1826), and when Silence acknowledges the quality of her own manliness: "Or sui jo moult vallans et pros" (2642) [Now I am quite valiant and honored].

Cil gros se trait al cuer en oire.
(1832-39)

So she separates from the crude the refined.
From this refined stuff she makes, without a doubt,
the good people and from the crude the worthless.
But if it should happen that Nature
becomes angry so that she hasn't a care,
if a little bit of coarse is blended with the fine
and is retained in the molding,
the coarse bran attacks the heart at once.

Repeating the words *délie* [pure, refined] and *gros* [crude] three times in shifting chiastic constructions emphasizes the uncertain relationship between the two grades of flour, and acknowledges a continuum of purity. Even in the bakery of Nature, flour is rarely encountered in an unmediated state, due to Nature's *corocie* [anger], a trait that aligns her with the traditional personifications of the goddess in medieval literature. Nature is given voice in poems such as *De Planctu Naturae* and the *Roman de la Rose* only because she is upset and must vent her complaint. This type of anger characterizes Nature as stereotypically female but also aligns her with the putatively male narrator of *Silence,* whose petulant digressions cause the matter of the romance to veer frequently away from its plot. And, as if on cue, *Silence*'s narrator launches into a twenty-line speech about the appearance of rich bodies [*riche cors*] with low-born hearts [*vil cuer et povre* (1843)] and vice versa. With this outburst, he seems to goad himself into questioning the relevance of the entire Nature episode. He shifts (and further mixes) his metaphor, claiming that "Li cors n'est mais fors sarpelliere, / Encor soit de la tierre chiere" (1845-46) [The body is mere sackcloth, / even if it's made from the dearest clay]. Even though this is a commonplace, his statement seems to deny the importance of Nature's work in building, which the past sixty lines have demonstrated.

Perhaps it is this denial of Nature's power that leads the narrator to examine the next step of the process of creating human forms: the imprinting of shape upon the dough she has sifted and prepared. The narrator moves from contemplating the inner substance of her creation to its outer form:

A son secré va, si descuevre.
Molles i a bien .m. milliers,
Que cho li est moult grant mestiers,
Car s'ele n'eüst forme c'une,

> La samblance estroit si commune
> De tolte gent, c'on ne savroit
> Quoi, ne quel non, cascuns avroit.
> (1886–92)

> She goes to her coffer and discloses it.
> She has nearly a thousand thousands of molds there,
> and she has a very great need of them,
> for if she had only one form,
> everyone would so much alike
> that no one would ever be able to tell
> who was who or what their name was.

Dame Nature begins the next step in the baking process by opening up (*descuevre*)[39] her own enclosed coffer (*secré*) in order to produce the formed pans that give her creations shape. In a bit of materialist detail that illustrates the allegorical vision of creation, Nature must have numerous shaped pans— a *.m. milliers* [a million] to be exact—in order to account for all the differences of human form. None are imperfect or accidentally misshapen: any sort of variation is a part of Nature's plan. Two implications can be derived from this description. First, contrary to what the narrator has said previously about her *corocie* (1836), which causes her to become less careful with her products' composition, Nature is now described as always being cautious with her molds, so that there is never anything wrong with her work (*n'a a blasmer rien*). Second, and more importantly, Heldris suggests that all human difference—big or small, handsome or ugly, *contrefaites* or *parfites*—is a matter of surface detail. These are superficial aspects, not metaphysical properties, pragmatically applied so that humans can distinguish between themselves, to know who they are and their names. Newman identifies the unexpected results of Nature's priorities:

> Heldris seems here to be making a distinction analogous to the Aristotelian dichotomy of form and matter, though with antithetical meaning. Silence's gender is signified by the inscription and coloring, or superficial form, stamped on that matter. His unusual privileging of matter over form explains why gender is more mutable than character.[40]

---

39. *Cuevre* [to cover, conceal] is an important word in *Silence*, and various compounds of it (*decuevre, recuevre*) are used as rhyme words twelve times in the poem, all of them paired with (*o*)*uevre* (work).

40. Newmann, "Did Goddesses Empower Women?" 144.

This is a startling reversal of the Aristotelian theory of conception, flipping its dialectic onto its head. *Materia* becomes the more substantial part of the process, while *forma* is reduced to just an outward appearance. However, the gendering of these forces is reversed as well, and the most natural, essential part of creation becomes gendered as male (the *vallant fleur*), and the female aspect only possible through the imposition of the mold.

The link between the *matyre* of the romance story and the floury *matere* of Nature's workshop is drawn further as the goddess sketches and forms the female features of the infant Silence. Not only does the goddess draw and inscribe her facial features just like the scribe draws characters on a sheet of parchment but also she employs the rhetorical practice of *effictio*, describing her creation from her shining blonde hair, "ki luisent cler par nuit obscure" (1907) [which clearly lights up the dark night] to her perfectly proportioned feet and toes (*piés et ortals a mesure*, 1944), following exactly the poet's prescription for praising the beautiful woman.[41] Femininity is a surface effect, glazed over this upper-class, masculine body, with the signifiers of the poetic blazon and the overdetermined language of artifice.[42] Silence is created to be delectable, a body consumable through (masculine) poetic efforts.

The evolution of Alain's or Jean's Dame Nature into that of Heldris not only involves altering her profession from blacksmith to baker. It also reimagines the allegorical possibilities extending from this personification. In the earlier two works, Nature is equipped with masculine hammers and feminine anvils—an image of carnal activity, of sex as the performance of strenuous work. The process of hammering out metal on an anvil is crudely symbolic, if not equally ironic, of the rhythm and sweat of male-superior intercourse. The transformation of Heldris's Nature into a baker proposes a different theory of the sex act, one which is polymorphous and not easily apprehended, defined by the process of blending and the mutuality of influence, rather than by the "correct" position and the collision's true stroke. It is a process that takes place behind the womblike oven's closed door.

The smithing Nature creates bodies that are not natural, but the baker of *Silence* creates something that is a sign of culture itself. Bread is the foodstuff that is most changed by its encounter with humanity. Inedible in its native state, grain must be ploughed, sown, reaped, winnowed, ground, mixed,

---

41. On the subject of effictio, Geoffrey de Vinsauf exhorts: "So let the radiant description descend from the top of the head to her toe, and the whole be polished to perfection" (*Poetria Nova*, trans. Nims, 36). This rhetorical practice is sent up in Chaucer's *Nun's Priest's Tale*, which deploys it to praise the figure of a handsome rooster (*Canterbury Tales* VII.2859–64).

42. The emphasis on the surface effects as gender identification may explain why Heldris always rhymes the word "halle" [sunburnt] with "malle" [male].

leavened, molded, baked, and then broken. Nature's products symbolize the human condition itself: that we are given to labor (see *Genesis* 3:19), liable to sin and penitence (eating nothing but bread and water), yet able to be united with God by way of the Eucharist. Bread reveals our connection with the world, mediated through labor, as we perceive it. Nature, at work in her bakeshop, garbed in her apron, is at the same moment her supposed opposite Noureture. Silence, the product of Nature's finest efforts, baked from the purest flour, imprinted and decorated with enough beauty for a thousand others, hardly has a natural body of her own. The outer decoration is superficial, not essential. That she is a woman has only to do with how her body is molded. The inner substance, the *vallant* flour, will determine her qualities and her worth; it is what Ebain will presumably recognize when he chooses her to be his next wife (though he has her stripped naked anyway, just to be sure).

3. COOKING WITH MERLIN

If the bodies of humans are merely stamped in the bakeshop with so-called "natural" gender distinctions, then it is no wonder that humans can so easily lead Nature's designs astray. Silence is rigorously educated in the pursuits of boys and exposed to the harsh elements, training which suffices to make a fine young man out of her, capable of fooling anyone. She even learns how to imitate socially inferior men by dyeing her face with herbs, a pose that allows her to travel Europe with a pair of wandering minstrels (2921–3476). Merlin, too, learns how to transform himself into a beast of the woods, where he roams free from human society. Not only binaries of female and male, aristocrat and commoner, but even human and animal seem to be little more than surface distinctions, vulnerable to Noureture's manipulation.

Himself an unnatural production—the child of a nun and an incubus—Merlin intervenes in historical events to make the unlikely come to pass, although these machinations tend to protect and ensure the proper patriarchal succession. He is not a member of the aristocracy, but he safeguards their values nonetheless, using his formidable powers of prophecy to rectify what goes astray. Merlin plays many roles in the texts in which he appears: prophet, magician, engineer, royal counselor, trickster, and wild man.[43] In *Silence* he wears several of these hats, but the most surprising is the toque—the puffy white cook's headwear he shares with Silence in the final episode of the story.

---

43. For an overview of and speculation about Merlin's many facets and interpretations, see R. Howard Bloch, *Etymologies and Genealogies*, 2–8.

Silence's capture of the wild Merlin is the culmination of her heroic quest, though it is neither the cessation of the romance's gender-bending energies nor the end of Silence's troubled path from cross-dressed child to "good" wife. Yet the transvestite heroine has already reached the apex of her masculine performance. Her bold exploits on the battlefield in the service of King Ebain (5185-647) exceed the finest knights of England and France in martial power and bloodthirstiness.[44] The sudden reversal of her fortunes in exile, and her seemingly impossible quest demanded on false pretenses, prevent her from discovering what more there is to life as a man beyond conquering hero. Twice caught in the snare of the wily Eufeme (who, furious at Silence's repeated refusal of her sexual advances, twice accuses Silence of attempted rape) (4071-148, 5747-78), Silence returns from exile in France only to be consigned to hunt endlessly for a Merlin gone bestial, pursuing a quarry who can only be caught (as he says himself) by an *engien de feme* (5803)—often translated as a "female trick," but it could just as easily be the "wit of a woman."

Silence herself must first be trapped, however, into taking up the search for Merlin. Eufeme tells Silence a lie about a symbolic dream she has had about the British king Vortigern and his rickety tower, which only Merlin can make stand upright overnight. Eufeme duplicitously begs Silence to find Merlin so that he can interpret this "dream," even as she glosses its literary and historical context—Geoffrey of Monmouth's *Regis Historia Britannia* (5779-80).[45] Eufeme assumes a narratorial role here: the tower that always falls in the night unites two plot-strands of the romance. It stands for the sexual and political challenges to Ebain's rule—the royal couple's childlessness, Eufeme's (attempted) adulteries, and the Count of Chester's rebellion.[46] These problems orbit around Silence's presence in Ebain's court: she is the object of Eufeme's desire, just as she is the hero who ends the insurgency. In both cases, the weakness of Ebain's reign is exposed and Silence's strength and desirability fill

---

44. Silence's activity and power in this scene is signaled by the *topos* of the arming of the hero (5334-68), traditionally used for (male) epic heroes. Lorraine Kochanske Stock compares this scene to Camilla's arming scene in the *Roman d'Aeneas* (ca. 1150), arguing that the author shows Silence not only meeting but exceeding her characterization as a masculine knight ("'Arms and the (Wo)Man' in Medieval Romance," *Arthuriana* 5 [1995]: 69-75).

45. Geoffrey of Monmouth, *History of the Kings of Britain*, 6.499-577, ed. Michael D. Reeve, trans. Neil Wright, 136-40. The cause of tower's fall proved to be pair of dragons fighting in a pool beneath the foundation.

46. Michelle Bolduc identifies the unity of these two characters: both give advice to Ebain but ultimately prove to be disloyal and wicked (187-90). The section of the poem containing their doubled infidelities (5557-878) is headed by a miniature of a strange creature that Thorpe identifies as a "bird with a griffin's head" (*Roman de Silence*, 8), but Bolduc perceives (more accurately, I believe) as a dragon (Bolduc, "Silence's Beasts," in *The Mark of the Beast: The Medieval Bestiary in Art, Life, and Literature*, ed. Debra Higgs Strickland, 191-93).

the resultant gap. The tower is an (im)potent emblem of Ebain's condition—at once Eufeme's sly comment on her husband's vulnerable rule, yet also a gesture toward ameliorating the situation.

Redemption is not in the cards for Silence, even though she will locate and capture the wayward magician. But the *engien de feme* that captures Merlin is not performed by Silence alone, but rather set into motion by Eufeme and helped along by Ebain. Silence is unusually passive during this important moment in this story; she is buffeted about by other forces, lost and confused. After a year of fruitless searching, and becoming more and more sure she has been sent on a fool's errand, Silence meets a mysterious old man in the woods. This old man (often identified by critics as Merlin in disguise)[47] greets Silence warmly and offers her hope in the form of an emblem:

> Amis, lasscier le dementer.
> Jo ai veü jadis enter
> Sovent sor sur estoc dolce ente,
> Par tel engien et tele entente
> Que li estos et li surece
> Escrut trestolt puis en haltece.
> (5915–20)

> Friend, let be your grieving—
> Formerly I have seen grafted
> often upon a sterile stock a sweet imp
> with such art and such application
> that the graft and the stock
> both increased to a height afterwards.[48]

The old man "up-writes" the falling tower with a new growth of grafted plants. In one sense, his prophetic words offer hope to Silence—that she will find Merlin, and also that she will flourish as a person of composite gender, despite her troubles in Ebain's court. The grafting represents possibilities that can bloom into prosperity, a fertile cooperation between the perpetually warring

---

47. This identification of the old man as Merlin stems from the story's parallel in the Grisandole episode of the *Estoire de Merlin* (ca. 1230–40), in which a white stag informs Grisandole how to capture the magician. The stag is later explicitly identified as Merlin. See Sarah Roche-Mahdi's examination of Merlin in *Silence* ("A Reappraisal of the Role of Merlin," *Arthuriana* 12 [2002]: 6–21).

48. Gloria Thomas Gilmore proposes a radically different, though feasible, translation of these words, arguing that the passage admonishes Silence to view things allegorically ("*Le Roman de Silence*: Allegory in Ruin or Womb of Irony," *Arthuriana* 7 [1997]: 113).

Nature and Noureture. Yet the "sterile stock" also recalls the suspended state of Silence's female body, which—according to cultural mores—requires a *dolce ente* (fresh shoot) in order to bloom.[49] The predetermined roles of wife and mother have lain dormant as she follows the third path of her own choosing.[50] Wandering in the wilderness, Silence's selfhood is detached from the discourses and performances by which she has created a masculine identity. Her fate is catching up with her, and she is beginning to fulfill her own prophecy: without an audience, she is both nobody and nude (*jo sui nus,* 2538), vulnerable to some new gender stamp. Just as Nature bakes her into a woman of the *gastial,* Silence's own cookery will have gendering effects, not only transforming Merlin back into a man but also bringing femininity unwittingly back upon herself. Her stock will bear fruit, but this is an uncertain boon that will leave her vulnerable to sexual consumption.

The recipe for baiting Merlin is not complicated, requiring only meat that has been heavily salted and three pots containing honey, milk, and wine. But, as with many recipes, presentation is everything. The meat must be cooked with a lot of smoke, so that the scent will spread through the woods and Merlin will notice it more readily. After he eats the salty meat, he will become thirsty and seek to drink from each of three pots, though the first two will only make his thirst for wine greater. The wine, in turn, will intoxicate Merlin and cause him to lose consciousness, allowing Silence to capture him. The key to the old man's recipe is the salt added to the meat. Commonly used as a preserving agent as well as a flavoring, salt was a valuable commodity that held a place of privilege upon the noble table, kept clean and dry inside a "salt-cellar."[51] Salt is a uniquely human product, either mined from the earth or evaporated from seawater, and used in specifically human ways. It signifies both the preservation of life and its pleasurable surplus. It interrupts natural processes of decomposi-

---

49. The double entendre recalls the narrator's statement about Silence as a boy: "poi en falt que il n'est malles" (2477) [little was lacking for him to be a male].

50. For a study of queer identities in *Roman de Silence,* see Waters, "Third Path." At the start of her adolescence Silence questions her gender identity, becoming trapped between the two possibilities presented by Nature and Noureture. Silence resolves the intellectual bind by following the argument of a third figure, Lady Reason, who appeals to the exterior advantages of manhood, such as the acquisition of superior social status (2497–656).

51. See Peter C. D. Brears, *Cooking and Dining in Medieval England,* 400, for a drawing of several examples of saltcellars. The "Lytyll Childrens Boke," a fourteenth-century courtesy manual, advises that a polite eater will not put his food directly into the saltcellar, but rather will scoop the salt out with the point of his knife (F. J. Furnivall, ed., *The Babees Book: Meals and Manners in Olden Time,* 18, lines 29–31). This courteous admonition is ignored in the romance of *Richard Coer de Lyon,* when King Richard, upon escaping from prison and bearing the heart of the lion that was supposed to kill him, confronts his captor at a banquet and dips the raw heart into the saltcellar before eating it whole (1103–9).

tion and transforms an edible object into a savory one. Precious (though not as dear as spices), salt is both a luxury and a necessity. Reputed to be an aphrodisiac due to its ability to warm the body into a state of arousal,[52] salt is the crystallization of surplus enjoyment, the very delight of eating.

Salted fish and meat would typically be found in a medieval kitchen throughout the year, and cooks developed ways to render preserved food more palatable by soaking it in water for several days.[53] For Silence to serve the meat as is—roasted and not boiled first—increases its dryness and suggests its use as a medicinal corrective for the humoral complexion of the wild Merlin, who has fed so long on the diet of a wild ruminant.[54] By eating like a beast, he has become one: "Cho est uns hom trestols pelus / Et si est com uns ors velus; / Si est isnials com cers de lande" (5929–31) [He is a man entirely covered with hair, / and so he is like a hairy bear; / he is as swift as the deer of the thicket]. Raw vegetables and grasses were considered to be humorally cold and dry due to their proximity to the earth, and so Merlin has become cold and dry as well, completely reversed from the ideal—hot and moist—masculine complexion.[55] He requires something to warm and moisten him into a human man again.

Silence's dinner party goes off without a hitch, and Merlin thirstily drinks from the three pots filled with honey, milk, and wine. Honey was considered hot and dry—its introduction into Merlin's already distempered system increases his thirst. Milk was deemed cold, moist, though volatile in the human digestive system, prone to corrupt and burn inside the stomach—it makes Merlin even more uncomfortable and more eager to drink the wine. Wine was often considered the perfect drink due to its humoral similarity to human blood, which allowed it to be swiftly and easily converted into spirits essential for bodily restoration.[56] It has a doubly transformative effect on Merlin, who drinks it to excess: his humors are realigned, and he falls asleep, losing (bestial) consciousness to awake as a human.

Although these are compelling medieval medical reasons for Merlin's recovery, the restorative recipe has culturally determined symbolic registers beyond its "natural" power to heal. Newman terms Merlin's cure a "Lévi-Straussian synthesis" between raw and the cooked foods, but notes that because meat and wine evoke the manly domain of the feast hall, these pro-

---

52. Albala, *Eating Right in the Renaissance*, 148.
53. See Brears, *Cooking and Dining in Medieval England*, 148–49, for ways to remove salt from meat.
54. See Albala, *Eating Right in the Renaissance*, 50–51.
55. Women were deemed to be colder and moister, a trait thought to explain their reputed lechery as a compulsive need to be warmed through sexual contact.
56. Albala, *Eating Right in the Renaissance*, 73–74; Adamson, *Food in Medieval Times*, 51.

cessed foods are more vital to Merlin's cure than the raw milk and honey, which correspond to the female body and primal nutrition.[57] Akbari stresses the humanizing power of the wine, which is the only item on Silence's menu found solely in the human world.[58] To assign these ingredients symbolic meaning, however, is to acknowledge their participation in the human domain of signifiers. Significance does not inhere in any foodstuff—the femininity of milk and honey is just as culturally conditioned as the manliness of meat and wine in the warrior's hall. All of the ingredients designate the imposition of human will. Milk and honey are gathered from domesticated animals, wine is subject to controlled spoilage, meat is cooked, and salt is cultivated.[59]

Merlin's powerful "cure" works its magic on the poem itself, reframing Silence's story. This is a narrative recipe as well as a culinary one, that orders the lines of the poem so that the feminine milk and honey is literally surrounded by the cultured and masculine wine and roasted meat: "vin, miel, et lait . . . / . . . et car bien fressce" (5944–45). The duality of Silence's sexual identity is writ large in the cooking process, allowing the restored Merlin to uncover her secret, to read her. Her female body, baked by Nature to be the most delectable and desirable of all her creations, is returned to the table. By enacting the old man's prescription, Silence sacrifices her masculine outer self, in effect feeding part of herself to Merlin in order to return him to humanity. Moreover, she re-empowers Merlin to determine the proper male succession in Ebain's court. She does this not only by being reborn, as Akbari suggests, as a female in her society[60] but also by consigning herself to a lower social status. In her own words, she does what she is unwilling to do *en son corage* [in her heart]—to "Irai desos, quant sui deseure" [to go down, when I'm above], to *honis* [disgrace] herself. This is exactly what Silence feared would happen as she contemplated ending her masculine performance at twelve years old (2639–42). As a cook, she loses both her masculinity and aristocratic status.

Despite being biologically equipped to provide the primal form of infant nourishment (both the blood that feeds the fetus in the womb and the milk that feeds the baby afterward), Silence has become conditioned to be more male in complexion than female. Not only has exposure to the sun and wind dried her body (again, as suggested by Heldris's common rhyme on *halle/ malle*) but she has also exercised her body in knightly combat and followed

---

57. Newman, "Did the Goddesses Empower Women?" 146.

58. Akbari, "Nature's Forge Recast," 44.

59. Silence's recipe does not include bread, but it is worth noting its similarly restorative power in medieval literature. In Chrétien de Troyes's *Le Chevalier au Lion,* the mad Yvain meets a hermit who brings him bread, even going so far as to acquire white bread in order to better suit Yvain's obvious nobility. The combination of cooked meat and white bread succeeds in bringing him back to his senses (ed. Staines, 261).

60. Akbari, "Nature's Forge Recast," 43.

the diet of a warrior. However, since the roles of mother and food provider are wholly governed by society, which has limited women of lower class to the roles of cook and nurse, Silence, as an aristocrat, is not destined to nurture anyone, not even her own child after it is born.[61]

At such a dramatic moment in the *Roman de Silence*—a story so obsessed with dialogue and verbal interaction that most of its manuscript miniatures only portray people talking[62]—further debate is unavoidable, and so once again Noureture and Nature meet to argue. The locus of inner turmoil, however, shifts from Silence to Merlin. In the final moments of the story, as Mary Ellen Ryder and Linda Marie Zaerr have observed, Silence's agency is diminished,[63] so much so that her internal dialogue—dramatized by the perpetual conflict between the allegorical figures of Nature and Noureture—lapses into their argument about Merlin. Silence is herself silenced in this last episode, both within and without, her destiny to be decided by others. Merlin and his violative performance of life outside society—like Silence, he was "noris en bos" (2354, 6003) [raised in the woods]—take the place of Silence's own nonconforming body. The fate of two men is at stake in this final debate, but only one is shown. Even the miniatures that accompany the Merlin episode do not feature Silence.[64] Merlin's occlusion of Silence presages her legal coverture to come, when she marries King Ebain at the end of the tale.

4. ROTTEN COUNSEL

The final debate between Nature and Noureture does not involve the fate of Silence—instead they restage the fall of Adam, grafting the ancient story onto the scene, creating a travesty both of the biblical narrative and of the old man's prophecy. The connotations of Eden are appropriate: even though Merlin is no Adam, he wills himself into a condition of renewed innocence.[65] Through his

---

61. Though medical authorities disapproved of the practice, Western European noble women often hired wet nurses to feed their babies, transforming the "natural" act of motherly breastfeeding through a cultural more.

62. See Thorpe's description of the miniatures (6–8), and Michelle Bolduc, "Images of Romance: The Miniatures of *Le Roman de Silence*," *Arthuriana* 12 (2002): 101.

63. Mary Ellen Ryder and Linda Marie Zaerr, "A Stylistic Analysis of the *Roman de Silence*," *Arthuriana* 18 (2008): 27.

64. The first, on fol. 218v, portrays a bird, apparently piercing its own breast like a pelican. The second, on fol. 221r, shows a Merlin-like figure sitting alone on a rock (see Bolduc, "Silence's Beasts," 193–96).

65. Merlin's storied assumption of the animal is traditionally explained in terms of madness, as it is usually presumed that one would have to be insane in order to want to take on a bestial life. However, the recent insights of animal studies question the reflexive assumption of animal inferiority and might encourage a reassessment of Merlin's act: might the magician just

diet of *herbes* and *rachines* he achieves a false state of prelapsarian nutrition, reversing the secondary and alienated relationship with nature that has been humankind's curse ever since the expulsion from paradise. Merlin eats without labor and without killing, yet this Edenic gastronomy is unnatural to him. Noureture recognizes this when she observes how the roasting meat tempts the bestial wizard:

> Or est Merlins en male luite.
> "Qu'as tu a faire de car cuite?"
> Dist Noreture, "Est cho dangiers?
> Herbes, rachines est tes mangiers."
> (6007–10)

> Now Merlin is in a painful struggle.
> "What do you have to do with cooked meat,"
> said Noureture, "Is this your whim?
> Herbs and roots are your food."

His "natural" predilection for meat interrupts Merlin's own self-discipline and the training he receives from Noureture, who teaches him to enjoy his greens. But appetite seems poised to betray him, a basic need that is indistinguishable from desire. Noureture cuts right to its effects on Merlin's body, the external forces by which he feels pulled in two. The word *dangiers* is slippery, meaning both caprice and compulsion;[66] it is a power outside of one's body that drives one to act. Food (*mangiers*) is the one thing that he cannot resist once he smells the meal laid out for him. He betrays his accustomed lifestyle on a whim of appetite.

Noureture attempts to bolster her weaker position with a rhetorical attack against Nature, invoking the incommensurability of men's bodies to their hearts, caused by the imperfections of Nature's process sifting and baking human forms. Noureture disavows her own power to improve a person with a bad heart, declaring that all bad men and women can be traced back to the first bad parents, Adam and Eve. Because no one came before them, their corruption must have come from Nature herself. Nature refutes this argument by retelling the story of the fall as an explicitly gustatory anecdote:

---

be playing at an imaginative refiguration of his life, a desire to experience what the world has to offer from many different points of view?

66. "Dangiers," s.v. Godefroy, *Dictionnaire de l'Ancienne Langue Francaise du IXme au XVIme Siécle*.

Cho dist Nature: "Or doi jo dire,
Cho sache Dex, li nostre sire,
Tu m'oposa del premier home
Ki pecha par mangier la pome.
Dex le fist certes com le suen,
Net, sans pechié, et biel et buen.
. . . .
Noreture, car te repoze?
Quanques Adans fist de rancure,
Fu par toi, certes, Noreture.
Car li diäbles le norri
Par son malvais consel porri.
Tant l'enaprist, tant l'enorta,
Que le pome le sorporta."
(6045–50; 6066–72)

Nature said this: "Now I must say,
God knows it, our Father,
You have opposed me since the first man
Who sinned by eating the apple.
God truly made him like one of his own,
Pure, without sin, both lovely and good.
. . . .
Noureture, why don't you give it a rest?
Whatever grievous acts Adam did,
It was by you, indeed, Noureture.
For the devil fed him
With his counsel, wicked and rotten.
So he taught him and encouraged him,
That he carried him away to the apple."

Nature argues that humankind fell by choosing the forbidden apple among all the other edible things available in Paradise, and the drastic effects have been carried down through history. Adam's drive for a kind of culinary innovation, the desire to eat something exotic, resulted in him imbibing (*norri*) the Devil's rotten counsel (*consel porri*). According to Nature, Noureture is born at this instant, appearing inside Adam at the moment of contact with the Devil: "Mais tolt lor vient de Noreture / Dont l'enemis Adan enbut / Quant par la pome le deçut" (6078–80) [But all that is due to Noureture / with which the

Enemy imbued Adam / when he deceived him with the apple].⁶⁷ Nature casts Noureture as an allegorical non-entity, a negative capacity equated with the Devil, with no power except for evil, to urge and confuse people to become contrary to nature. At that, Noureture turns pale and disappears—and Merlin (and Silence) revert to their "natural" identities.

Just as Silence seems to disappear from the scene of Merlin's fall, so too there is no Eve in Nature's retelling of the Fall. The narrator is silent upon the feminine at this piviotal moment—abandoning even the baiting, misogynistic diatribes that he seems to relish so much.⁶⁸ This omission is strategic, however; it is meant to imply more than he could say about the subservient role of women in the story. Nature's version of the Fall, mustered to deny her responsibility for Adam's disobedience, is exculpatory, meant to argue for a male nature that is not flawed at its core, but rather misled by circumstance. Nature's emphasis upon God's creation of the first man—and thus Adam's necessary goodness—is the crux of her argument. Eve, whom Nature does not mention, may be a different case: she was first tempted by the Devil and failed to resist him, eating the apple and then giving it to Adam. Nature's position on Eve is unclear: perhaps she was simply the first victim of the Devil/Noureture; or perhaps she—and consequently all women—are inherently "bad."

Playing the part of the absent Eve in this scene, Silence assumes the role of perfidious food provider, giving Merlin the food that causes a second fall from innocence. This is no tragedy of biblical proportions, however, but rather an episode of uproariously comic gluttony. Merlin's submission to the smell of roasted meat results in his punishment through a series of painful slapstick pratfalls. Victorious Nature treats Merlin like a *maleöit fol* (6091) [wretched fool], dragging him by the scruff of the neck through the brambles and bushes, tearing and scratching the wild man in the process of celebrating her triumph. By chastising the wayward wizard, Nature demonstrates the cost of betraying one's "natural" identity. Merlin is afflicted with a great burning desire, a ravenous appetite not only for meat but also for his own displaced human identity. This hunger leaves him vulnerable both to Silence's trap and also his own machinations. The setup is farcical, the action burlesque. Merlin is all gluttony in his single-minded fixation "de la car" [by the meat], a phrase repeated three times (6109–15). Regardless of the pain it causes him, he tears into it, not caring if it is "Cuite u crue, salee u fresce" (6113) [raw or cooked, salted or fresh]. Merlin ignores Nature, Noureture, and saltiness here—all he cares about is his hunger. Salt is the activating agent for the trap that catches

---

67. Translation by Roche-Mahdi.
68. See the narrator's comments after Eufeme is rebuffed by Silence (3901–24), or when she learns Silence is coming back to England (5222–41).

both Merlin and Silence: it is a feature of the meat that is not immediately visible, especially after it has been roasted. Merlin cannot know the nature of the meat until he takes a bite first. In the same way, Silence's body, like Silence's meal, is both salted and fresh, her true nature concealed from sight.

The comic description of Merlin as he drinks the pots is a further jab at his gluttony—the physical torment of his indigestion that the narrator hopes will provoke belly-laughs from the audience:

> Ki donc veïst enfler Merlin!
> Com plus en goit, plus en puet boire,
> Et si ne fait fors lui deçoivre.
> Ki donc veïst home a mesaise!
> Merlins crieve d'anguisse enaise.
> Il voit le lait, si en boit donques.
> Or n'ot il mais tele angoissce onques.
> Ki donc veïst ventre eslargir,
> Estendre, et tezir, et bargir,
> Ne lairoit qu'il n'en resist tost!
> (6120–29)

> Then you should have seen Merlin swell up!
> The more he swallowed the thirstier he got—
> all he accomplished was his own undoing.
> You never saw a man in greater discomfort;
> Merlin was nearly dying with agony.
> He saw the milk and drank it then.
> He had never been in such pain!
> If you ever saw how his belly swelled up,
> expanded, inflated and dilated,
> you would have burst out laughing![69]

The repeated lines "Ki donc veïst" [you should have seen] make Merlin a spectacle to be gawked at: his belly swells up like a balloon in a parody of overeating. The absurdity of the display is emphasized by the piling-on of synonyms for swelling of the stomach (*enfler, eslargir, estendre, tezir, bargir*). Both his inflation and his agony suggest that Merlin is experiencing a kind of pregnancy, shifting between the male and the female in his tormented state. He gives birth to himself as a human, just as he will "engender" Silence.

---

69. Translation by Roche-Mahdi.

At this point, the compound identities both of Silence and Merlin are reaching their breaking point; the paradoxes inherent to being "norris en bois" [raised in the forest] are becoming more and more intolerable. As Merlin succumbs to Silence's edible snare, we realize that neither of them can escape their culturally conditioned selves. Merlin's inclination to consume the products of human labor drags him out of the forest and back into society. One can be nurtured in the woods—the chaotic space outside the court—only in the complete absence of others. Merlin, in his solitude, has managed to defy Nature for a long time, so long that he can exist without labor in the woods, gathering the simplest of foods. He is no longer a man because he has moved beyond the human dependence on labor. Silence, too, was raised in the forest, "solitive et solitaire" (2154) [solitary and alone], hidden away from the pressures and performances of aristocratic life. She was able to labor to become a man in this isolation, free from discourses that would feminize her. Yet unlike Merlin, whose bestiality frees him from humanity, Silence is nothing without a stage upon which to work at her masculinity.[70] Social humanity cannot find escape from culture in the woods, for it brings its political constraints and feels its absence. Just as the body wears culture's requirements, so the mind toils under its burdens.

5. THE POT BOILS OVER

Just as Silence drops out of the final debate between Nature and Noureture, so she will take a secondary role in the *dénouement* of the *Roman de Silence*, reduced to the status of an observer in her own life story. She reacts inwardly but never initiates action in the poem's last scenes, subject to Ebain's and Merlin's speech acts. Merlin takes over the tale. The account of his irrepressible laughter at the other characters' predicaments (and his own) replaces the introspection of Silence, his extroversion dominating the final events of the romance. What only has been thought is spoken aloud; what lies hidden will be dragged to the surface. Secrets are made into proclamations, and clothed inscrutability becomes naked exposure.

Merlin always gets the last laugh. Silence has captured him and Nature humiliated him, but the prophet and trickster, who knows the ends of all

---

70. Silence, as a knight and vassal, is a social creature who feels her exile profoundly. However, this is not the only attitude to take toward life in the forest. The eagerness shown by Cador's kinswoman, the widow who attends Eufemie as a midwife and then raises Silence in the woods, embraces the possibilities of being a *femme solée* away from court and its patriarchal culture (2155–74).

things, is the one giggling when it is all over. Merlin's hilarity, the marriage of King Ebain to Silence, and the king's reversal of his edict that no woman can inherit land, close *Silence* on a comic note. Comedy restores all its energetic disruptions to the original status quo. Nothing seems to change in this comic mode; its reparations seem to smooth over the story's ideological challenges and innovations. Merlin, the supporter and guarantor of the masculine values of society, performs this comic labor; his ability to see into the future often leads affairs to mirror the way they were in the past.

Exposed to the gawking eyes of crowds, Merlin labors as well as laughs. He is a cook preparing a special dish: "Il tienant or Merlin por sot, / Mais il decoverra le pot, / Si fera telis i a maris (6185–87) [They took Merlin now to be a fool / But he would uncover the pot, / And make many of them there uncomfortable]. Even while reduced to a fool and a prisoner, Merlin cooks up his revenge, uncovering the kettle and stirring the brew so that its contents do not boil over prematurely. He masks the fruits of his efforts until the perfect moment, when King Ebain calls out for the dinner of his comeuppance—the revelation that Silence is a biological woman.

Throughout the *Roman de Silence,* the labor of cooking does not merely alter the flavor of a foodstuff: the spice reveals its inner nature only to counteract or alter it. Cookery is a practice of revelation, exposing the truth behind appearances. Nature's bakeshop concocts Silence's composite and confused identity, a product of *vallans* flour (that is, aristocratic and masculine matter) in the form of femininity. In trapping Merlin, Silence lays bare the strong roots of his humanity, concealed but not negated by his bestial practice and animal diet. She exposes herself as well: for both, cooking is apocalyptic in the root sense of the word (from the Greek: *àpo* + *kalyptein* = to disclose, uncover). The dish reveals the eater, uncovering truths that have lain hidden or unacknowledged.

While Silence's culinary act was restorative, feeding the human in Merlin so that it can reemerge and take its rightful place, Merlin's is emetic, forcing the truth out of those who have internalized their deception for so long:

> Merlins, ki siet desos le lanbre,
> Ki voit et set trestolte l'uevre,
> Destemparra ancui tel suevre,
> Ki sera tels i a moult sure
> Anchois que viegne nuis obscure.
> (6408–12)

> Merlin, who sat beneath the carved paneling,
> Who sees and knows the entire work,
> Was mis-tempering that very day so spicy a sauce
> That would make many bitter bellies
> Before the dark night fell.

This is the only place in the poem that the *(o)uevre* (work) does not rhyme with some form of *cuevre* (to cover). *Uevre* is most often used to describe Silence herself—not only the secret of her gender but also the efforts by which she has concealed it. This work, which has been covered, uncovered, and recovered, finally reaches a stage where it must be laid bare. The baked body of Silence is ready to be consumed by masculine society. What better way to serve it than accompanied by the *suevre* that Merlin concocts, the spicy sauce of prophetic revelation?

The verb *destemper* (or *destremper*), as Terence Scully notes, is used to signify the process by which dry ingredients such as spices were mixed with liquids in order to create a humorally balanced mixture that could be added to a dish or used to form the base of a sauce.[71] Medieval cooks had to be quite careful of the balance of these blends, ensuring that their cooking did not make their patron ill by disturbing his complexion. The act of creating gastronomic equilibrium, then, is synonymous with cooking. Merlin, however, is not a chef that is interested in soothing anyone: he cooks to uncover the truth, and so Merlin's dish is the romance equivalent of the angel's book in Revelations 10:10: "And it was in my mouth, sweet as honey: and when I had eaten it, my belly was bitter." His stew is a purgative medicine, meant to go down sweetly but burn inside the stomach, intended to purge Ebain's court of its complacent acceptance of corruption and deceit. Ebain, who has labored long to cover up Eufeme's schemes and maintain his honor, will no longer be allowed to look the other way. Merlin is the final chef in the sequence of *Silence*'s cooks; his meal is prophecy distempered and barely palatable, but vitally necessary to disgorge the deceptions that surround the English king.

Merlin's cathartic revelations seem to reset the romance, to replicate its opening circumstances. King Ebain is single again, just as he was at the start of the tale. He renounces his onerous prohibition of female inheritance (the rationale for Silence's cross-dressing in the first place) and makes peace with one of his land's most prominent families through a marriage with their daughter. But these apparent resolutions are impossible to digest without a bitter belly. Silence's extraordinary *aventures* as a man must come to a halt: she

---

71. Terence Scully, "Tempering Medieval Food," in *Food in the Middle Ages: A Book of Essays*, ed. Melitta Weiss Adamson, 6–7.

must step down while she's on top. And though she exemplifies the narrator's closing admonition for all women to be led by Noureture from their originary *malvaise* (6684–701), her gender laboring thwarts the ideological status quo and throws its binary logic into chaos. Class, gender, sexual identity, even the human/animal distinction has been threatened by her performance and the world has been revealed as an eminently queerable place. Yet this queering is also theorized as a means to resist political injustice and thrive in a poorly led kingdom. Category crisis has liberated its players in an unjust world—if only temporarily. This is too much for Heldris's conservative narrator to bear: he labors to tamp down these menacing exceptions to the dreary rule. The method for ending this carnivalesque reign of binary play is hegemonic, the king himself acts unilaterally to bring the world back into dyadic alignment. Confronted with the accusation that his most reliable retainer is a woman, and his wife has a male lover right under his nose, and to have these allegations bruited before his entire court, King Ebain does the only thing he can do. He works to displace his own burning shame onto someone else, ordering that the "nun" and Silence be stripped naked in front of everyone. They are punished by exposure for their transgressive behavior, all treacheries to gender being equal. The only verification he will accept—despite the fact that Merlin has been right about everything else—is the naked "proof" of biology. The story is boiled down at its conclusion to an imposition of the unadorned truth of Nature (a word that can mean "genitalia" in Old French). Despite its earlier philosophical exploration of a laboring goddess Nature and a gender that is just skin-deep, the narrator seems to deny his imaginative work, copping out to the established order of things. Yet his theory of bodies lingers: if gender is just molded onto a body, then how can Ebain ever know what Silence "really" is, even if he sees her genitals for himself. Isn't he just assuming he knows what they mean?

The final miniature in the manuscript illustrates the indeterminacy of this crude test of veracity: the king is shown facing an empty silhouette of a woman. The manuscript itself seems to deny resolution in a poignant coincidence or perhaps an intentional alteration: the paint that once represented the miniature woman's nakedness has either flaked away or been scraped off, leaving an empty outline to represent the truth of the transgressive heroine of the *Roman de Silence*. What is left is the account of labor, of performance, and in the end that is all a reader can trust in a world riven by category crises.

The possibility of category crossing, seemingly so common yet so menacing to traditionally androcentric, patriarchal forms of civilization, foregrounds ideas of the naturalness of human bodies thought to be inherently marked by both gender and class identities. Heldris de Cornuälle, if any such English author actually existed, has exulted in his proto-postmodern attack on the prediscursivity of these bodies, refusing to accept the constraints of cisgender assumptions and recognizing, like Judith Butler does so famously, that performance is a powerful political force in society. The more obviously political romance of *Havelok the Dane*, explored in the next chapter, also probes a related question: in a world in which class identity was thought to be even more determining than gender, what happens when the sovereign must actually perform the role of the servile? *Havelok* approaches this delicate, disruptive question in a manner parallel to Heldris. That is, the anonymous author stages his intervention by means of food, revealing perhaps the most compelling example of the force of political appetites in the romantic imagination. *Havelok* demonstrates that social order is made legible through what its members can eat, founded upon and edified by culinary distinctions. It is not just a matter of kings having more to eat than the peasants: eating itself is an expression of political power. Sovereignty, as opposed to servility, is manifested through privileged consumption of human products, and is therefore dependent upon the labors of suffering, toiling humanity.

CHAPTER 3

Havelok the Dane

Food, Sovereignty, and Social Order

> The daily fight in which the human body is engaged to keep the world clean and prevent its decay bears little resemblance to heroic deeds; the endurance it needs to repair every day anew the waste of yesterday is not courage, and what makes the effort painful is not danger but its relentless repetition.
>
> —HANNAH ARENDT, *THE HUMAN CONDITION*

1. THE GENRE OF LABOR

THERE IS a generic problem inherent to the story of the struggle of the working class, as Arendt suggests in the above passage. In myths, humans labor heroically against nature and find victory and glory in their efforts. Even when a hero performs a seemingly ordinary act—for example, cleaning out a stable or competing in a swimming contest—the stakes are magnified far beyond what any other person could expect to achieve. For everyone else, there is only a "relentless repetition" of the struggle against disrepair and chaos, entangled in an interminable battle to maintain life itself. The circularity of labor, which must immediately reincorporate some part of what it produces in order to continue working, forestalls the question of heroism as much as its grinding endlessness overflows narrative bounds. To be recognized as extraordinary, a hero must wrest surplus into one's possession, a feat that demonstrates one's excellence among others. In the narrative of productive work, there are few of the remainders—wealth, honor, or glory—that allow a tale to be pushed toward climax, conclusion, and repose. Labor-power as material phenomenon or human condition exists beyond the horizon of aristocratic genres, like tragedy, epic, and romance, and this exclusivity renders these literary forms unable to represent the actual source of the political power they celebrate.

The romance of *Havelok the Dane* (ca. 1295) is an experiment in generic frontiers, an attempt to look into the vanishing point that is the unrepresentable space of work. It is a narrative profoundly concerned with the human body's distressing vulnerability in a world of sweat and hunger. It is a story pitched at the grand scale of international political maneuvering, of dynasties and usurpation, of invasion and restoration that nonetheless characterizes its own themes in a decidedly more local context, describing itself as a story of "Hw he weren born and hw fedde" (2987).[1] Such a homely assessment seems overly modest for such a rich, complex, and magnificent tale, yet it is literally true. In charting the course from Havelok's exile in infancy, youth of toil, and ultimate reclamation of his inheritance, the romance never stops watching his body, and his efforts to sustain himself during his exile stand in for the more standard set of adventures of the knight-errant. Havelok is a conspicuously physical hero, remarkable not only for his great size and strength but also for a physicality bound up in the quotidian, in the "relentless repetition" of daily struggle for sustenance.

The story of *Havelok* operates on a continuum between deprivation and labor at one end, and superabundance and effortless acquisition at the other. Havelok's life moves between these extremes of subordination and sovereignty in a relationship intelligible mostly through the consumption of food. The conspicuous presence of eating in *Havelok* is not an attempt to court the tastes of middle-class readers: rather, food is vital to the romance's inquiry into political theory. *Havelok* has long fascinated and puzzled readers with the wealth and realism of its portrayal of working-class life and its apparent lack of traditional romance *topoi*. It is unique in its disregard of the courtly realm of tournaments and quests, of lover-knights and damsels in distress, a generic panoply that "never pretend[s] to give an accurate picture of life in their times," yet that radiates from these conditions all the same.[2] Instead, the first thousand lines of *Havelok* abound with details of working-class life and economic conditions, and create explicitly a "rags-to-riches" journey for Havelok. As he climbs the social ladder, we see fish, meat and bread produced and exchanged, starvation lingering a step away from plenty, and unemployed boys knocking each other down in order to gain work.

This emphasis on the quotidian in a genre otherwise renowned for its fantasies of courtly life has led to serious misgivings about the author, audience,

---

1. *Havelok*, ed. Smithers. Citations of *Havelok* are from this edition. Editorial marks (italics and brackets) have been removed for ease of reading, but otherwise spelling has been maintained.

2. Ramsey, *Chivalric Romances*, 36

and purpose of *Havelok*.³ Many critics have argued that the homely details of the story could not possibly have appealed to a genteel audience, and therefore found it inconceivable that the poem could have originated anywhere within the aristocracy. The preeminent expression of this sentiment belongs to Derek Pearsall: "The manner of the poem is rough, but the handling of the story bears witness at every point to deliberate purpose, and *Havelok* has a claim, if any English romance has, to be regarded as the genuine expression of popular consciousness."⁴ By contrast, Susan Crane reminds that "our only evidence of the story's transmission prior to its appearance in *Havelok the Dane* finds it within the circles of power," and these more courtly versions also contain antecedents of the same homely details.⁵ The story of Havelok is first found at the beginning of Geoffrei Gaimar's *L'Estoire des Engleis* (ca. 1150), a chronicle written for Constance fitz Gilbert, an Anglo-Norman noblewoman of Lincolnshire.⁶ Much critical ink has been spilled arguing these class sympathies back and forth, an exchange outlined by Christopher Stuart.⁷ Michael Faletra makes a persuasive refutation of the populism of *Havelok*, mobilizing postcolonial ideas to understand the proto-nationalism of the story. The effect of this incipient collective awareness is to create a "profound mystification" that subordinates class complaints to a growing nationalist sentiment in England, and that "employs this new expression of group identity as a means of combatting potentially dangerous tensions within medieval English society, tensions that would come to a head in post-plague England with the Peasant Revolt of 1381."⁸ The fantasy of an England united best serves the powers that be, and

---

3. Critical opinions about the English romance have traditionally upheld Chaucer's *The Knight's Tale* as an apotheosis of its courtly ideals and intentions. In this magnificent poem, Duke Theseus prolongs chivalric contest in order to grant himself a greater and greater jurisdiction over the untidiness of life and death in order to magnify and celebrate the values of the aristocratic class. This celebration of knightly display systematically suppresses what is carnal or appetitive in humanity. This final point is suggested by Kathryn Lynch in "From Tavern to Pie Shop: The Raw, the Cooked, and the Rotten in Fragment 1 of Chaucer's *Canterbury Tales*," *Exemplaria* 19 (2007): 122.

4. Derek Pearsall, "The Development of Middle English Romance," in *Studies in Medieval English Romances: Some New Approaches*, ed. Derek Brewer, 19.

5. Crane, *Insular Romance*, 43.

6. Geoffrei Gaimar, *L'Estoire des Engleis*, ed. Alexander Bell. A translation is available in idem, *Lestorie des Engles solum la translacion Maistre Geffrei Gaimar*, ed. and trans. Sir Thomas Duffus Hardy and Charles Trice Martin, *Rerum Britannicum Medii Aevi Scriptores*, vol. 91. The only other extant analogue is the Anglo-Norman *Lai d'Aveloc* (ca. 1150–200), and found in *Le Lai d'Haveloc and Gaimar's Haveloc Episode*, ed. Alexander Bell.

7. Christopher Stuart's excellent summary can be found in "*Havelok the Dane* and Edward I in the 1290s," *Studies in Philology* 93 (1996): 349–51.

8. Michael Faletra, "The Ends of Romance: Dreaming the Nation in the Middle English *Havelok*," *Exemplaria* 17 (2005): 355–56.

allows them to suppress or ignore the complex interweaving of class interest that existed in late thirteenth-century England.

Interestingly, none of these arguments address the provenance of Oxford, Bodleian Library MS Laud Misc. 108, the sole extant manuscript of the Middle English *Havelok,* and they choose instead to determine an audience by characterizing the relative appeal of its poetic features, categorizing these elements as belonging to "high" or "low" literature. This manuscript, however, tells a more complex story. It is constructed in two separate parts, the first dominated by a version of the *South English Legendary* (ca. 1265), an important and widely disseminated collection of hagiographic materials, and the second mostly filled by the romances of *Havelok* and *King Horn* (ca. 1270).[9] This overwhelmingly devotional context has led some critics to consider *Havelok* and its romance neighbor as "homiletic romances."[10] Ownership of MS Laud 108 is unknown for its early history, though Andrew Taylor posits that various pieces of the manuscript were copied in the same Oxford-area bookshop and commissioned perhaps for a well-to-do East Anglian patron.[11] However, an inscription late in the manuscript can be dated to the mid-fifteenth century, which attests to a possible owner, Henry Perneys, a London guildsman and draper, whose father John was one time the mayor of London.[12] While not settling the question of *Havelok*'s ideal audience for certain, the provenance of the codex suggests that it found a home among the prosperous urban bourgeoisie who were in the process of becoming the dominant economic force in late medieval England, a social class whose perspective on cultural and political power would have been quite pragmatic.

The socioeconomic interests of *Havelok* should be considered as evidence of the artistic integrity of the story—and its political sophistication—rather than a distressing example of the inferior tastes of an English vernacular reader. Furthermore, the source of the English nobility's political power was largely economic, not military—as a consequence, there would have been a

---

9. *Havelok,* xi–xii; A. S. G. Edwards, "Oxford, Bodleian Library, MS Laud Misc. 108: Contents, Construction, and Circulation," in *Texts and Contexts,* ed. Bell and Couch, 25.

10. The attribution "homiletic romance" was first made by Dieter Mehl in *Middle English Romances,* 5. Kimberly Bell reads *Havelok* and *King Horn* in the context of the kingly saints' lives contained in the *South English Legendary* ("Resituating Romance: The Dialectics of Sanctity in MS Laud Misc. 108's *Havelok the Dane* and Royal *Vitae*," *Parergon* 25 [2008]: 32–38).

11. Andrew Taylor, "'Her Y Spelle': The Evocation of Minstrel Performance in a Hagiographical Context," in *Texts and Contexts,* ed. Bell and Couch, 76–80.

12. This inscription appears on fol. 238v and reads "iste liber constat Henrico Perneys testantibus Iohanni Rede presbiteri William Rotheley et alijs" [this book belongs to Henry Perneys by the testimonies of the priest John Rede, William Rotheley and others]. This attribution is discussed by Smithers, *Havelok,* xiii; Edwards, "Oxford, Bodleian Library," 29–30; and Christina M. Fitzgerald, "Miscellaneous Masculinities and a Possible Fifteenth-Century Owner of Oxford, Bodleian Library, MS Laud Misc. 108," in *Texts and Contexts,* ed. Bell and Couch, 87–89.

great deal of interest in and familiarity with the common objects and practices of everyday life that create and maintain power.[13] The implications of the nobility's interest in the operations of their own households are explored in the work of Vance Smith, who argues that romances are deeply invested in economic problems such as surplus and exchange, and that they reflect this interest in narrative and symbolic choices as they adapt continental romances to insular forms. *Havelok* presents an interesting case within Smith's paradigm: the poem explicitly imagines economic relations rather than wrapping them in symbolic language.[14]

The overt, material representation of food in *Havelok* is central to its purpose, and it is only through food practices that the author can most effectively explore the fundamental connection between the individual laborer and the body politic, as incarnated by its ruler. Yet food is only occasionally noticed by critics of the poem, often as presence favoring its middle-class affinities. This omission is especially interesting since the continuous focus on Havelok's eating is not found in the Anglo-Norman versions of the legend. Robert W. Hanning was the first scholar to dwell at any length upon the edible in *Havelok*, explaining this extended interest with the statement: "All human strength and growth depend upon sufficient nourishment, and therefore repeated feasts accord well with the poet's constant interest in Havelok's progress from an impotent child to a strong adult."[15] In Hanning's paradigm, food is primarily a means to an end, a material consideration that justifies the romance's emphasis on its hero's remarkable physique. Yet Hanning does not explore these feasts for their social and political ramifications, and in fact, underplays the import of the story's first two meals (those given by Grim and Leue and by Bertram the cook) because of the reduced circumstances of Havelok. To Hanning, their desperation precludes their political interpretation. Dayton Haskin relates the tale's emphasis on food as part of its structure of Christian generosity and Matthean judgment, subordinating the material aspects of the poem to its religious ideological interpretations.[16] As a result,

---

13. Crane, *Insular Romance*, 6–7. Margaret Wade Labarge, *A Baronial Household of the Thirteenth Century*, confirms many of these observations. A parallel situation could be seen in the *Islendingasögur* or "family sagas" of the Icelandic tradition, which often show the oligarchical, landowning "gentry" of the Icelandic countryside engaged in the daily activities of their farmsteads, whether mowing hay or flensing beached whales, activities seemingly shared with their enslaved laborers. This connection is intriguing given the Scandinavian affiliations of Havelok the Dane.

14. Smith, *Arts of Possession*, xiv–xv, 5–8.

15. Robert W. Hanning, "*Havelok the Dane*: Structure, Symbols, Meaning," *Studies in Philology* 64 (1967): 599.

16. Dayton Haskin, S. J., "Food, Clothing and Kingship in *Havelok*," *American Benedictine Review* 24 (1973), 204–13.

food does not become very specific in his argument. This chapter moves past these early studies by elevating the status of food to a powerful social object in its own right, one whose production, circulation, and consumption play an important role not only in forming political bodies but in distinguishing them, as well.

In voyaging from the incipient sovereignty of his infancy (the suprasomatic quality that overflows Havelok's body through his blazing mouth) to the utter servility of his youth, Havelok observes firsthand how the material wealth of the land is produced, exchanged, and altered through the labor power of his rightful subjects. Recent critics have explored the *Havelok*'s inclusive perspective of society as the precocious ideological stirrings of the modern English nation-state.[17] Without refuting this idea, I argue that the story's integrated and inclusive view of social order explores a more fundamental problem of political theory: the definition of sovereignty, the ineffable right to assemble a political body to rule. While most romances tell the story of how a youthful but unprepared nobleman achieves self-knowledge and his birthright, none attempts anything as radical as to erase the hero's aristocratic identity completely.[18] By taking this extreme step, the *Havelok* poet attempts to represent the moment that subordination is transformed into sovereignty, to discover the act that distinguishes one from the other. *Havelok* recognizes that eating, the same action that unites all humans despite their position in society also divides an overlord from his many servants. Georges Bataille, exploring the definition of sovereignty in *The Accursed Share*, makes a similar observation:

> What distinguishes sovereignty is the consumption of wealth, as against labor and servitude, which produce wealth without consuming it. The sovereign individual *consumes and doesn't labor*, whereas at the antipodes of sovereignty the slave and the man without means toil and reduce their con-

---

17. Most recently in Thorlac Turville-Petre, "*Havelok* and the History of the Nation," in *Readings in Medieval Romance*, ed. Carol M. Meale, 121–34, and *England the Nation: Language, Literature, and National Identity, 1290–1340*; Robert Rouse, *The Idea of Anglo-Saxon England in Middle English Romance*, esp. 70ff; and Faletra, "Ends of Romance," 348.

18. There are some romances that come close, like *Octavian* (ca. 1350), which places Florent, its noble foundling, in a burgher's house, yet derives much of its comic energy from the boy's unconscious affinity for aristocratic values. *Isumbras* (ca. 1320–50) turns its knightly hero into a blacksmith, though this is done as part of a humbling penitential regime and keeps him close to the material register of the military class. The *Tale of Gamelyn* (ca. 1350–70) may be the romance that comes the closest to *Havelok*; its hero reaches out to outlaws and subverts legal society in order to redress his brother's attempts to dispossess him.

sumption to the necessities, to the products without which they could neither subsist nor work any longer.[19]

The sovereign is recognized by his ability to "truly enjoy the products of this world," that is, by consuming what others produce.[20] He never has to experience labor himself, but exists in a state of absolute leisure and enjoyment. His pleasure in eating is not limited by the pain or effort of expending himself in order to produce the objects of his delectation (since to offer up one's own labor-power would expose oneself to the consumption of someone else—and as soon as that possibility exists, one no longer can be recognized as sovereign).[21] The world of sovereignty is not just conspicuously engaged with surplus: as "life beyond need" it is surplus itself.[22] This privileged location of consumption sits in fundamental opposition to the "antipodes" of "necessities" and "subsistence," but is hardly separable from it. The terms that Bataille sets forth are extremely useful to illuminate *Havelok*'s transition between the lowest and highest positions in society. In the wake of dynastic and legal failure, represented in the text by the usurpations of the wicked noblemen Godrich

---

19. Bataille, *Accursed Share*, 3.198 (emphasis in the original). His discussion of sovereignty versus subordination recasts Hegel's Lord/Bondsman dialectic into terms explicitly engaged with political theory. By doing so, he seems to be reading Hegel in a way congenial with the insights of Andrew Cole's argument of the feudal context of the Lord/Bondsman dialectic ("What Hegel's Master/Slave Dialectic Really Means" [*JMEMS* 34 (2004): 577–610]).

20. Bataille, *Accursed Share*, 3.198. Bourdieu suggests that the cultural elites actually endeavor to consume their rightful commodities in a different manner than their subordinates: "The denial of lower, coarse, vulgar, venal, servile—in a word, natural—enjoyment, which constitutes the sacred sphere of culture, implies an affirmation of the superiority of those who can be satisfied with the sublimated, refined, disinterested, gratuitous, distinguished pleasures forever closed to the profane" (*Distinction*, 7).

21. That the king may not have been capable of producing the food he eats is the question lurking behind the classic and amusing anecdote of King Alfred's disguise, as he is questioned by a cowherd's wife after allowing cakes to burn over the fire, found first in the *Annals of St. Neots* (ca. late tenth century, once thought to be written by John Asser, the biographer of the king) and then later interpolated by Matthew Parker into his 1574 edition of Asser's *Life of Alfred* (893), and which becomes popularly recounted in many subsequent histories and chronicles. (For the Latin text of Asser and the *Annals of St. Neots*, see *Asser's Life of King Alfred*, ed. William Henry Stevenson, 136, and a modern English translation in *The Medieval Life of King Alfred the Great*, trans. and ed. Alfred P. Smyth, 25.)

22. Surplus is directly related to exceptionality, an idea that forms the core of Carl Schmitt's classic definition of sovereignty: "Sovereign is he that decides on the exception" (*Political Theology: Four Chapters on the Concept of Sovereignty* [1934], trans. George Schwab, 5). This powerful and paradoxical statement is revisited and elaborated in Georgio Agamben's *Homo Sacer: Sovereign Power and Bare Life*, trans. Daniel Heller-Roazen, esp. 15–29. Though he does not name him directly in the third part of *The Accursed Share*, Bataille is certainly responding to Schmitt. Whereas for Schmitt, the exception is a juridical problem mystified by political mythology, Bataille engages sovereignty as an economic condition made mythological.

and Godard, the rebuilding of social order must begin at its most fundamental level, with the simple act of feeding a hungry child.

2. FOOD IN THE BODY POLITIC

The English king Athelwold, a description of whose reign opens the poem, offers a paradigm for the ideal relations between food and political authority. The narrator's extended encomium portrays him as a bountiful provider, creating laws that are just and appropriately enforced, roads that are safe from robbers, and giving protection to the poor and helpless (27–105). The poem pointedly lingers on Athelwold's guardianship of his people's nutrition. His strength holds off invaders and prevents the people from starving due to warfare: "Was non so bold louerd to Rome/ Þat durste upon his londe bringhe/ Hunger ne here—wicke þinghe" (64–66). His virtues are hardly limited to the military; they are matched and even exceeded by his largesse toward his people:

> Hauede he non so god brede
> Ne on his bord non so god shrede
> Þat he ne wolde þor-wit fede
> Poure þat on fote yede.
> (97–101)

This description of the king's generosity comes near the end of a nineteen-line tirade (an extended run of verse that repeats a single rhyme), praising Athelwold's readiness to fight his opponents and his obedience to the church. His culinary charity is another form of kingly magnificence, which expresses both his strength and his holiness, an act of charity that is simultaneously a conspicuous display of wealth and power. Feasting upon the best of his people's products, which he does not produce himself, he can afford to redistribute the leftovers to the needy of his kingdom. His generosity is only enhanced by the excellence of the food he is willing to send out as alms. Athelwold dines in a manner that enforces his claim to rule his nation, but with the happy result that all have enough to eat.

This vision of peace and plenty, the nutritional process of good rule in England, is imperiled by Athelwold's impending death without an adult heir, a situation that will be repeated in Denmark with Havelok's father Birkabeyn.[23]

---

23. I read the abbreviated account of Denmark's political situation as an effort to show the two countries as twinned entities, equivalent legal bodies, with Birkabeyn's Denmark more or less possessing all of those qualities evinced by Athelwold's England. However, this interpreta-

Both kings attempt to ensure that their kingdoms will be safe, and their heirs provided for until they come to their majority, but Athelwold's own inability to eat in his final sickness (146) is a sign that a chain of sufficiency has been broken. Despite the kings' laudable attempts to create a legally binding consensus to ensure the continuity of their realms, deprivation will soon follow. The betrayal of their regents' oaths is not long in coming, and both Godrich and Goddard manifest the renunciation of their vows with acts that deprive the heirs of food: their charges will "greten ofte sore/ Boþe for hunger and for kold" (415–16). The implications of tyrannical rule go beyond mere starvation, as displayed by the bloody actions of Birkabeyn's usurper. Having imprisoned the king's children in a tower and arrived to check on their misery, Godard receives a precocious request for increased maintenance from the three-year-old Havelok:

> "For us hungreth swiþe sore,"
> Seyden he, "we wolden more:
> We ne have to hete, ne we ne have
> Her inne neyþer knith ne knave
> Þat yeveth us drinke ne no mete,
> Haluendel þat we moun ete—
> Wo is us þat we weren born!
> Weilawei! Nis it no korn
> Þat men micte maken of bred?
> Ws hungreth—we aren ney ded!"
> (455–64)

The tiny child and heir appears to know exactly, though intuitively, what he and his sisters are entitled to under the agreement their father made with Godard. In his grammatically convoluted concluding statement, "Nis it no korn/ Þat men micte maken of bred," Havelok recognizes the intimate connection between sustenance and service that is required to preserve them as figures of authority. Godard, in response, carves Havelok's sisters "al to grotes" (472), into little pieces of flesh, and by doing so provides a terrifyingly literal response to Havelok's request for food. The horrifying opportunity for cannibalism shocks the audience with Godard's monstrosity; it also illuminates

---

tion is questioned by Robert Rouse, who suggests that Denmark is a "legal vacuum," and the effect of Havelok's rule over both countries is to import an English form of a legal golden age into the less developed partner (*Idea of Anglo-Saxon England*, 104–5). My reading is confirmed by Gary Lim, "In the Name of the (Dead) Father: Reading Fathers and Sons in *Havelok the Dane, King Horn*, and *Bevis of Hampton*," *JEGP* 110 (2011): 26–27.

the paradox of sovereignty: that it can never be self-sustaining. Havelok can no more feed upon his sisters' flesh than his royal identity can allow him to make his own food.

Fantasizing about the limits of sovereign consumption was not uncommon in medieval historical texts. In several instances, chroniclers noted moments where the appetite of the king was less than wholesome, and constructed potent critiques for those unsavory hungers. In Benoît de Saint-Maure's *Chronique des Ducs de Normandie* (ca. 1150), William II of England was reputed to have been punished for his presumptuous, and by some accounts, irreligious rule by suffering a freak accident while hunting in the New Forest in 1100. The night before his death, according to Benoît, the king had a prophetic dream of being lost in the forest and suffering a great hunger. There he finds an empty church and enters to find a slain deer on the altar ("Un mult grant cerf qui ert ocis" [40, 562]), and he begins to eat its flesh.[24] To his horror, the body is transformed into a human, but William finds himself unable to refrain from continuing his meal.[25] Robert Mannyng of Brunne, an East Anglian writer active just before the *Havelok*-author, described the strange anthropophagic meal of King Cadwallon of Britain in his *Chronicle* (1338), a provision that sets the king apart among his subjects. While at war with a rival king, Cadwallon of Britain falls ill and feels that he must have venison in order to be cured of his ailment. His hunters go forth into the woods, but find no game. So one of his vassals "schare a pece out of his thee" to give to the king.[26] Cadwallon eats the human flesh and finds it quite sweet (15,066), and is subsequently restored to health, free to pursue the war. One of the most intriguing examples of sovereign cannibalism is found in the expanded A text of the romance of *Richard Coer de Lyon* (ca. late fourteenth century), which features not one but two instances of King Richard I's reputed anthropophagism—most shockingly when he serves the severed and roasted heads of Saracen captives to a delegation from Saladin.[27] These three anecdotes illustrate the potential outrage in spectacular sovereign consumption, that kings could and did eat foods unavailable to their people.

The full implications of Godard's shocking crime do not become fully apparent in the narrative until Havelok unwittingly reveals his birthright to Grim and Leue one hundred lines later. Whereas the fisherman and his wife look at Havelok and witness his royal potential overflowing through his

---

24. Benoît de Saint-Maure, *Chronique des Ducs de Normandie*, ed. Francisque Michel.

25. The portent turns upon an oneiric pun, "cerf" (deer), and the implied "serf" of the human meal.

26. Robert Mannyng of Brunne, *The Chronicle*, ed. Idelle Sullens, 15,061.

27. *Richard Coer de Lyon: Der mittelenglische Versroman über Richard Löwenherz*, 3580–89.

burning mouth, Godard sees only flesh-and-blood children, whose need for physical comfort provides him an opportunity to thwart the rightful succession, and whose material bodies can be reduced to meat and blood that will never manifest their divine authority. If, as Christopher Cannon suggests, this romance is not so much about the actual person of the boy king, but "rather, the *extent* to which [Havelok] exceeds the bounds of personhood, that which is in him . . . which exceeds what any person *could* be,"[28] then the moment of Godard's shocking crime reveals the perils of this formal, definitional misconception: Havelok's destiny and power are entirely derived from his exceptionality, his immaterial qualities that have the power to reach out and reorganize the material world. This exceptionality, the very core of sovereignty, is what prevents Godard from finishing off the heir himself. He is moved by a "miracle fair and god" (500), something that neither he nor the narrator can explain, but which forces the usurper to delegate responsibility for the heir's death.

Godard's cruel bargain with his lowest thrall, the fisherman Grim, appears to be the final step in the dreary collapse of society. Instead it results in restoration and the reintroduction of food into political life. The fisherman's cold determination to perform his end of the exchange is shattered by the miraculous revelation of the young Havelok's heritage. The bright light that flames from the boy's mouth announces that Havelok's tiny body is both helpless child and imperiled polity, the twinned person of kingship.[29] The light, and its supplementary "kynemerk"—a cross-shaped birthmark of red gold (as it will be described) reminds Grim and his wife Leue that the true source of sovereignty is not yet destroyed.[30] The blazing mouth of lordship itself, and the hope it betokens, demands that his subjects give it food, and so the couple perform a pledge of loyalty that centers on the nutritional: "Louerd, we sholen þe wel fede/ Til þat þu cone riden on stede" (622-23). Grim and Leue's words

---

28. Christopher Cannon, *The Grounds of English Literature*, 182.

29. The *locus classicus* for this idea remains Ernst Kantorowicz's groundbreaking study *The King's Two Bodies: A Study in Mediaeval Political Theology* (1957). Although he analyzes the similarity between the iconography of Christ and Otto II seated in majesty (see ch. 3, esp. 61–66), there does not seem to be any mention of a flaming mouth as a sign of sovereignty.

30. *Havelok*'s blazing mouth as a sign of kingship is unique among other English romances, with the only parallel scene found in the legend of Piers Tollere, from the Life of St. John the Almoner and retold in Robert Mannyng's penitential manual, *Handlyng Synne* (1303), ed. Idelle Sullens, who transforms himself from a miser to a man of saintly charity and is seen by a beggar with a mouth blazing with light (5575–946). It may also be intended to recall the fiery mouths of the Apostles at Pentecost (Acts 2:1–4), a symbol of divine presence communicable beyond language. Mannyng's *Chronicle* also contains a version of the *Havelok* legend based on the *Estoire des Engleis*. Bell links Havelok's illuminated mouth to miraculous lights observed in the *South English Legendary*'s *vita* of King Edward ("Resituating Romance," 45).

are the first step toward reestablishing an ideal system of loyalty and hierarchy, binding themselves to an agreement that revivifies the former society out of its broken pieces. Their words reinstate the social bonds unraveled by usurping regents who have starved their charges and reneged on their promises. Overwhelmed by the awesome display of birthright, they renounce the false bargains of Godard and perform a declaration of servitude. The term of this new state of thralldom is highly specific: Grim and Leue swear to *feed* Havelok until he is old enough to ride and wield weaponry, and perform the functions of knight and king (620–25).

Just as Havelok's birthright becomes conspicuous in a miraculous flash of light, so his first meal is remarkable in its quantity and quality:

"Wel is me þat thou mayth hete!
Goddoth!" quath Leue, "I shal thee fete
Bred an chese, butere and milk,
Pastees and flaunes—al with swilk
Shole we sone thee wel fede,
Louerd, in this mikel nede."
(642–47)

The catalogue of dishes given here is surprisingly varied: the food that the fisherman and his wife make spontaneously produces an entire bakery case in response to the miraculous opportunities afforded by Havelok's glowing mouth. Although cheese, bread, and milk probably formed the bulk of the peasant diet at the best of times, there is an element of luxury in the other items Leue provides.[31] The "pastees" (meat pies) and "flaunes"[32] are food items that would exceed the capabilities of the average peasant house. Since most

---

31. Thorold Rogers romantically affirms that English peasants lived in a "coarse plenty" (*Six Centuries of Work and Wages: The History of English Labour,* 63), while Stephen Mennell suggests more "monotonous" choices available to the working poor (*All Manners of Food,* 2nd ed., 40). Regardless of the amounts posited between these two extremes, the average peasant probably ate very little meat, as most domestic animals were more valuable and productive while alive, and hunting was reserved for the landed classes. Peasants would largely have depended on milk, eggs, and fish for their intake of animal protein. Christopher Dyer suggests that at the best of times only the most prosperous of peasant families (in fourteenth-century southern England) could have afforded to purchase fresh meat and prepared foods ("Did the Peasants Really Starve in Medieval England?" in *Food and Eating in Medieval Europe,* ed. Martha Carlin and Joel Rosenthal, 59–60).

32. This dish is not exactly the same as the baked custard dish that we are used to eating, but instead is a type of pie or cake. The cookery book known as the *Diuersa Servicia* (ca. 1381) provides a recipe for "Flownys in Lente," which consists of pie shell (or "cofyn") filled with almond milk, rice flour, figs, almonds, and dates (Hieatt and Butler, eds., *Curye on Inglssch,* 78).

cooking was performed with an open fire or hearth, very few peasant homes would have had facilities for baking.³³ Therefore, pasties and flans would have to be purchased from a baker or cookshop, an expenditure that is unlikely given the late hour and Grim's abject social position. Leue's provision, however, is more than enough for Havelok's needs, but sufficiency is not the point here. Havelok's nascent sovereignty spontaneously produces marvelous excess, food that can potentially support a "life beyond utility." Bataille states that this type of life is precisely the realm of the sovereign, of "the enjoyment of possibilities that utility doesn't justify (utility being that whose end is productive activity)."³⁴ The pasties and flans appear at Havelok's first meal because they represent a kind of surplus expenditure that a plate of salted herring would not. Grim is a fisherman after all, and the presence of fish in this context would indicate nothing more than a balanced account, a household completely sufficient in itself. But, at this moment, Havelok's presence causes Grim and Leue to suddenly, magnificently exceed the capacity of their own possessions—just as the freedom and reward for fostering the true heir will outstrip what was offered by the usurping regent.

The manner in which Havelok eats Grim's provender further exposes the intimate connection between eating and nobility: "Anon he bigan to ete / Grundlike, and was ful bliþe" (651–52). The adverb "grundlike" describes a meal that is both serious and delightful, pleasurable and desperately needed, nutritional and political. It is derived from "ground" and originated in the sense of the ground as the lowest part, the basis or foundation of an edifice, landmark, or idea.³⁵ To describe Havelok's eating as "grundlike" here is to suggest that he acts according to his most fundamental identity; that Havelok affirms himself to be the heir to the kingdom just by eating. The *Havelok* poet literally grounds sovereign identity in the child-king through a connection to activity upon the earth: the ground that is worked to produce food is the same ground the possession of which underwrites nobility. In this context, the word communicates the layers of social complexity in the scene, connot-

---

33. Massimo Montanari, describing the growth of a "new" cuisine in the thirteenth and fourteenth centuries, cites the fad for cakes and pies as a development "dependent upon, or at least favoured by, the presence of an oven, and so one that transcended the domestic environment" (*The Culture of Food*, trans. Carl Ipsen, 66).

34. Bataille, *Accursed Share*, 3.198.

35. *MED*, s.v. "ground," 1–14. Compare "groundli," adv. (a) "Strongly, violently, vehemently," and (b) "exceedingly, thoroughly, completely, fully," to (c) "basically, fundamentally," and "groundli," adj., meaning (a) "firm, solid," or (b) "fundamental, thorough, well-grounded, learned." Smithers, in the glossary to *Havelok*, gives the definition as "(1) solemnly; (2) in good earnest; (3) vigorously," definitions that remain close to the connotation of ground or foundation inherent in the word (190).

ing both solemnity and heartiness, marking Havelok as inherently noble even at a young age. The word "grundlike" will be repeated four more times in the poem, though always describing actions involving Ubbe (a Danish nobleman who will become Havelok's right-hand man), particularly the tone of the oaths he makes to the rightful king.[36] Yet the word will never be used to describe Havelok again, indicating that Havelok is at his most noble during this first meal given him by his subordinates.

Havelok's first meal in the story is much more than simply the start of a chain of meals that structures the romance, an example relegated to inferior significance due to its desperate circumstances and domestic setting. In the humble abode of Grim and Leue, the political body of Denmark rises again from its foundation, taking root in the very base of society. It is a domestic beginning to a new political entity: the body politic begins anew, restructured by the family meal.[37] Indeed, Havelok's first meal becomes an important political lesson in the sovereign's need for recognition from his subordinates. By subjecting themselves to the child king, Grim and Leue make themselves subjects to Havelok's authority and submit themselves to the miraculous possibilities that are not their own. Their struggle, both in Denmark and after the family's flight to England, makes sovereignty possible, even if they will never directly benefit from its realization.

3. THE ROMANCE OF VOCATION

Grim's hurried flight into exile separates Havelok from his inheritance by not only physical space but also by social and economic distance: by moving from Denmark to England, he also moves from perilous recognition to anonymity and backbreaking work. In the domain of subordination represented by England, food can only be represented through effort and exchange: it no longer appears miraculously in response to need, as did Havelok's first meal. Grim's life in England is solely depicted in terms of labor and commodities:

---

36. Ubbe demands the people make oaths to serve Havelok on three occasions: at 2012–15, 2267–71, and 2304–10. The final repetition describes Ubbe's fight with Godrich: "Grundlike here swerdes ut-drowen" (2660), signifying the puissance and vigor of their battle. Again, in all of these instances, the descriptor signifies action according to one's basic identity: the people swear oaths; noblemen, even villainous ones, draw swords and fight.

37. Julie Nelson Couch affirms the vital connection between childhood and kingship: "The Middle English *Havelok* begins and ends with an attention to children that equates their good keeping with the proper, orderly continuation of the kingdom" ("The Vulnerable Hero: *Havelok* and the Revision of Romance," *Chaucer Review* 42 [2008]: 334).

> Grim was fishere swiþe god,
> And mikel couþe on þe flod—
> Mani god fish þer-inne he tok,
> Bothe with neth and with hok.
> He tok þe sturgiun and þe qual,
> And þe turbut and lax withal;
> He tok þe sele and þe hwel—
> He spedde ofte swiþe wel.
> Keling he tok and tumberel,
> Hering and þe makerel,
> Þe butte, þe schulle, þe þornebake.
> (750–60)

The so-called "catalogue of fish" is an odd inversion of a traditional feature of epic poetry. Whereas classical epics like the *Iliad* or the *Aeneid* use the catalogue as a way to amplify and embroider descriptions of the power of princes or the magnitude of battles, this one lists commodities as made comprehensible through effort. The fish are not simply inert parts of the list: they are wrested from of the mysterious depths of the sea, a fact emphasized by the repeated phrase "he tok" and the invocation of the tools Grim uses to catch them ("with neth and with hok" [753]; "se-weres" [785]). The poem itself depends on Grim's toils, as the fish can only be named through his efforts, their presence as literary artifacts dependent upon human action. Their presence here serves to describe another kind of power: the economic potential of the "mikel couþe" of Grim, the skills and knowledge of a fisherman who can create prosperity from the water. The catalogue is deliberately structured—the fish that head the list, the sturgeon and whales, were often associated with the nobility, while the last items are the flatfishes that dwell on the bottom of the sea. There is no apparent hierarchy in the middle of the list, however: for instance, herring and cod [*keling*] were the most common food fishes of the region, and would seem to merit a higher position.[38] The catalogue expresses the abundance of fish around the mouth of the Humber, and ties the representation of food to the application of human labor. The catalogue of fish, as Roy Michael Liuzza observes, is "not a gratuitous detail; it is the object of Grim's hard work and the source of his prosperity. Inseparable from material motivation or production, the catalogue of fish is part of a system in which money

---

38. Several of the fish listed are difficult to identify, as they are either *hapax legomena* [*tumberel*] or probable scribal repetition [*qval* to *hwel*, both meaning "whale"].

rather than chivalric honor is the source of value."[39] Just as honor has no value without another person to recognize it, this commercial system has no coherence without acts of exchange. The fish are commodities in motion, sent forth into time. They have a present and a future, destined for the marketplace, to be bartered and sold, and transformed into some other commodity. The symbolic power of the catalogue of fish lies precisely in its transitory readiness to be exchanged for another plethora of verbal signs and material objects. The next twenty-four lines constitute yet another catalogue, describing the items that Grim and his three sons earn at the marketplace for their fish: the bread, beans, and wheat that form the staples of their diet (768–71). Their economic status is dramatically enhanced when Grim can catch an especially marketable fish, the lamprey, which can be sold for cash and used to purchase the other commodities, the meat, rope, and finer types of bread that the family needs in order to thrive (772–85). Nevertheless, whether receiving money or barter for their product, Grim's family is undeniably subordinate, not just socially but materially, as well.

Although the town of Grimsby will be founded around the site of Grim's earthen house (as related at 734–49), there seem to be no people outside of the family in *Havelok*'s account of life in England. There are towns and granges, but they are places only, potential markets where commodities come and go. The strict materialism about Grimsby is disturbing in its tacit substitution of things for people. The romance here portrays the rise of market relations in what was economically fallow land, revealing the moment when the social relations between humans become expressed through the public action of exchange.[40] Though the narrative has not yet reached the lowest moments in the trajectory of Havelok's servility, this life of market exchange represents a shocking departure from realms of sovereignty and the genres that represent it. In this antipodean world, men do not have ownership over their possessions, and to survive by these things is to become subordinated to the process of their exchange.

Even so, the strict materialism of Grim's life does not feel that desperate. In fact the family can support the boy king in a manner that more or less befits his noble status, preserving his "life beyond utility."[41] Havelok continues to eat

---

39. Roy Michael Liuzza, "Representation and Readership in the Middle English *Havelok*," *JEGP* 93 (1994): 510.

40. This world of commerce fits Marx's description: "It is nothing but the definite social relation between men themselves which assumes here, for them, the fantastic form of a relation between things" (*Capital*, 1.165).

41. Bataille, *Accursed Share*, 3.198. Havelok is a child during this time, but childhood was usually no exemption from the average working family's labors.

in a sovereign manner, but he eventually realizes the inequality of the arrangement, and the injustice that these circumstances precipitate:

> Hauelok was war þat Grim swank sore
> For his mete, and he lay at hom—
> Þouthe, "Ich am nou no grom!
> Jch am wel waxen and wel may eten
> More þan euere Grim may geten.
> Jch ete more, bi God on liue,
> Than Grim an hise children fiue!
> (789–95)

At this moment, Havelok realizes the hardship in which his own appetite places his family: that his ability to eat more than "Grim an hise children fiue" will eventually outstrip even Grim's extraordinary resourcefulness. He recognizes that his massive capacity for consumption should be converted into an equally massive potential to perform productive labor. Not only can he bear four times as much fish as his brothers, he can also sell them for silver more easily (815–24). Havelok "submit[s] to the useful" in such a way that estranges himself utterly from his own innate sovereignty, a privileged state that his foster parents have attempted to maintain.[42] Acknowledging his subordinate condition, Havelok decides to live according to the terms of his life. The boy king, turning his back on his own sovereignty, proclaims, "Swinken Ich wolde for mi mete— / Jt is no shame for to swinken" (799–800), an affirmation literally bounded by work and toil.

The story of Havelok has become thoroughly imbued in the material, where idealistic motives have no role in inspiring action. In the *Lai D'Haveloc*, Grim sends Havelok to Lincoln in order to instill his foster son with the social graces his status will require, and sends his sons with him to act as servants.[43] In the English version, however, natural and economic disaster forces Havelok to leave Grim's house. A great famine ("dere") shatters the careful balance that Grim has managed to create and forces Havelok to travel to Lincoln to seek employment, clad only in a "couel" cut from an old sail (859). This begins a quest for vocation that is wholly unique to the Middle English *Havelok*, and

---

42. See ibid., 3.226–27.

43. *Le Lai d'Haveloc*, ed. Bell, 166–84. This episode does not appear in the *Estoire des Engleis*. The relationship of food to acquisition of such social graces is very important, as conduct manuals, for example "Stans Puer ad Mensam" or the "Urbanitatis" (both ca. 1400) define manners almost entirely by behavior at the table. The political resonances of conduct manuals are explored in the following chapter.

does not appear in the known analogues of the poem. Whereas other dispossessed heroes, such as the hero of *King Horn,* assume a humble disguise in order to further their cause, their day-to-day existence is never dominated by the need to work. In making Havelok actually toil, the story reveals an unusual quality of the mundane and sympathy for the lower classes in the representation of the city, and this clarity of perception cuts through the conservative generic expectations of romance narrative. Havelok actually becomes a poor worker, and as a result the story is transformed from a tragedy—the genre of princes and their inevitable fall—to a sort of desperate realism, a place of arbitrary misfortunes and impoverished people. Havelok does not deserve his hardships any more than the other people on the streets of Lincoln do, and his successes are as randomly encountered. This drastic reduction in circumstance has the effect of portraying life at its least miraculous and most abject.

On the streets, Havelok reaches the nadir of his relationship with well-fed sovereignty. Now he must confront desperation and death utterly unlike anything encountered by romance's more martial heroes. Heroes like Beowulf or Roland, for example, often confront the possibility of death, but the perils they face are notable and worthy of narrative: their demise will ultimately unite a textual community. Theirs is a sovereign death, wasteful and glorious, and faced without hesitation. Bataille compares the difference between this experience of death and the one experienced in the subordinate world:

> From the viewpoint of the sovereign man, faintheartedness and the fearful representation of death belong to the world of practice, that is, of subordination. In fact, subordination is always grounded in the alleged need to avoid death. The sovereign world does have an odor of death, but this is for the subordinate man; for the sovereign man, it is the world of practice that smells bad; if it does not smell of death, it smells of anguish; its crowds sweat from the anguish provoked by shadows.[44]

If the state of servility, as Bataille describes, is "grounded in the alleged need to avoid death," then to preserve one's livelihood, to apply effort to maintain oneself, is the death of sovereignty. Havelok faces utter ignominy in perishing, a nameless death that perpetuates nothing, but he has already died as a sovereign body. And death certainly seems to be the only end anticipated from Havelok's experience in Lincoln. He spends two days without eating and then earns a piece of bread for bearing meat into the Earl of Lincoln's castle, a job

---

44. Bataille, *Accursed Share,* 3.222.

he acquires only by shoving other hopefuls down into the mud (889–91). It is two more days before the opportunity to work again arrives. There is a painful irony to the transaction, a heart-breaking incommensurability between paucity and plenty: Havelok can carry an entire cartload of food, yet in return he receives only a "ferþing wastel" (879), a tiny piece of fine bread insignificant in either monetary or nutritional terms. The exchange of labor for food, which Grim had balanced for a time, now only leaves Havelok in arrears. He can never receive enough food to restore the strength he expends to earn it. This is not a romanticized, happy working class, nor is the bustle of Lincoln's streets anything Havelok can enjoy.[45] There is nothing here but fear, hardship, and a slow descent into starvation and death.

There is food for Havelok in Lincoln, but it exists in the bounded space of the Earl's castle, a place from where the administrative apparatus of the sovereign reaches out to bring in more. The household's open mouth, a conduit constantly cycling in commodities, voraciously consumes foodstuffs as if there were no famine, using all it takes in to perpetuate its display of political and economic power. Having only come into contact with abundance while bearing huge loads of fish in exchange for insufficient pay, Havelok faces an easy choice: to serve in the noble kitchen and live, or die of hunger on the streets outside.

4. THE WORLD IN MINIATURE

There is plenty in the midst of dearth, and it exists in the bounded space of the Earl of Lincoln's castle. Its great administrative apparatus grasps the stuff of life from the city's streets and markets and drags it inside, holding it out of the reach of those that need it most. In exchange for the life it snatches, it leaves behind only death by starvation. The household has its own uses for what it has seized, utilizing what it has taken to perpetuate the display of its political and economic supremacy. The kitchen, as the inward conduit of the household, constantly cycling in commodities, voraciously consumes foodstuffs as if there were no famine at all. In fact, in these meager times the culinary demonstration of executive privilege becomes all the more important, its waste and glory all the more wasteful and glorious; the potlatch fires glow all the brighter in the lean circumstances that surround it.

The kitchen is the locus of political display, a workshop where sovereignty is assembled and served. Medieval England was primarily an agrarian society,

---

45. See Liuzza, "Representation and Readership," 509.

its economic production based in food, the labor of many bodies concentrated into a single set of commodities. The banquet not only feeds a lord and his household but also demonstrates political power in a tangible, empirical way. The privileged enjoyment of food occurs in a wasteful gastronomic spectacle, showing off the finest that can be produced locally in concert with what the lord's purchasing power can provide in more distant commodities, whether from the Midlands or the Moluccas. The feast manifests the lord's power, for the entire world appears on the table, altered into a shape that the cook sees fit. Brillat-Savarin was keenly aware of the link between food and power:

C'est la gastronomie qui inspecte les hommes et les choses, pour transporter d'un pays à l'autre tout ce qui mérite d'être connu, et qui fait qu'un festin savamment ordonné est comme un abrégé du monde, où chaque partie figure par ses représentants.

It is gastronomy which so studies men and things that everything worth being known is carried from one country to another, so that an intelligently prepared feast is like a summing-up of the whole world, where each part is represented by its envoys.[46]

Gastronomy, according to Brillat-Savarin, is the knowledge of the globe and its arrangement upon the table. It presents political and economic power in very real terms. Indeed, by giving it so much agency as to state that it "inspecte les hommes et les choses," Brillat-Savarin claims that gastronomy is a kind of political power in itself, a panoptic force that demands that the world and its things offer themselves up to be discovered, arranged into "un abrégé du monde" and ultimately consumed. More importantly, the feast is a symbolic demonstration of sovereign privilege, the right to seize and manipulate commodities, and to waste or use them as one sees fit.

The creation of a "world in miniature" is not an easy or clean process, and the crispness of Brillat-Savarin's description does not take into account the messy metamorphosis that transforms commodities, both common and exotic, into the spoils of gastronomy and brings them to the table. The medieval kitchen could be an infernal place, as penitential manuals often observed, comparing it to a perverse kind of church, replete with the sacrifice of animals and the prayers of gluttons seeking to alleviate their swollen bellies and the pains of indigestion.[47] Images of Hell in religious art often resembled the

---

46. Brillat-Savarin, *Le Physiologie du Goût*, 60. Translation: M. F. K. Fisher, *Physiology of Taste*, 53.

47. See especially the *Fasciculus Morum*, ed. and trans. Siegfried Wenzel, 630–31.

organized entropy and aestheticized horror of the kitchen of the great house, capturing the similarity between the destructive and torturous activities of demons and cooks.[48] Unless specially designed to alleviate these problems,[49] the kitchen was often a dark and smoky place, with little fresh air or natural light to be had, filled with sweaty bodies toiling and the smells of cooking, from the appetizing (a spit of roasting meat or fresh mixture of spices) to the offensive (burned food, rank garbage).[50] This is the hell at the center of the production of social value, presided over by its demonic lord, the cook. The destructive, violent nature of the kitchen's frenzied efforts was well known, for instance, as observed by Chaucer's Pardoner: "Thise cookes, how they stampe, and streyne, and grynde, / And turnen substance into accident / To fulfille al thy likerous talent!"[51] The metamorphic processes of cooking operate to extract the essences, the intangible qualities hidden within a foodstuff that represent not only the very identity of a commodity as use-value but also the labor expended to produce it as surplus-value, an excess that is immediately convertible into social capital. The symbolic transmutation places not just food on the table for consumption but also the appropriated labor power of the peasant—the effort of living bodies now "deadened" through exchange. Waste, surplus, and excess are served as objects of gastronomic pleasure.[52]

As the yawning maw of the house, the kitchen represented the greatest day-to-day liability of balanced expenditure. The majority of a household's purchases would have been made for the kitchen, and its operations, however necessary for sustenance and display, required tight administrative control.[53] Commodities, both common and exotic, were brought into the house for use in the kitchen, and each had to be carefully accounted for. Meals were to be made for the lord and his guests, his retinue and household employees, and whatever was left over was expected to go out as alms. The cook assembled this panorama and orchestrated this demonstration of secular power, and the

---

48. Such a comparison is made explicitly in Dante's description of the punishment of the Grafters in *Inferno* 21.55–57, as demons hold the bodies of the damned beneath burning tar: "Just so cooks make their scullions plunge the meat down into the cauldron with their forks, that it may not float" (Trans. Charles Singleton).

49. See Brears on the archaeological remains of these innovations, such as louver-board vents, chimneys, and permanent drains (*Cooking and Dining in Medieval England*, 173–201).

50. See Scully, *Art of Cookery*, 86–89, on the layout of the medieval kitchen.

51. Chaucer, *The Pardoner's Tale*, VI.538–40. This is an ironic repetition of Pope Innocent III's *De miseria humane conditionis*: "One cook mashes and strains, another mixes and churns, and together they turn substance into accident, make nature into art" (*On the Misery of the Human Condition: De Miseria Humane Conditionis*, trans. Donald Roy Howard, 45).

52. Marx, *Capital*, 1.270–73; Smith, *Arts of Possession*, 46–47.

53. See Kate Mertes, *The English Noble Household, 1250–1600*, 81–83.

kitchen was his workshop. However, the manorial cook must have suffered under the paradoxical demands: he had to be able to transform "an overwhelming mass of raw material" into dishes deemed palatable by his lord, and to account minutely for each transformation.[54]

Havelok is employed at the filthy, abject root of social power, in a type of hell that generates the symbolic power of sovereignty. As the "descent to the underworld" stage of his journey, his employment in the kitchen provides a valuable, chthonic lesson about social power and where it originates. Work in this theater reveals how political life is manifested, at the pulsing heart of the aristocratic house, though he is little more than a slave to its demands.[55] There is still a great distance between him and noble eating, yet within the walls of Lincoln's castle, he has some connection to the magical (and terrible) process through which sovereign display is created. But Havelok is a minor figure in the kitchen, given the most menial tasks in the symbolic presentation of social power:

> Fir and water I wile you fete,
> Þe fir blowe and ful wele maken;
> Stickes kan ich breken and kraken,
> And kindlen ful wel a fyr,
> And maken it to brennen shir.
> Ful wel kan ich cleuen shides,
> Eles to turuen of here hides;
> Ful wel kan ich dishes swilen,
> And don al þat ye euere wilen.
> (913–21)

He is given only tasks that require him to lift and carry raw materials: wood, water, kindling, and enormous loads of fish and meat (see aforementioned lines, as well as 933–41), while receiving only food in exchange.[56] He becomes practically dehumanized while working for Bertram, more beast of burden

---

54. Labarge, *Baronial Household of the Thirteenth Century*, 85; *Fleta*, vol. 2, Publications of the Seldon Society, vol. 89, ed. and trans. H. G. Richardson and G. O. Sayles, 75. The "strict practicality" of household account books takes on a different form in the surviving medieval cookery books, which rarely provide any definite measures for ingredients, especially the extremely expensive spices.

55. Arendt recognizes this brutal circumstance of household economics: "To labor meant to be enslaved by necessity" (*Human Condition*, 83).

56. Christopher Stuart interprets Havelok's refusal of cash wages for his work as a moment that belies the middle-class origins of the romance: "We must wonder how many peasants ever fantasized about working tirelessly for only their board and clothing. On the other hand, many monarchs must have had dreamed of having subjects as manageable as Havelok" ("*Havelok the Dane* and Edward I in the 1290s," 355). According to Labarge, Havelok would have received little

than man, clad poorly and suffering from his endless efforts (944–67). The scullion was often considered the filthiest and least privileged of the household's many workers, at the very bottom of the social ladder.[57] Here he still must work so that his masters may consume the products of their privilege, but at least he receives enough to eat.

The kitchen is Havelok's escape from the desperation of incommensurable toil. It is also the gate through which the channels of food and power flow, a threshold between realms of sovereignty and servility. The kitchen is the place where labor creates the miraculous forms of extravagant living, where the material objects that the two realms share—that is, effort versus entitlement—receive the imprimatur that distinguishes them forever from their humble roots. The cook's craft is the material process of sovereignty's confrontation and supersession of the subordinate: the art of cookery enacts the struggle of the lord to overcome his dependence on its bondsman, to reconstitute that dependence as its opposite and proclaim triumph over the merely material circumstances.[58] Cookery arranges the world to suit the sovereign, and it objectifies everything that serves that arrangement by rendering it edible, as stated by Bataille: "I forget that the existence within men continually obliges me to treat as a thing that which I eat, that which serves me, and myself or my fellow beings, as a subject, who eats, who serves himself."[59] Entitlement, the sovereign relationship of the self to everyone else, is enabled by one's position at the table. Edibility is tied to servility; what the sovereign eats also serves the sovereign. Either way, the laborer and the dish are consumed through service (in the word's dual sense of servitude and silverware), and both allow the ruler to achieve recognition.

The originary nobility of Havelok, even when he is socially powerless, manifests itself through his contact with the materia of power: as he works, all who see him admire his humility and lament the acutely visual injustice of such a noble-looking boy serving in such debased conditions. This recognition of his innate quality transforms the narrative itself, and the representation of arbitrary toil is exchanged for a series of fortunate chances that reintegrate the disordered pieces of the social order and push Havelok toward the realization of his destined role.

---

else for his efforts if he refused cash wages, as the scullion tended to be hired on an ad hoc basis and paid off whenever the household moved (*Baronial Household*, 69).

57. The low repute of the scullion may be discerned from Chrétien de Troyes's *Le Chevalier au Lion*, when the giant Harpin du Montagne declares that he wants to force the afflicted vavasor's daughter into "the company of a thousand naked, filthy fellows, vagrant scum and scullion boys" (*Complete Romances*, trans. Staines, 306).

58. Hegel, *Phenomenology of Spirit*, §§179–81.

59. Bataille, *Accursed Share*, 3.238–39.

5. BANQUETS (AND DREAMS) OF POWER

Havelok's exertions estrange him from any but the most vicarious experience of lordship. The banquet—the end point of so much labor, the culminating moment of political display—is precisely what he is lacking in the account of his employment in the kitchen: he suffers (949) but never toils toward any particular social function. Instead he endures an endless process of work upon a feast that he can never attend. If Havelok is to regain his lost sovereignty, then he must rediscover the enjoyment of eating as well as the social performance of the banquet. Havelok must be able to eat once again in a "grundlike" manner: with the satisfaction of hunger accepted as a political necessity by others, a recognition that establishes both the political system and his sovereign identity atop it.

Godrich's evil plan to disparage his ward Goldeborw, the dispossessed daughter of King Athelwold, by marrying her to the lowly Havelok unexpectedly places the Danish heir back into contact with the possibilities of sovereignty. Chosen only for the conspicuous gap between his great height and base circumstances, which allows Godrich to fulfill his oath (made at 199) to marry Goldeborw only to the "heste" ("highest") man in England, Havelok nonetheless is empowered by the union to choose a new life for himself and his wife. Aware of the humiliating conditions awaiting his new wife in the kitchens ("Men sholde don his leman shame" [1192]), Havelok decides to escape from the kitchens of Lincoln and the servile life that sustains him. The regent's malicious act immediately redounds to great good, as Havelok gives up the job that keeps him subordinated to aristocratic power and frees Goldeborw from her imprisonment. Flight from sovereignty's terrible workshop also places Havelok back into a trajectory where he will be the guest of honor at a banquet—three, in fact, and each of increasing size and importance. These feasts are dramatically different in the way they represent Havelok eating: food and labor become separated from each other as Havelok climbs up the social scale, but as the work disappears, so will the means by which food can be represented in the poem. Havelok, the hungriest hero in Middle English literature, will cease eating as he assumes his throne.

The first of these banquets carefully recreates Grim and Leue's meal for the young Havelok back in Denmark. That first meal was modest and familial though vitally important: the exchange of food restarted the social order broken by Godard's betrayal. Again, a social order has been broken with Havelok's renunciation of subservience, and again, the family initiates a new order. Back in Grimsby, the community now named for his foster father, Havelok's family embraces him through a feast thrown in his honor. The children of Grim reiterate their father's pledge to serve the Danish heir and place their lives and possessions at his disposal. A homecoming feast follows this pledge of loyalty:

> Hwan he þis ioie haueden maked,
> Sithen stikes broken and kraked,
> And þe fir brouth on brenne;
> Ne was þer spared gos ne henne,
> Ne þe hende ne þe drake:
> Mete he deden plente make—
> Ne wantede þere no god mete,
> Wyn and ale deden he fete,
> And hem made glade and bliþe;
> Wesseyl ledden he fele siþe.
> (1238–47)

The action of a single person is given up here for verbs in the third person plural: "he" (they) is repeated throughout the passage, but their identity is not entirely clear and not important. The collectivity of the feast is what gives it significance. Havelok at this point is just another member of the family, enjoying their hospitality and sharing their board. The lack of pronoun referents and passive verbs emphasize the lack of actors in this scene, creating the image of faceless servants even as they recall Havelok's anonymous labors as a scullion (when his duties included tasks like hauling and breaking firewood, 913–21). We remember the hero's backbreaking efforts in the kitchen but are not given the opportunity to identify with anyone else performing that work. Havelok no longer toils in the kitchen but, ostensibly, on the level of language, neither does anyone else.

The elision of the laborer also operates to conceal Grim's family's frantic sacrifice: they instantly alienate themselves and give up all of their possessions to Havelok. They offer to be given away in marriage or sold as slaves if needed ("þou mithe us boþe yeue and selle / þou mayt us boþe selle and yeue," 1219–20), and the poem describes this act of submission as if it were a perfectly natural, unremarkable thing. The account of the foodstuffs given up to their brother's enjoyment (geese, chickens, ducks, and lots of alcohol) recalls the property that Grim was forced to sell in order to enable his desperate escape from Denmark (700–703), as well as the catalogues of Grim's economic activity that supports the family (750–85). The family's abandoned resources symbolize their utter sacrifice of a secure future to that promised by Havelok's ascension, a desire to spend their surplus magnificently to exalt and celebrate their royal foster brother. The abasement of Grim's family before

Havelok marks an important moment in his quest to achieve his lost birthright: they recognize themselves as his rightful subjects and proclaim their submission—but submission does not automatically make Havelok a lord.

To become transformed from kitchen boy to king, Havelok must also recognize himself as the sovereign, the subject to whom everyone else is object. Although he possesses genealogical and theological claims to the throne of Denmark, represented by the birthmark on his shoulder and his illuminated mouth, he has no consciousness of their significance, or has seemingly forgotten his heritage through a lifetime of toil and struggle. The *Havelok* poet here raises the same epistemological question pondered by Georges Bataille: How can sovereignty know itself? He notes:

> To know is always to strive, to work; it is always a servile operation, indefinitely resumed, indefinitely repeated. Knowledge is never sovereign: to be *sovereign* it would have to occur in a moment. But the moment remains outside, short of or beyond, all knowledge.[60]

Knowledge and sovereignty do not coexist. But sovereignty must know itself in order to achieve identity. This paradox confronts the *Havelok* poet just as it confronts Bataille, and it creates an opportunity for startling innovation in the traditional story of Havelok, allowing the poet to depart dramatically from its extant sources in order to answer this question. In all three versions of the story, the missing information is relayed through a portentous dream. The dream vision in medieval literature represents a type of knowledge that is not governed by reason or logic—it is spontaneous and revelatory, but it is not sovereign knowledge. A dreamer can ascend through the planes of the universe and see the very throne of God, but that experience does not convey sovereign knowledge once it has been analyzed and written down.

Gaimar and the *Lai d'Aveloc* avoid the paradox by distancing Havelok from the vision, instead giving the prophetic dream to Argentille (Goldeborw's counterpart) and placing its interpretation in the hands of a convenient hermit. The dream itself is an ornate pageant of wild animals: a wild bear stalks Argentille and Havelok between the sea and the forest. Pigs and boars come to their aid and fight the bear along with the foxes that accompany Havelok. A great boar then slays the bear and the foxes submit themselves to Havelok. The trees salute him and the sea rises, and finally a pair of lions arrive, killing the remaining beasts but kneeling before Havelok. The flooding woods are then

---

60. Ibid., 3.202 (emphasis in original).

filled with frightful noise and Argentille awakens to see her husband's mouth emitting bright light.[61]

The noise and violence of Gaimar's scene stands in marked contrast to *Havelok*, where the predominant tone is stunned quiet and youthful innocence, the imagery simple and powerful. The *Havelok* poet adapts the portentous dream from his sources but transforms the convention through the powerful simplicity of the vision he gives Havelok. The dream is a conscious and daring attempt to step outside of overwrought allegory, like that seen in Gaimar, and into a more symbolic, as well as philosophically ambitious, mode of representation. Havelok's dream provides a glimpse of what sovereign knowledge might look like. The heir to Denmark understands his destiny and birthright without strife or struggle, in a fleeting moment that stands in dramatic contrast to the bustle and flurry that have identified Havelok's life so far.

Havelok can work to achieve many things, but he can never work to attain sovereign knowledge. He needs to experience a revelation that will invert his self-awareness and pull him out of his subordinate circumstances and back to the romance narrative of his lost inheritance. The Grim family's ritual of remembered allegiance rekindles Havelok's self-knowledge—and the spending of their labor and the glorious waste of their sacrifice provides the raw material for it to occur. Others work; Havelok is brought to self-recognition. So that night as he sleeps and Goldeborw witnesses the flaming light pouring from his mouth, Havelok experiences a "selkuþ drem" of sitting atop the tallest hill in Denmark, where he can see the whole world spread out beneath him:

> Als I sat up-on þat lowe
> J bigan Denemark for to awe,
> Þe borwes and þe castles stronge;
> And mine armes weren so longe
> Þat I fadmede al at ones,
> Denemark with mine longe bones.
> And þanne Y wolde mine armes drawe
> Til me and hom for to haue,
> Al þat euere in Denemark liueden
> On mine armes faste clyueden;
> And þe stronge castles alle
> On knes bigunnen for to falle—
> Þe keyes fellen at mine fet.
> (1292–1304)

---

61. Gaimar, *L'Estoire des Engleis*, 195–238.

The image is one of disarming innocence: a childlike Havelok looks down on the panorama beneath him and amuses himself with the contrast in perspective. Everything else is small, but his outstretched arms appear enormous so he can embrace their entirety (*fadmede al at ones*). The word "fathom" in this context is rich and complex. It signifies intimate physicality, to embrace or encircle with one's arms, the enjoyment of close relations to family, friends, and other social equals. It also is the act of a parent or superior to a child or dependent; it is nurturing and protective, physical reassurance communicated through the tactile awareness of superior size and stature. A fathom is also a measure of height or depth, the space marked between a grown man's outstretched arms, an extension of the body that makes spaces comprehensible by humanizing distance. There is a cognitive dimension to fathoming, as well: one encircles a concept with one's mind and understands it. So Havelok embraces Denmark, measuring it in terms of his own body and comprehending his realm in relation to himself. He experiences his birthright in a "grundlike" manner: his body symbolically united with the earth that forms his rightful inheritance, and he solemnly becomes the corporeal equivalent of the entire country he is destined to rule.

The illusion of scooping up distant castles and towns, however, is not broken when he tries to clutch them to his body—in the dream, perspective becomes reality. Havelok recognizes Denmark as his own, and Denmark recognizes him in return. His kingdom returns his embrace as child clings to its parent: "Al þat euere in Denemark liueden / On mine armes faste clyueden" (1300–1301). The act is somatic and performative, and most importantly, it is consensual. The mutuality and willingness of the parties here surely recalls the absence of consent at earlier stages of the story: Godrich's authoritarian rule of England ("Al Engelond was of him adrad, / So his þe beste from þe gad," 278–79) as well as Goldeborw's forced marriage to Havelok. The people cling to him, and the castles, by kneeling and dropping their keys at his feet, submit themselves to his protection, an oneiric return to the perfect state constructed by Athelwold at the poem's beginning. The emphasis is not on the nation as a single body, but on the individual entities of that nation at the moment that they are incorporated. The scene is ecological: a unity and interrelation of multiple bodies that share the same political space, all taken into account as an assemblage, all acting with the mutual interests at heart.[62] Arranged spatially below the heir and made common through their shared geography,

---

62. Alexis Kellner Becker presents a forceful reading of Havelok as an ecologically focused poem ("Sustainability Romance: *Havelok the Dane*'s Political Ecology," *New Medieval Literatures* 16 [2016]: 83–108). Joseph Taylor remarks upon the ecological valences of Anglo-Norman sovereignty, uniting the dead body of the king with the beasts (and people) of the realm in

the different parts of the country of Denmark are formed into a whole by Havelok's action. By embracing them and being embraced in turn, Havelok becomes aware of his sovereignty. Furthermore, the act of extending and contracting his arms to collect his birthright, as well as the use of several words that signify both height and depth ("fadmede"; "lowe" [a hill or depression[63]]) makes this vision peculiarly Havelok's. Havelok is destined to climb to power from the depths of the social order, and he has done so through Grim the fisherman's ability to draw life and meaning from the depths of the ocean. But where Grim used tools and his great skill (*mikel coupe*, 751) to win sustenance for his family and attain economic sufficiency, Havelok can gather his birthright with his arms alone—from the breadth of the land rather than the depth of the sea. Without effort or sweat he attains the sovereign knowledge he will need to triumph over his enemies and restore his rightful rule.

The remainder of the story is in some sense an anticlimax after the spectacular dream: Havelok's victory over his oppressors is a foregone conclusion once he recognizes himself and returns to his homeland. The narrator is doggedly determined, however, to present the entire process of returning to rule, from winning the favor of Ubbe, the local magnate (1626–714) to a bone-crunching brawl with a gang of thieves (1767–1920) to his recognition by Ubbe as the rightful heir to the throne (2086–312). Within this account are two more feasts that mark Havelok's final ascent to power, and these two occasions reveal a startling change in his relation to food: the assumption of his noble identity is also the end of Havelok's hunger. The first of these final meals occurs on Havelok's first night in his homeland, when Ubbe is given a fantastically valuable gift, a ring bearing a stone valued at hundred pounds (1633–34), by the mysterious Havelok and his beautiful wife. The compelling nature of the ring and the apparent nobility of its giver[64] demands that Ubbe provide a gift in return, and so he responds with a gracious invitation to dinner:

Þanne he were set and bord leyd,
And þe beneysun was seyd,

"Sovereign Ecologies: Managing the King's Bodies in Anglo-Norman Historiography," in *The Politics of Ecology*, ed. Randy P. Schiff and Joseph Taylor, 179–209.

63. *MED*, "loue," n. (1) & (3); "loue," adj. Etymologically, "low" as in "low places" is derived from the ON *lagr* (low), while the other comes from the AS *hlæw*, a funerary mound or barrow. There are extant uses of either meaning in texts contemporary with *Havelok*.

64. A folio is missing from the manuscript at this point in the story, and therefore the rationale for Havelok's disguise and the circumstances of his encounter with Ubbe are unknown. The *Estoire* and the *Lai* introduce a magic ring that belonged to Gunter (Birkabeyn's counterpart in these versions) that gave its wearer invulnerability, which Sigar Estalre (Ubbe) recognizes as belonging to the departed king.

> Biforn hem com þe beste mete
> Þat king or cayser wolde ete:
> Kranes, swannes, ueneysun,
> Lax, lampreys, and god sturgun,
> Pyment to drinke and god clare,
> Win hwit and red, ful god plente—
> Was þer-inne no page so lite
> Þat euere wolde ale bite.
> Of þe mete forto telle
> Ne of þe win bidde I nout dwelle.
> (1723–35)

In contrast to the feast with Grim's family, all mention of dinner preparation is elided except for the setting of the table. This meal is conspicuously a display of political power, an act of a lord's generosity to a potential retainer. Ubbe demonstrates his economic wherewithal as a lord who can properly feed and care for those in his service. Accordingly, the meal is exceedingly noble in its meats: crane, swan, venison, salmon, sturgeon, even the lampreys that represented monetary wealth back in Grimsby. Although political power is intended to radiate around Ubbe, Havelok is spontaneously served the food that fits him best, even when the host does not fully recognize his guest. Decorum seems the most important aspect of the meal: the formality of setting the table for dinner; the "beneysun" said before the meal as much a part of the form as the consumption of the rhyming "ueneysun." There are still some traces of the servants here though, in the image of the smallest servants ("no page so lite," 1733) getting their share of the ale going around the table. But while there are dishes on the table and drink to be had, there is no indication of their enjoyment by the guests. In this new domain of political maneuvering and sovereign plenty the feast becomes more of a performance and ritual, and less nutritive in its focus.

Feasting as social ritual is even more important for the banquet Ubbe holds to gather the people of Denmark so they can recognize Havelok as their king. The scene is a literal realization of Havelok's dream; the stretching out of his arms to his people is revealed to be a call to dinner. But here the transformation of Havelok's position is revealed, a change signaled by the way that the feast is described. Decorum dominates the event—forty days of spontaneous merrymaking on the occasion of Havelok's coronation, its participants curiously unconcerned about the usurping regent still at large. Furthermore, the visceral representations of food that were so important in previous feasts are at this moment almost an afterthought. There are many entertainments for the guests, comprised of both high- and low-brow activities, all exhaustively catalogued: jousting, wrestling, stone-throwing, minstrelsy, games of chance, reading of romances, and the baiting of bulls and boars (2321–32). But the menu is related in a few curt lines:

> þer was swiþe gode metes
> And of wyn þat men fer fetes,
> Rith al so mik and gret plente
> So it were water of þe se.
> (2341–44)

These lines do little more than note the presence of food and wine, and to assure their oceanic amounts. We do not read how merrily or heartily the guests consumed this food, nor are we given invocations of wassailing and toasting that followed each of the two previous feasts. At such a triumphant moment, plenitude is the only criteria. The overflowing board of Athelwold is reconstituted in the final moments of the poem by Havelok's plenteous regal fare, promising a return to sufficiency and a smoothly run government for the whole of Denmark and England.

6. EMPTY FEASTING

The final moments of *Havelok* promise a banquet of good rule to come but never actually include the feast. Food remains in a state of suspension between exchange and enjoyment: we are assured of plenty but never see that abundance in use. After the feast with Grim's children, Havelok is never again shown eating, and after Denmark recognizes its true king, no one seems to eat. Even the wicked Godard invokes in vain the meals he provided his retainers: "Jch haue you fed and yet shal fede— / Helpe me nu in þis nede" (2421–22). His promises of food can do nothing to stem the tide of Havelok's conquest. A final banquet is held after England has been liberated and Godrich punished, but it passes in a mere three lines (2949–51), suddenly the event is of little imaginative interest, an afterthought to the triumphal rush of the romance to its conclusion. The fullness of the legend itself has squeezed out all other images of plenty. Even Havelok's own enormous and overabundant body, once defined by its boundless capacity for mighty exertions, has been subsumed into the status of a figurehead. As the unchallenged ruler of England and Denmark he is transformed into a true Leviathan, the living symbol of political power.

The disappearance of eating in a story where it has previously been so important is vexing, especially when the narrator will finally insist that this story originates in the account of "Hw he weren born and hw fedde" (2987). This bald statement seemingly grounds the entire international drama in simple acts of nurture, in moments of eating that would be unexceptional except for Havelok's royal birth. The duality suggested in this line, however, indicates that there is something more important to the story than just consumption. It proposes that sovereignty functions as both a diachronic fact of lineage and a synchronic practice of recognition. If sovereignty is distinguished by its claim to consume what it does not produce, it does not follow that simply eating is enough to demonstrate its manifestation. In untangling the strands of epistemology and economics that are woven together in the problem of political power, Bataille argues for the need of recognition by those that are ruled. "Traditional sovereignty," he states, "also presupposes that the masses see the sovereign as the subject of whom they are the object."[65] Some other person or persons must objectify themselves and make their labor available for the sovereign's consumption. Someone must feed the royal child in order for him to grow up to be a king. The act of nurture that follows recognition is the common denominator in the progression of the five meals I have followed through *Havelok*: every time a person recognizes their obligation to the boy king, whether consciously or not, they feed him and nurture him. Recognition followed by food allows Havelok to be revealed as "grundlike"—solemn, noble, foundational—as he was as a tiny child on the floor of Grim and Leue's hovel (652). This is also why his blazing mouth is always observed in close proximity to not just food but also to those with the means to act upon the light's bright promises. Lack of recognition, or else a refusal to recognize, as is evident in the horrors of Godard or the brutality of the streets of Lincoln, results in starvation. Each time the scene of a meal is repeated, the circle of recognition is extended until it encompasses the entire land that Havelok is destined to rule. If recognition by others, by the people, by the subjects of one's rule, results in the production of food, then what the sovereign is truly hungry for is that recognition. By the time that Havelok has conquered both Denmark and England, there is nothing left for which to hunger: two nations recognize his right over them and will strive hereafter to satisfy his every need.

---

65. Bataille, *Accursed Share*, 3.239.

At this level, the story demands to be read conservatively: the romance is perfectly reparative and the violations of the social order it celebrates are seamlessly restored as soon as born heirs regain their rightful place. Such a reading would accord with the generic expectations of the romance, which usually portray an aristocratic hero's quest for self-realization that will enable the perfect possession of one's birthright. According to this model, Havelok's journey through the working world reveals the mechanisms by which the power he is entitled to wield is produced and distributed, a revelation that brings him into full self-consciousness of what that power means and how to use it. The distribution of power, and the food that attends upon it, is uneven by nature, but so long as the proper figurehead stands atop the system, the apparent inequities in the social order are revealed as harmonious and necessary.

To view *Havelok*, however, as a story of traditional political systems that operate in perfect harmony is to smooth over the disturbing implications of the degradation and tortuous work experienced by the hero at his lowest moments. His travail is terribly real within the story, the injustice of his compelled servitude the equal of even the worst crimes committed against him by Godard. Havelok thoroughly experiences the burden that faces humanity in the postlapsarian world: he must "do [his] mete to þigge / And ofte in sorwe and pine ligge" (1374–75).[66] Julie Nelson Couch observes a "ubiquitousness of vulnerability" suggested by the invocation of the hero's bodily endangerments: if Havelok can suffer the travails of starvation and labor, then anyone can.[67] The genre of romance is notable for the automatic satisfaction of its heroes' bodily needs; invisible servants generate sustenance that is consumed without being any more visible. *Havelok* violates this expectation by making the nutrition itself the object of a quest. The story weaves together food, servitude, and pain in order to elevate quotidian needs into a heroic pursuit. But this pursuit is not in itself heroic: labor is circular, and a body that has earned its bread through sweat will be hungry again soon. Havelok may obtain a

---

66. The potentially religious identification of Havelok's suffering, connected as it is to the martyrdom narratives of the *South English Legendary*, is made by Bell: "Havelok himself emerges as a Christ-like hero who shares more affinities with Christ and the saints than he does with other romance heroes," and later, "the journey in *Havelok* is much more closely related to the saints' quests for heavenly perfection found only through torment, affliction, and humility" ("Resituating Romance," 28, 43). See also Couch for a discussion of religious affect as reading and representational practice for users of the miscellany that contains *Havelok* ("Defiant Devotion in MS Laud Misc. 108: The Narrator of *Havelok the Dane* and Affective Piety," *Parergon* 25 (2008): 53–79).

67. Idem, "Vulnerable Hero," 346.

surplus that allows him rest and conclusion, but the vast majority will never find either. To represent work as heroic in the romance of *Havelok* is to beg that the same dignity be given to all those that suffer and starve around the dispossessed heir. Havelok's travails reveal the deep injustice in the political and economic systems the poem claims to celebrate, inequities that only radical change may redress. *Havelok*'s victory is primarily a victory for its ability to consolidate aristocratic power away from the story's extended and deeply sympathetic view of the working classes.

The suffering necessary to create sovereignty, and the compassion this pain invokes, create an uncomfortable remainder in the story. The need to repress this surplus sympathy perhaps explains the ultimate disappearance of food from the field of representation. Havelok eats as much as he can as he struggles toward his inheritance, but once he has achieved it, any focus on his food is indecorous, a distressing reminder of irresolvable injustices. The status quo that is restored with Havelok's reign is ideologically reciprocal, but this reciprocity can only hold true on the largest scale: portraying what the true king eats recalls Havelok's own harrowing existence as a starving laborer. It reminds us that those workers are still starving and serving in order to bring food to the tables of the powerful. The kitchen, the gastronomic machine that transmutes subordinate food into sovereign life, still grinds and stamps and strains, still extracts surplus-value out of expropriated commodities. It can only be hoped that the appetites of those it serves are moderate in their demands. *Havelok*, though essentially a conservative text, has raised provocative questions about sovereignty and sufficiency that trouble the reestablishment of an ideal political system, calling attention to inequities of appetite, labor, and deprivation that differentiate highest from lowest, even as it yearns for a golden age of proportionality that preserves the best features of that economic system.

This sensitive recognition of social inequity and keen philosophical sustenance gives way to the savoring of a more jaded, acerbic repast. Although a localized tale of belligerence and psychopathy, the romance of *Sir Gowther*, subject of the next chapter, contains several important continuities with the vast dynastic movements of *Havelok the Dane*. First, the two poems both start with the implications of the birth and fostering of their heroes, a common enough initiation for any Middle English romance, but one that explicitly creates continuities between identity, infancy, and ingestion as a political force. Second, they both explore the nature of "right rule," interrogating the virtues that render a monarch qualified to dominate a group of people (which is also reflected in the critique of King Ebain's rule in the *Roman de Silence*). But where *Havelok* investigates the very nature of sovereignty as a philosophical problem, *Sir Gowther* tackles the issue as a matter of education, of the painstaking process, here represented as penitential labor, of cultivating good manners. The display of this kind of socially instantiating "nortur" performs aristocratic entitlement, and acting gracefully and correctly in that conspicuous arena of political action—the banquet hall so desperately sought by the servile Havelok—encourages others to recognize their ruler's superiority.

CHAPTER 4

Sir Gowther

Table Manners and Aristocratic Identity

Les animaux se repaissent; l'homme mange; l'homme d'esprit seul sait manger.

Animals feed themselves; the man eats; but only the man of spirit knows how to eat.

—Brillat-Savarin, *The Physiology of Taste*

1. THE MAN OF SPIRIT

BRILLAT-SAVARIN ENVISIONS a world divided by dining, though the content of one's meal does not seem significant. What is more important is the manner in which one eats. The animal merely grazes, eating to live, fixated solely on the act. Humanity is distinguished by the capacity to dine according to an established set of rules. Even so, quips the gourmand, only the most illustrious eaters—aristocrats of the edible—actually live by these practices, thereby showing that they deserve to rule both the gastronomic and political worlds. Brillat-Savarin's aphorism reflects the lessons of the anomalous romance *Sir Gowther* (ca. 1400), which tells the tale of a demonic, rapaciously violent duke who is turned from his evil ways by the imposition of a bizarre penance: the Pope enjoins him to eat "no meyt bot þat þou revus of howndus moþe" (279).[1] *Sir*

---

1. Citations of *Sir Gowther* are from Cornelius Novelli's parallel-text edition (*Sir Gowther: An Edition*, PhD diss., Notre Dame, 1963), and are of the Advocates version (contained in Edinburgh, National Library of Scotland MS Advocates 19.3.1, sometimes called the Heege Manuscript), in consultation with a facsimile of the original (Phillipa Hardman, ed., *The Heege Manuscript*), unless otherwise noted. The Advocates version, with its vigorous alliteration and vivid descriptions of Gowther's savagery, has generally been the preferred text for recent scholarship. The only other extant version (hereafter the Royal version), also dating from the late fifteenth century, is contained in British Library Royal MS 17.B.43.

Gowther posits that consumption, even as a disgusting travesty of aristocratic manners, reconfigures the terrible appetite into something tamed and tractable, redeemable not only spiritually but socially as well. In order to become a *homme d'esprit*, Gowther must first experience what it means to eat like an animal. The romance, vicious as well as viciously satirical, deploys this message subtly by crossing the anti-heroic poem with a context of the literature of courteous instruction. The *Gowther* author thereby valorizes the fundamental importance of table manners in the construction of virtuous, redeemable humanity, erecting an edifice that distinguishes the proper consumer both from the animals and the infidels that surround and permeate society.

The scene of such edification is the same as *Havelok the Dane*: the banquet hall, where dining room tables, dinnerware, and delicious fare constitute a massive assemblage of polite society that "relates and separates" all humans at the same time, to quote Arendt, placing human bodies as well as material objects into social circulation with each other.[2] But where the dynastic romance's view of the feast occasion and its massive set of performances and rituals bring Havelok into greater focus, in *Sir Gowther*, the untidiness and haphazard nature of this process is instead emphasized. The sovereignty enjoyed by Havelok, which is augmented by food and service, fragments and dissolves in the legend of Gowther's career, called into question by the enormous effort applied to acquisition of decent manners. The grand concert of the feast is shown to be a much messier affair, in ways congruent with the speculations of J. Allan Mitchell: "A dining table is a scene of bodily incorporation and physical absorption, where incommensurable things cross, catalyze, and consume one another in ways that are considered productive and sometimes perverse."[3] Gowther's grotesque performance of inverted (if not perverted) manners show that the banquet cannot be so carefully orchestrated, and that its spectacular opportunities for sophistication and distinction are always contingent and fragile, eternally needing to be replayed and reaffirmed by future performance.

The wayward nature of the meal ensures that not just corporeal appetites are satisfied during its many courses, but the political appetites of its participants are, as well. Given the frequency of conduct book injunctions not to gorge oneself (or even fully satisfy oneself) at the table, it might seem that the social hunger for status and recognition is the primary drive behind it all.[4] So long as the penitent Gowther battles for table scraps with the dogs of the

---

2. Arendt, *Human Condition*, 52.

3. J. Allan Mitchell, *Becoming Human: The Matter of the Medieval Child*, 142.

4. See John Lydgate's "Dietary, and a Doctrine for Pestilence," in *The Minor Poems of John Lydgate*, part 2, ed. Henry Noble McCracken, 137–38; and William Caxton's *Book of Curtesye*, ed.

hall, the poem endorses this political performance as a drive toward social as well as religious reintegration. In fact, the poem is rather clear-eyed about a fundamental truth of society: consumption, even if fantastic and bestial, influences the practical operation of the body politic. By couching Gowther's weird penance as a social phenomenon, the poem's gruesome excesses become an imaginative instruction in the courteous graces necessary to be a legitimate member of convivial society. Penitential regimens are equal parts ideological submission and bodily performance, although critics have tended to focus on religious aspects of the Pope's strange prescription to the exclusion of the political and social ramifications of its requirements. E. M. Bradstock first identifies *Sir Gowther* as penitentially focused, revealing it to be more powerful and purposeful than previously granted, while Andrea Hopkins commends the poem for its "spare, lean, cryptic, allusive," penitential narrative, which allows the "two great movements of sin and atonement at its core" to stand out clearly.[5] Such scholarship has redeemed *Sir Gowther* from its traditionally low critical estimation and authorized its study, though still with varying assessments of its value. George Kane commends the romance only for the honest simplicity of its hero once he recognizes his penitential obligations: "If a man is to be the son of a demon, and he is to purify himself, this is how we would have him behave."[6] Joanne Charbonneau is not convinced by the transformation at the heart of the poem's plot, positing that Gowther's saintly end is not commensurable with the demonic violence of his former life.[7] Michael Uebel is unique in diagnosing no change at all in Gowther, that the "psychopathologies" that wind him in their folds prevent him from exceeding his originary perverse condition, even in death and sainthood.[8] Alcuin Blamires admires *Sir Gowther*'s "surface crankiness and drastic speed" and reads the tale politically as expressing anxieties over "breeding and dynasty" endemic to early fifteenth-century England.[9] Most recently, Anna Chen describes the romance

---

F. J. Furnivall, 19. Stephanie Trigg states this perennial requirement well: "The art of fine eating is the art of not seeming to need to eat" ("Learning to Live," in *Middle English*, ed. Strohm, 468).

5. E. M. Bradstock, "The Penitential Pattern in *Sir Gowther*," *Parergon* 20 (1978): 3–10; Andrea Hopkins, *The Sinful Knights: A Study of Middle English Penitential Romance*, 145 and 150.

6. Kane, *Middle English Literature*, 32.

7. Joanne Charbonneau, "From Devil to Saint: Transformations in *Sir Gowther*," in *The Matter of Identity in Medieval Romance*, ed. Phillipa Hardman, 21–28.

8. Michael Uebel, "The Foreigner Within: The Subject of Abjection in *Sir Gowther*," in *Meeting the Foreign in the Middle Ages*, ed. Albrecht Classen, 96–97, 110. The difficulty of overcoming the destiny of categories can be felt in *Sir Gowther* even in its generic designations: the poem identifies itself as a "law of Breyten" [a Breton *lai*] (15) yet indulges in both hagiographic, romance, and even *chanson de geste* elements.

9. Alcuin Blamires, "The Twin Demons of Aristocratic Society in *Sir Gowther*," in *Pulp Fictions*, ed. Nicola McDonald, 45–47.

as "structured by two competing cultural imaginaries of childhood as socially brutish but also spiritually redemptive, whereby Gowther simultaneously eats his way out of one model of childhood and back into the other."[10]

As these last two critics show, *Sir Gowther* is fixated upon the problem of human identity both as produced by birth as well as formed through nurture. Blamires claims that the romance "focuses key anxieties of society's dominant group at such a pitch as to project a kind of worst-case threat to dynastic stability," a menace to the polity that takes demonic form in the poem's imaginative register.[11] By contrast, in comparing the romance to its manuscript contexts of childhood play and instruction, Chen observes that "eating can be learned, and education can be eaten, as Gowther demonstrates when he eats with dogs in order to learn to become human."[12] Parallel to the educational emphasis in Chen and others, I argue that Gowther's atonement demonstrates that the decorous practice of eating shapes aristocratic bodies and feeds the desire to belong to a social unit. Required to cleave to the court, Gowther's penitential regime makes him both a fool (355) and a dog, and these recognizable, though abased, positions in the household redeem him and ultimately teach him how to be a healthy, conforming nobleman. Although Gowther is rendered bestial, his performance is compared to human social rituals. By skirting the boundaries of the animal, eating like the beast into which he has made himself, Gowther is reincorporated into the body politic.[13] Animals contextualize human behaviors, even the rambunctious dogs that beg and fight for tasty bits, a fact anticipated by the story of the Canaanite woman who famously begs Jesus for assistance in Matthew 15:25–28, winning his aid through her politically savvy response to his first rebuff. The animal is an always-present possibility in the inculcation of social graces, as well: the child who is not properly trained in them resembles nothing more than a "beast," according to William Caxton.[14]

As *Sir Gowther* reveals, however, belonging to the human social order does not only mean eating in the right manner but also deploying violence to the proper degree and against the appropriate targets—not only the dogs

---

10. Anna Chen, "Consuming Childhood: *Sir Gowther* and National Library of Scotland MS Advocates 19.3.1," *JEGP* 111 (2012): 361.

11. Blamires, "Twin Demons," 46.

12. Chen, "Consuming Childhood," 377.

13. Karl Steel argues, "Nothing in this penance threatens the distinction between humans and animals, for it is because the Pope and Gowther alike think animals are degraded that the penance works *as* penance" (*How to Make a Human: Animals and Violence in the Middle Ages*, 238). Yet there is something noble about the dogs, who, by pursuing their natural inclinations to fight over bones under the dinner table, become agents of God's instruction in the romance.

14. The sentiment can be found in William Caxton, *Dialogues in French and English* (ca. 1483), ed. Henry Bradley, 9.

of the hall but also the "hethen hownd" of the Sultan and his Saracen army (376). The demonic duke is not redeemable despite his penchant for bloodshed, but perhaps paradoxically because of it, and his unusual penance could be seen as both a lesson in social decorum and a strangely effective training regime. Standard penitential fare, a diet of bread and water, might leave the demonic knight too enervated to defend Christendom against its foes. Yet fighting with dogs is just the sort of thing to prepare him for battling the foreign threat and dragging Europe as well as an emperor's daughter out of the jaws of peril. The *Gowther* poet recognizes what kind of knight his society needs in a time of imperial crisis, and he drives the poem to redeem the duke regardless of the savagery Gowther has inflicted upon church and country. The poem ultimately comes to a shocking conclusion: romance can express betrayed urges for decency, but even in those thwarted expectations of social decorum, the political work of the genre still functions. By altering its drives almost at will, it incorporates every conflicting image of generic propriety and social edification into an uncomfortable, satiric whole. *Sir Gowther* turns its apparently religious focus on its ear, and what seems on its surface to be a penitential poem is actually a political one in its preoccupation with the proper sort of knight at the turn of the fifteenth century: a good consumer as well as a doughty fighter.

2. THE CONTEXT OF COURTESY

The allure of reading of *Sir Gowther* as penitence derives in no small part from the romance's association with religious texts in MS Advocates 19.3.1 (otherwise known as the Heege Manuscript), such as the *Vision of Tundale*. However, as Phillipa Hardman points out, the contents of the entire codex tell only part of the story. She explains that the Heege Manuscript is comprised of individual quires or "booklets" that were only bound together into a single volume sometime in the late fifteenth century.[15] Before then, they were a self-contained series, each carefully constructed according to a deliberate pattern. In particular, the three romances in the anthology—*Sir Isumbras, Sir Amadace,* and *Sir Gowther*—appear to have been carefully edited for use as educational tools, and each is paired with a short didactic poem to further that purpose.[16] It is important, therefore, to consider the context of the individual quires when examining the contemporary reception of the poems now

---

15. Hardman, ed., *Heege Manuscript*, 3. See also Chen, "Consuming Childhood," 362ff.
16. Mary Shaner, "Instruction and Delight: Medieval Romances as Children's Literature," *Poetics Today* 13.1 (1992): 5–15; Hardman, ed., *Heege Manuscript*, 22–25.

contained in the Heege Manuscript. Thus, although *Sir Gowther* appears with the *Vision of Tundale* in both its manuscripts, in the case of the Advocates manuscript, the pairing is coincidental. More important to consider, in terms of how this booklet would have been used by its first owners, is *Sir Gowther*'s pairing with the conduct poem known as the "Urbanitatis" (ca. 1375–400).[17]

Conduct books are didactic poems that teach the art of polite living, usually focusing on highly formulaic precepts of bodily control and comportment at the table. They are found throughout Western European medieval literature, with texts extant in most vernacular languages as well as in Latin. As Stephen Mennell observes, the promulgation of treatises that instruct their users in the appropriate methods to consume (the "civilising of appetite," as he calls it) are doubtlessly enabled by the growing stability of the food supply in Western Europe, in terms of amount and variety.[18] The audience for these etiquette manuals was varied, with versions directed both at men and women, masters and servants, aristocrats and bourgeoisie alike. A venerable genre handed down through the Middle Ages, conduct books enjoyed a boom in popularity in fifteenth-century England, about the time *Sir Gowther* was copied into its extant manuscripts. This trend was fueled by the ever-increasing social stature and literacy of the prosperous middle classes as well as the recent innovation of paper manuscripts, which led to the increased availability of written works.[19] Kathleen Ashley and Robert L. A. Clark describe the power of conduct books in this period to provide "a guide for literate readers to negotiate new sets of social possibilities," the necessity of which attests to the mobility of the upper ranks of the middle class.[20] The sheer number of conduct books suggests that they had an overwhelming presence in the imagination of readers at the time, and many fifteenth-century manuscripts that contain romances and other popular genres have accompanying courtesy manuals.[21]

---

17. There is no edition of the "Urbanitatis" more recent than Furnivall's *Babees Book*, 13–15. The Heege MS version bears the header "stans puer ad mensam," which identifies the poem as a member of a family of related courtesy poems to which it does not properly belong. Most editors of *Sir Gowther* and cataloguers have perpetuated the misidentification of the "Urbanitatis." See Jonathan Nicholls, *The Matter of Courtesy: Medieval Courtesy Books and the Gawain-poet*, 177–95, for a catalogue of the various courtesy books and their manuscript traditions.

18. Mennell, *All Manners of Food*, 32.

19. See Claire Sponsler, *Drama and Resistance: Bodies, Goods, and Theatricality in Late Medieval England*, 54.

20. Kathleen Ashley and Robert L. A. Clark, introduction to *Medieval Conduct*, x.

21. See for instance Oxford, Bodleian Library MS Ashmole 61 (compiled in the fifteenth century), which contains four conduct books (*How the Wise Man Taught his Son* [item 3], *How the Good Wife Taught her Daughter* [4], *Stans Puer ad Mensam* [7], and *Dame Courtesy* [8]) along with numerous Middle English romances (including *Sir Isumbras* [5] and *Sir Orfeo* [39]). See George Shuffelton's edition *Codex Ashmole 61: A Compilation of Popular Middle English Verse*.

Readers of the *Sir Gowther* booklet in the fifteenth century would have had to confront a shocking discrepancy—a brutal and violent story alongside a genteel courtesy manual—and to attempt to synthesize the two extremes into an instructive whole. One way to do so is to assume that both texts, on a basic level, are concerned with the creation of a well-behaved man, a proper consumer fit for polite society, who knows his rightful place and eats according to courteous expectations. The "Urbanitatis" does this explicitly, proclaiming that the assiduous application of good conduct will not only train the pupil to become a full-fledged citizen of the world of politesse but also will have the power to make him an entirely new man, despite social background or parentage:

> Leyt not þy cowntenanes þer with abate,
> For gud nortur wylle saue þy sta[t]e;
> Fadur & modur, what euer þei be,
> Wele is þe chylde þat mey the
> In hall in chambur, whedur þou gon,
> Gud maners maken a man.
> (27–32)[22]

Although the final line closes with a slant rhyme and a metrical clang, its lesson rings clear: correct social bearing reconstructs the subject, purging him of the limitations of blood or family, revealing him to be a legitimate member of convivial society. The import of this passage can be applied both to the nameless pupil of the "Urbanitatis" and to the monstrous child of *Sir Gowther*. Just as the successful application of table manners (which would demonstrate one's "gud nortur") enables the child of modest birth to succeed among those of exalted station, so too will Gowther's grotesque courtesy lessons beneath the table allow him to pass, and eventually to thrive, as a fully redeemed member of the social body.

How one comports oneself at the table determines one's place at it—and these behaviors structure human society. They evince the reception of social imperatives "whispered by the *habitus*," as Sponsler puts lyrically, referring to Bourdieu's renowned concept of cultural dispositions that structure human

---

22. Citations from the "Urbanitatis" are based on my transcription of the poem as it appears in the Heege Manuscript in Hardman's facsimile, in consultation with Furnivall's edition, which is derived from the version in British Library MS Cotton Caligula A.ii. All contractions have been silently expanded for ease of reading. The manuscript reads "stake" at line 28, which is likely an error.

practice, more or less unconsciously obtained.²³ The tenor of conduct book lessons resonates with the implications of *Sir Gowther*. Good manners discipline the individual and qualify him or her to become a member of a larger social body. Conduct literature polices bodily performance in order to shape an ideal, aristocratic human society. It is the prandial engine of social distinction, the "judgment of taste," which as Bourdieu argues, is a privileged demonstration of desires, objects, and behaviors that vibrate with economic domination among classes warring for cultural preeminence.²⁴ This battle over political supremacy, fought on the field of courteous performance is just as serious and dangerous as any violent conflict. The troubled reign of the Lancastrian Henry VI, marred by bouts of mental disability and Yorkist usurpation, was made all the more complicated by the relatively impoverished king's impotence to perform the social display of regality to any degree respected by his aristocratic subjects, many of whom could afford to demonstrate their power much more effectively. The unfortunate king was described as entering "more lyker a play than the shewyng of a prynce to wynne mennys hertys, ffor by this mean he lost many and wan noon or Rygth ffewe."²⁵ His royalty resembling more a stage play than actual sovereignty, Henry VI failed to assert his ineffable right to rule through a failure to ostentatiously perform it. The *Liber Niger* (ca. 1471), an ordinance book attributed to the household of Edward IV, one of Henry's Yorkist rivals, begins by providing a venerable historical justification for the political importance of prandial majesty. Citing the effect that the household management of King Solomon had on the visiting Queen of Sheba, the book explicitly links the ordering of the banquet hall to the sober guidance of the state:

> Also when she sawe the habundance, varied, and maner of disposicion of such metes as cam to king Salamonis, hit smote her from any sprite to speke, thus seyng that queen, that the trouth of Salamon is wortines was more than his fame did expresse; semyng also to her that euery master officer in his sober demenyng, his honestee, his riche araye, and of all theyr mannerly cerimoniez don in that court, that eche of hem miȝt be lykenyd to a king of her cyuntree . . . this caused the wise queen to maruayle more hugely,

---

23. Sponsler, *Drama and Resistance*, 67. For Bourdieu's ideas of the *habitus*, see his *Outline of a Theory of Practice* (1972), trans. Richard Nice and *The Logic of Practice* (1980), trans. Richard Nice.

24. Bourdieu, *Distinction*, 11. See also 386–87.

25. *Great Chronicle of London*, ed. Robert Fabyan, A. H. Thomas, and Isobel Thornley, 215.

she tho3t there that euery officer in vnitie of loue aplyed to excuse other by seruyce and attendaunce, that any man no fawte cowed aspye.[26]

The book goes on to recognize other, more recent, and English regal households before laying out its own precepts for the management of the king's *domus*. In every case, the demonstration of royal magnificence, the orderly and well-considered display of commensality to both guests and strangers alike, is an outward sign of virtuous governance. A well-kept household signifies the reasonable and equitable rule of the country, with aristocratic courtesy the hand on the tiller of the ship of state.

The elite do not just hunger for different, more refined commodities in the social realm, they yearn and enjoy them in an entirely distinct fashion, enjoying them as a "pleasure purified of pleasure," elevating their *savoir* (a word that denotes both knowledge and taste) into the sphere of high aesthetics.[27] A change in the manner and the method of eating alters appetite, and subsequently identity. Hunger itself becomes educated so that the consumer no longer acts in an unsanitary, greedy, and thoughtless way. Proper, aristocratic society is imagined as a convivial community, bound by rituals of eating together, and it is this communal body that Gowther must infiltrate, and by which he must be accepted in order to be redeemed. Even by devouring his food in an appalling parody of proper conduct—by tearing it from the mouths of dogs—Gowther will be able to renounce his demonic patrimony and reconstruct himself as a powerful warrior for the cause of Christian Europe. His story, as nasty and violent as it is, is in fact a romance of manners. *Sir Gowther* operates as an inverted sort of conduct poem, an educational example complemented by the "Urbanitatis." Both texts explore the way that etiquette operates as a political force—culturally hegemonic yet self-mobilized—to mold individual behavior in a social context.

3. "GUD MANERS MAKEN A MAN"

Norbert Elias's groundbreaking *The Civilizing Process* examines the connection between the growth of conduct literature in early modern Europe and the development of a sense of *civilité,* based in class, which accompanies new forms of political and social organization arising in the sixteenth and seventeenth centuries. Elias claims that a new sort of social contract is conceived in this era, and that the conduct book—particularly Erasmus of Rotterdam's

---

26. *Liber Niger,* in A. R. Myers, ed., *The Household of Edward IV: The Black Book and the Ordinance of 1478,* 81.

27. Bourdieu, *Distinction,* 6.

De civilitate morum puerilium (1530)—both creates and expresses this new understanding.[28] Elias charts the conduct book's work in evolving the ideal of the human body, *homo clausus,* as self-contained, discrete, and closed to other human bodies surrounding it, while at the same moment the entire social order is altered to accommodate this new sense of personal space. As Mitchell observes of Elias's view of manners: "Attempting to transcend environmental contexts and animal functions, the human is supposed to come into possession of himself at the table, surrounding himself with so many buffers against nature."[29] To Elias, human practice and self-control are meant to differentiate the self from the other, from the chaos of the world, as well as from the untidiness of past ages and identities, creating in effect a newly convivial, civilized humanity. This thesis is a masterpiece of cultural materialist scholarship, yet it ignores the fact that the evolution of self-governance via the conduct book had been underway for four hundred years or more by the time Erasmus wrote his treatise, and that several medieval conduct books provided Erasmus with his mannerly precepts.[30] In the years since the publication of Elias's seminal work, scholars of medieval literature have filled critical gaps regarding the nature and importance of the courtesy manuals of the Middle Ages, and have also incorporated twentieth-century cultural theory—the work of Bourdieu and Michel de Certeau, for example—to broaden the understanding of social power exerted through the conduct book, revealing the operation of hegemonic discourses through the manuals' seemingly banal precepts.

As Sponsler and Mark Addison Amos have demonstrated, the operations of the structures and forces that drive quotidian existence are expressed as overt discourse in medieval courtesy literature as early as the mid-twelfth century, if not earlier, in both monastic and secular contexts.[31] This assertion reveals that there was a continuity of interest in the techniques of bodily control and social engineering throughout this period, despite its profound cultural and economic changes. The medieval forebearers of Erasmus initiate a new understanding of the body in society, as Sponsler reveals of the conduct book: "Its focus is on the individual body, understood as an engine of consumption—not just of food, but also of emotions, thoughts, other personal

---

28. Norbert Elias, *The Civilizing Process* (1939), trans. Edmund Jephcott, 1.47–52.

29. Mitchell, *Becoming Human,* 141.

30. Elias himself acknowledges this, yet it does not alter the periodizing assumptions of his argument. The basic content of *De civilitate* is carried over from the medieval conduct book, though Erasmus's style is characteristic. See Appendix C to Nicholls, *Matter of Courtesy,* 198–201, for notes on the continuities and differences between Erasmus's work and medieval conduct books.

31. Sponsler, *Drama and Resistance,* 53; Mark Addison Amos, "'For Manners Make Man': Bourdieu, de Certeau, and the Common Appropriation of Noble Manners in the *Book of Courtesy,*" in *Medieval Conduct,* ed. Ashley and Clark, 30.

activities, and even social relations."³² The courtesy poem recognizes the social obligations of all citizens, that is, to be open to a variety of attitudes, acts, and commodities as well as to consume them correctly, and properly defines the human subject in consumer society not as *homo clausus* but instead as *homo circumferens*—a humanity in motion. Though not legislated explicitly, manners, usually indoctrinated through what Bourdieu calls a "hidden persuasion of an implicit pedagogy," enforce a law of the consumer in an edible world.³³ Michel Foucault identifies a similar imperative to bodily discipline, and though he locates it much later in European history, the obligations and regimes of the conduct book are much the same. Courtesy instruction just as surely "increases the forces of the body (in economic terms of utility) and diminishes these same forces (in political terms of obedience)."³⁴

Proper comportment, and the necessity of properly inculcating it, is consistent for nearly four hundred years. The most important alteration to this social imperative is who comprised polite society, as the bourgeoisie grew in prestige and power, demanding its share of luxuries traditionally enjoyed by the aristocracy and religious elite. The courtesy book negotiates a world of commensal relationships, demonstrating the proper way to exist amid socially important commodities—food and other trappings of spectacular social living. It sets standards by which the public display of identity can be measured and policed, and which encourage, as Sponsler claims, the "willing conscription of the individual into the cultural work of social conformity and bodily control."³⁵ By reading the courtesy book, each guest at the feast assumes full responsibility for disciplining his or her own public behavior. Yet free choice is mitigated by the rigidity of the pressure to conform to these mores. This atmosphere of socially imposed self-censure discourages defiant acts of "incorrect" or willful usage of commodities—"poaching" society's products, to borrow a term from de Certeau—acts that foster resistive, disruptive identities within hegemonic systems of production and consumption.³⁶

The medieval conduct manual carves a space for consumption as a force in political economy, an avant-garde acknowledgment of the economic power of consumption that anticipates Marx's "Introduction to the Critique of Politi-

---

32. Sponsler, "Eating Lessons: Lydgate's 'Dietary' and Consumer Conduct," in *Medieval Conduct*, ed. Ashley and Clark, 6.

33. Bourdieu, *Outline of a Theory of Practice*, 94. He continues: "The whole trick of pedagogic reason lies precisely in the way it extorts the essential while seeming to demand the insignificant" (94–95).

34. Michel Foucault, *Discipline and Punish: The Birth of the Prison*, trans. Alan Sheridan, 138.

35. Sponsler, *Drama and Resistance*, 53.

36. de Certeau, *Practice of Everyday Life*, 1.xii.

cal Philosophy" (1857).[37] Here Marx describes a tightly bound cycle of economic action, where producer and consumer are inextricably locked together, each dependent on the other for fulfillment and perpetuation. Each side is not only "immediately its opposite" but also mediates the other. Production makes commodities to be consumed, but consumption produces the subject who will give the products their "last finish." Without a consumer to complete the cycle, a product remains a mere potential, a thing that does not need to be reproduced.[38] Therefore, production must produce not only the object to be consumed but also the consuming subject:

> Production also gives consumption its specificity, its character, its finish. Just as consumption gave the product its finish as product, so does production give finish to consumption. *Firstly*, the object is not an object in general, but a specific object which must be consumed in a specific manner, to be mediated in turn by production itself. . . . Production thus produces not only the object but also the manner of consumption, not only objectively but also subjectively. Production thus creates the consumer.[39]

Production without consumption is a creative force without a raison d'être, and consumption is merely raw desire without production to refine it. All of them produced phenomena, manner and need align with practice and desire, and each consequently does its part to shape human identity as consumers in a political economy. The exchange of a product or "finish to consumption" completes the cycle: the commodity draws flame in its consumption, becoming fascinating and spectacular to its consumer, whose desire for it is reborn.[40] The consumer moves forward to yearn for new items to be produced and exchanged, sending them back into the realm of practice, where products wear their manner of use upon their commodifiable sleeves.

The conduct manual's role in this cycle of self-regenerating and perpetual production is to denote the rules and proprieties by which commodities must be consumed. Mitchell observes, "Such voluptuous texts are also communicating practices for future reference and reenactment, generating new and lively multisensory occasions."[41] Courtesy literature records and prolongs perfor-

---

37. Marx, *Grundrisse*, 83–111.
38. Ibid., 91.
39. Ibid., 92 (emphasis in original).
40. The Hegelian implications of the commodity's moment of flashing into reality is explored in Andrew Cole's "The Sacrament of the Fetish, The Miracle of the Commodity," in *The Legitimacy of the Middle Ages: On the Unwritten History of Theory*, ed. Cole and D. Vance Smith, 81–82.
41. Mitchell, *Becoming Human*, 161.

mance, rendering the continuity of acts into something themselves consumable, themselves a guarantee of future delicious banqueting. Body and text become united through the act of articulation, and both are joined to the edible realm of the material. And with the precepts of comportment spun into practice, every body moves in precisely the right way, every object is properly mobilized, every morsel of food or sip of drink decorously taken inside. The political appetites of the social order are sent into circulation through somatic harmony, every consumer submitting themselves to its logic and ensuring its vitality through voluntary conduct. Political society itself is produced through proper, expected orders of consumption.

Knowing how to eat one's food is central to the consuming identity and the concordance of its reign. Yet Marx complicates his own argument in an aphorism that moves inward, from the consideration of consumption as a category of human economic behavior, to consumption as the literal ingestion of food. No longer a metonymy, the simple though powerful reference to ingestion and bodily needs suggests the unraveling of the entire circle of production:

> Hunger is hunger; but the hunger that is gratified with cooked meat eaten with a knife and fork is a different hunger from the one that bolts down raw meat with the aid of hand, nail, and tooth. (92)

The inner tensions of this sentence seem ready to implode: Hunger is not just hunger: there are as many kinds as there are ways of satisfying it—some socially condoned, others violative. Different eaters experience their food in different ways, based on their choice of the array of social practices available to them. Hunger matters because hunger is fundamentally the product of political economy—to hunger is a political act in itself, a yearning for involvement in the world around. To crave a foodstuff, regardless of how it is eaten, integrates the consumer into the cycle of production and consumption, and compares the self to a circle of other eating citizens. One becomes a consumer through appetite, but each consumer individuates that identity by the manner in which one satisfies it. Even if the producer has determined the means by which the consumer takes in the product, placing him or her, for example, in a world of "knife and fork," the consumer still can choose to violate that compact.[42] What is at stake is recognition and conformity: gnawing with "hand,

---

42. Medieval Western Europe was largely not a land of the knife and fork, and diners preferred to eat with their hands, scooping up sauces with bits of bread or with shared spoons until the early seventeenth century, though forks had been used in Byzantium and destinations eastward for some time before that.

nail, and tooth" would identify this consumer as refusing to conform, as lurking dangerously or disgustingly outside the realm of proper consumption.

Considering the power of the chain of production that determines so much of the individual's experience of commodities, it seems questionable whether this toothy resistance is even possible. De Certeau claims that it is: that consumers exist who do not passively ingest the products of dominant society, but rather create a powerful, but temporary, relationship with commodities, which registers their individuality and agency in mass society. Such "poaching" is a form of tactical defiance of the totalizing strategies exerted by hegemonic society to create docile, passive consumers for its products.[43] There is no need to assume that this paradigm of resistance only holds true for contemporary, mass-market society: Marx's ideas of the circularity of consumption and production describe general human behavior, observable in any possible economic order, and de Certeau's most powerful example of creative "poaching" is derived from indigenous cultures adapting themselves to Spanish colonial domination in the early modern era.[44] The existence of conduct books proves that the usage of commodities was policed just as carefully in precapitalist eras. Consumption, as de Certeau argues, has never been a passive act; rather, it is capricious and powerful. Consumers wrest products into their control and shape their own bodies and identities for the brief moments of their use. Production can create the products needed by consumers, but it cannot always dictate how they actually use them. While resistive consumption can invent subversive identities, it is still dependent on possession of the object in order to exert this force. One is not a consumer unless there is something to consume, and so even the poacher relies upon the structures of productive society to express his or her resistance.

Sir Gowther is about an eater who violates the dominant structures of eating, yet who carves out a space for himself in polite society despite devouring meat with his hands, nails, and teeth. Gowther moves through several modes of consumption, from a demon child to a fool among the dogs, from an animal to an homme d'esprit—and in each case, he exerts and manifests his identity via the products available to him. The romance constructs its ferocious anti-hero through attention to his "poaching" consumption, yet only to show how this defiant consumer can be brought around to proper eating—and even proper violence—by his eventual participation in the established social order. In its fantastic legend of evil redeemed, *Sir Gowther* communicates the power of appropriate consumption—expressed by Mitchell's tabular assem-

---

43. For "tactics" versus "strategies," see de Certeau, *Practice of Everyday Life*, 35–37.
44. Ibid., 31–32.

blage—upon the privileged imagination, and posits that social renovation is possible through the application of specific behavioral precepts. This power is reflected in the condensation of an entire realm of ethical expectations into a single milieu—the banquet hall—that becomes the stage of the good life. In this way, the poem parallels the "Urbanitatis," which advises that identity should be articulated through the proper use of material objects and mediated by the practices of conviviality. The lesson of political appetites is made clear through the synecdoche of *hall* for *world*: the substitution actually accesses a truth of society, that its ways are foodways, that its best practices first begin in the refectory.

4. "IN IS YOTHE FULL WYLDE SCHALL BE"

The circle of his world limited by his tiny, barely formed body, Gowther is nonetheless imbricated right away into a world of political eating. His demonic childhood foreshadows his utter lack of a convivial social model, but, as Jacques Derrida claims, "One never eats entirely alone."[45] The baby feeds, according to the customs and precepts of his pediatric culture, as a singular being though even this life of focused alimentation is undeniably part of the social order. His father, the Duke of Estryke, at first brings in the wives of his vassals to nurse his "son" (Gowther is the issue of a demonic rape), submitting the child's nutrition to common Western European practice. But this requirement is itself a demonstration of his sovereign prestige: he flaunts his economic wherewithal among his inferiors.[46] By claiming the bodily productions of his knights' wives, and thwarting their fecundity for his own benefit, the Duke hoards the reproductive potential of his entire household. The avaricious vanity of the Duke's privilege, however, redounds to his misfortune when the infant Gowther begins to kill his nurses:

> þo duke comford þat Duches heynde,
> And aftur melche wemen he sende,

---

45. Jacques Derrida, "Eating Well, or The Calculation of the Subject: An Interview with Jacques Derrida," in *Who Comes After the Subject?*, ed. Eduardo Cadava, Peter Connor, and Jean-Luc Nancy, 115.

46. This does not accord well with what is known about medieval wet nurses; that is, that they were hired on the bases of geographical proximity and financial need, and were most likely to be peasants or servants rather than gentry. Studies of wet-nursing emphasize that this practice was increasingly common among noble women through the Middle Ages, even though most medical authorities stated in no uncertain terms that the milk of an infant's own mother was the most beneficial to the baby (Valerie Fildes, *Wet Nursing*, 32–35).

>   þo best in þat cuntre,
> þat was full gud knyghttys wyffys.
> He [Gowther] sowkyd hom so þei lost þer lyvys,
>   Sone had he sleyn thre!
> þo chyld was yong and fast he wex—
> The Duke gard prycke aftur sex—
>   Hende harkons yee:
> Be twelfe moneþys was gon
> ix norsus had he slon
>   Of ladys feyr and fre.
> (97–104)

Gowther's feeding is a perverse realization of influential ideas about the nature of humanity: in *De miseria humane conditionis* (1194–95), Pope Innocent III censures the grotesquerie of fetal development:

> Hear now on what food the child is fed in the womb: actually on menstrual blood, which ceases in the female after conception so that the child in her womb will be nourished by it. And this blood is reckoned so detestable and impure that on contact with it fruits will fail to sprout, orchards go dry, herbs wither, the very trees let go their fruit; if a dog eat of it, he goes mad.[47]

Innocent III feeds into common perceptions of the cursed nature of female bodies, demonstrating that the moral condition of the fetus actually partakes of corporeal uncleanness, so that every human shares in this primal state of blighted physicality. The infant Gowther, by sucking down life as well as nurse's milk (which was believed to be a corporeal refinement of blood), extends the horrifying terms of mortal misery, continuing an execrable parasitic existence outside the womb. Structurally, the stanza is a masterful example of how form can be used to evoke horror: the quick passage of time matches the lines exactly. In twelve lines, twelve months pass, and nine of these lines describe nine slain nurses, one line for each one killed. The narrator's coldly detached tone gives only the barest hint of the baby's gruesome sustenance, leaving a terrifying suggestion to stand in for the agonizing death of each nurse drained of her life force. The infant Gowther completes the gesture of domination performed by his father—the Duke pushes his lordly prerogative upon his subordinates to an unreasonable degree, but the baby ends it in horror. The symbolic gesture is made terribly literal. Gowther cannot be satisfied with the

---

47. Pope Innocent III, *On the Misery of the Human Condition*, 9.

nutritive power of mothers' milk, sucking in more and more until he takes in human life itself as nourishment. In a precocious and horrifying version of the previous chapter's vision of sovereign consumption, he despoils and destroys what he eats, in an awful scene that far outstrips the poem's sources in its sensationalism.[48]

The nursemaids are human life and labor-power reduced to material substrate, bare life rendered edible by preposterous and awful literality. The fanatical desire for power in the Duke only leads him to search for one after another female body to serve after the previous one is drained of life. Only after a confrontation with his aggrieved vassals does the Duke give up on the nursemaids, requiring his own wife to suckle their baby instead. But this act ends in terror too:

> His modur fell afowle unhappe,
> Upon a day bad hym þo pappe,
>   He snaffulld to hit soo
> He rofe þo hed from þo brest—
> (111–14)

Again, the poet creates a shocking effect with simple means: a disjuncture between expectation and its savage result, created by the innocent-seeming word "snaffulld." Possibly a *hapax legomenon*, it seems to mean "suckled."[49] Such a homey, wholesome word creates the image of a baby's sweet reaction to its mother's breast, a tiny gurgle in anticipation of its meal. This cuteness, however, is cruelly reversed in the nearly unimaginable sadism of the next line: "He rofe þo hed from þo brest."[50] By biting off her nipple, Gowther not only rejects her as a nourisher[51]—perhaps unfairly punishing his mother for the unnatural process of demonic rape that led to his birth—but also asserts for himself a new role as consumer. The infant Gowther will no longer be satisfied with maternal nutritive power. Unable to be suckled any longer, his own mother having fled in

---

48. In *Robert le Diable* (ca. late thirteenth century), a probable source for *Sir Gowther*, the young Robert is born after a particularly long labor, and then kicks, scratches, and bites his nurses so much that he can only be fed by means of a hollow piece of horn (E. Loseth, ed., 105–12).

49. *MED*, "snaffelen" (v.). *Sir Gowther* is only example of usage provided in this entry.

50. The B version is slightly less sadistic at this point, saying that Gowther only "tare the oon side of hire brest" (130).

51. Gowther attacks his mother at the very source of her maternal identity—the word for mother (*mater*) was thought to be derived from the word for breast (*mamma*), according to thirteenth-century scholar Bartolomeus Anglicus's *On the Properties of Things* (1240), trans. John Trevisa, ed. M. C. Seymour, 6.vii.

terror from her monstrous progeny ("Scho fell backward and cald a prest, / To chamber fled hym froo [115–16]), Gowther is hurriedly weaned and given "rych fode" (120) to eat, the diet of a nobleman. However, the taste for death and pain is firmly established in the infant—it is all that he will crave from now on.

The inadequate substitution of "rych fode" for mother's milk drives the swiftly growing child to precocious violence, his penchant for harmful action evolving with his rapid development ("In a twelmond more he wex / þen odur chyldur in seyvon or sex" [129–30]). As a baby, the only power he had to harm others was through his mouth, but as he achieves adolescence his appetite becomes sublimated into a zest for rapine and murder. Symbolizing this redirected desire, he forges himself a falchion "boþe of styll and yron" (126), which projects his hostility outward and gives him an awful tool with which to act upon his wicked desires. It is a terrible weapon, whose single-edged blade is most effective for hacking and chopping rather than stabbing or slashing. Gowther's new weapon reveals a transfer of the story's fixations from oral to genital and introduces a new phase in his violent lifestyle. Now that he carries a weapon—now that he is literally "armigerous"—all he needs is the cultural authority to declare war upon society; an authority given by his hapless father, who knights him out of a misguided intention of correcting his son's unruly behavior, and who then dies of sorrow.[52] Impotent in every important way, the old Duke bows out of the story, leaving Gowther's mother to cope with her terror of their monstrous child. Now "Sir" Gowther as well as the Duke of Estryke, he is no more constrained by the expectations of correct knightly behavior as he was by the "Name-of-the-Father."[53] He is driven to "wyrke is fadur wyll" (160), submitting to patrimonial urges he does not fully understand, obeying a father he is not wholly conscious of.

His awful hunger lingers, motivating his future actions and evolving with his rapid development. Gowther misunderstands many aspects of the ritual appropriation of the trappings of aristocratic life, using gratuitous violence when other forms would serve. It is unsurprising, then, that he would perversely perform that important signifying practice of noble life, the hunt. Like any good knight, Gowther loves the chase "aldur best," but fails to hunt in the appropriate spaces: "Parke, wodd and wylde forest, / Boþe be weyus and street" (162–64). Here the tail-rhyme, which sounds as though it were merely

---

52. Or maybe not so misguided, since there were manuals aimed at instilling knightly codes of conduct, such as Ramón Llull's *Libre del Orde de Cauayleria* (ca. 1290), which existed in a Middle English translation, later printed by William Caxton (ca. 1483–85). (For Caxton's translation, see *The Book of the Order of Chivalry*, ed. Robert Adams).

53. See Francine McGregor, "The Paternal Function in *Sir Gowther*" on the application of Lacanian psychoanalysis to the story (*Essays in Medieval Studies* 16 [1999]: 67–78).

a formulaic verse-filler, actually exposes the truth of Gowther's hunting. Parks and woods and wild forests are good places to hunt, but finishing the list with roads and streets invokes an image of a highwayman. The tail-rhyme subtly creates the image of a Gowther who uses the hunt as an excuse to rob and kill. This liability to depredation is confirmed by the next stanza's horrors:

> He went to honte apon a day,
> He see a nonry be þo way
>   And þedur con he ryde;
> Þo pryorys and hur covent
> With presescion ageyn hym went
>   Full hastely þat tyde;
> Þei wer full ferd of his body,
> For he and is men boþe leyn hom by—
>   þo soþe why schuld y hyde?—
> And syþyn he spard hom in hor kyrke
> And brend hom up, thus con he werke;
>   Þen went his name full wyde.
> (165–76)

The brutal acts of Gowther and his men are contextualized by the formal rituals of the aristocratic hunt—but this sanctioned process of death instead becomes the naked application of terror and force. All violence being the same to the young duke, it is unsurprising that he should stumble upon a convent along his way and want to raze it to the ground. The pleasures of the chase, which end in the decorous consumption of its spoils, are intermingled with Gowther's raw thirst for brutality. The desire for the pursued object constitutes what might be considered an unproblematically noble identity in other hunters, but for Gowther, the target and his desire for it only further enhance his identity as a bloodthirsty killer. He needs to destroy the convent and its unfortunate inhabitants in order to perpetuate this perverted and misdirected self-construction.

However, the connection between hunting and violent eroticism is not merely the product of a diseased, sociopathic mind: it is a common trope in medieval literature. The "love-hunt" *topos* is found in a broad array of texts, from the spectral hunter and hounds of Filomena's story on the fifth day of Giovanni Boccaccio's *The Decameron* (1350), to Jean Froissart's genteel "lamoureuse cache" in the *Paradys d'Amours* (ca. 1360s), to the link between romantic longing and the death of a loved one in Chaucer's *Book of the Duchess* (ca. 1368), to the game of exchanges in *Sir Gawain and the Green Knight* (ca. 1390).

Even when the ultimate moment of killing the prey is absent or underemphasized, these stories conflate the pursuit of love with hyper-masculine competition and rape. *Sir Gowther*, in this instance, is remarkably clear-sighted and noneuphemistic. There is no way that the actions of his hunting party can be mistaken for anything but ultra-violence. In this way appetites, whether for food or other bodily needs, drive the young Gowther into greater and greater enormities of behavior, converting the gentility of the romance genre into its savage negation in brutal life-narrative.

5. "ÞAT ÞU REVUS OF HOWNDUS MOÞE"

This first movement of *Sir Gowther*, chronicling the young duke's sociopathic *aventures*, speculates upon the link between consumption and identity. Gowther produces bloodshed as if he relishes the taste, producing in turn a persona that savors horrible deeds and hungers for more. Since identity, according to Marx and de Certeau, is produced and reproduced through consumption, Gowther is locked in a cycle of consumptive violence that compromises his role as duke and knight, and endangers the political entity that his body is meant to guarantee. His awful devoration reveals his misunderstanding of how a social body is constituted. The dreary pattern, however, is interrupted by the intervention of a "nolde erle of þat cuntre" (189), who gives the duke a paternity to match his ferocious performance.[54] In a clever parody of standard romance structure, Gowther's new identification as "sum feyndus son" (193) matches his reality—there is no longer any discrepancy between the name of the hero and his actions. But the poem itself defies the romance trope of recovered identity as its final resolution; this dubbing comes in the middle of the poem rather than the end, and the name so discovered is the very essence of evil. Gowther finally realizes how others see him; that his solipsistic existence has consequences in the outside world, and that he has constructed a terrible political realm around his ferocious appetites. This self-recognition transforms the daydream of Sigmund Freud's "family romance" into a nightmare, with Gowther's inadequate father supplanted by the more powerful yet terrible figure of the engendering demon.[55]

---

54. This is a good example of the tendency in medieval English romance to externalize psychological aspects of the protagonist. In *Robert le Diable*, Robert's revelation is wholly internal; a realization that despite the fact he tries to do good, some force within him turns whatever he does to evil (369–403).

55. Sigmund Freud, "Family Romance" (1909) in *Collected Papers*, ed. and trans. James Strachy, 5.74–78.

The twofold revelation of his parentage (by the earl and by his mother, who confesses it at the point of her son's falchion [204–7]) is the romance's turning point, and the patent, demonic truth is finally articulated. He must face, as Jeffrey Jerome Cohen describes, "the elemental nonsensicality of his coming into being"; the incoherence of the world, driven by acts of violence, that he has constructed around him.[56] Sovereign prerogative comes crashing down around his ears, inspiring in him a rage that threatens both the earl and his mother, but ultimately leads him to share his tears with her. As Margaret Robson notes, these tears are the first thing he has shared in his entire life,[57] and they "glyde" down his cheeks just as his sword was ready to "glyde" through his mother's heart. Gowther's reaction is to seek an outside to his circumscribed existence, to find another father figure who will dare to discipline him and force him to undergo the change that he now seeks.

Yet even after finding this new paternal ideal in the Pope, Gowther's anticipated new identity does not change very much from his previous one, as signified by his refusal to set aside his awful falchion (273–78). After his conversion, Gowther continues to be a fighter and a knight, but this military role does not seem to be countenanced by the Pope's prescribed penance, which instead focuses on him as a consumer:

> Wherser þu travellys, be northe or soth,
> Þu eyt no meyt bot þat þu revus of howndus moþe
>   Cum thy body within;
> Ne no worde speke for evyll ne gud,
> Or þu reyde tokyn have fro God,
>   Þat forgyfyn is þi seyn.
> (279–84)

This extraordinary penance combats Gowther's penchant for violence by redirecting his literal appetite. The Pope understands that by eating in a different manner, the young duke will be forced to realign his social body, changing who he is, in effect, through his mouth. Once able to win the food that no other class could obtain, now he must live upon what no other person would touch. The hypermetricality of line 280, which has five stresses instead of the usual four, jumps out of the verse pattern to underscore its outrageous

---

56. Jeffrey Jerome Cohen, "Gowther Among the Dogs: Becoming Inhuman c. 1400," in *Becoming Male in the Middle Ages,* ed. Bonnie Wheeler and Jeffrey Jerome Cohen, 228.

57. Margaret Robson, "Animal Magic: Moral Regeneration in *Sir Gowther,*" *Yearbook of English Studies* 22 (1992): 149.

requirement.[58] If it were for not the final, overflowing stipulation "of howndus moþe," Gowther's appetite might not be that different from what it has been during his life. The Pope recognizes the awful truth of the penitent's desires, emphasizing its unwholesome nature by using the word "revus." The verb *reven* signifies a swift and savage action with which Gowther is all too familiar, meaning "to plunder," "to snatch," and "to obtain love by force,"[59] and is closely related to the modern English verbs "bereave," "raven," and "ravish." Just as the infant Gowther "reft" his mother's nipple from her body, the matured penitent must continue to eat in an appropriative and violent manner.

Required literally to drag the food out of another creature's mouth, Gowther must become even more of a brute in order to allay his brutishness. It is not a matter of simply changing his diet. If it were, then a regimen of bread and water would be sufficient to humble the proud and dangerous duke. Instead, how Gowther eats is more important. The Pope recognizes that Gowther has no taste at all for nurture as it can ordinarily be obtained through human relationships, from one hand to another, and so he must be restored at a bestial remove from these socially instantiating bonds. The mouths of dogs are therefore a mediating step that intervenes between Gowther and the rest of mankind.

The Pope's prescription resonates with the precepts of conduct literature in form as well as content. The medieval reader of the poem would likely respond to the similar feeling and sound of the instruction in *Sir Gowther* when confronted with the Pope's corrective prescription. Yet this educational context is invoked precisely to subvert expectation. Take, for example, this passage from the "Urbanitatis":

> yf þu sytte be a worþeer mon
> Þen þi selfe þu art won
> Suffur hym first to toch þo meyt
> Or þat þu selfe þer any wylt geyt
> To þe feyrst morsell þu mey not stryke
> Thoffe þat þu do hit wele lyke.
> (43–48)

The instruction of the Pope seems to set the conduct book's advice on its ear. In the "Urbanitatis," deferring to a "worthier" supper-mate is a way to demon-

---

58. Here, the B version reads: "And gete thi mete owt of houndis mouth" (283), which Karl Breul adopts in his edition of *Sir Gowther*, dropping the important clause "þat þu revus." (*Sir Gowther*).

59. *MED, reven* (v.) def. 1(a), 2(a), and 3(b).

strate one's respect for the social hierarchies of the dinner table. In *Sir Gowther,* the duke's meal-partner is not human, and so the duke must acknowledge his new status as lower than canine. Furthermore, the Pope's instruction to "reave" food from a dog's mouth contradicts the conduct book's edict to select one's portions carefully and deliberately, and not to "stryke" out at the meat one wants to eat. From this perspective, the Pope gives Gowther a penance that looks and sounds like a deformation of proper, acceptable table manners. Just as his life has been a dark parody of the chivalric ideal, so Gowther's cure is equally parodic and inverted. However, the primary lesson of the romance and the conduct book are ultimately the same: by eating from the mouths of dogs, Gowther is meant to learn that the world and its inhabitants are both distinguished and connected through rituals of eating.

6. "A GREYHOWNDE BROGHT HYM MEYT"

The convivial aspect of his atonement is not immediately available to the penitent Gowther. He has closed the door on his antisocial ways, his private hell of uncontrollable behavior, and taken the first steps toward starting a new life and a new identity. He has willed himself to become a bodily work in progress—a creature yearning to change his very existence. However, he must locate the proper public venue in which to practice his penance. He starts by taking a bone from a random dog on the streets of Rome and then ventures on foot in an unknown direction, uncertain about what he is seeking.

Along the way to this unknown fortune, Gowther discovers a quiet place in the wilderness, and, resting there, his life takes a turn for the miraculous:

He seyt hym down undur a hyll,
A greyhownde broght hym meyt untyll
    Or evon yche a dey.

Thre neythtys þer he ley:
þo grwhownd ylke a dey
    A whyte lofe he hym broȝht;
On þo fort day come hym non,
Up he start and forþe con gon,
    And lovyd God in his thoȝt.
(294–302)

In this mysterious moment, the tempestuous existence of the young duke melts away into hushed silence, a marked contrast to the clamor and violence of his former life. The greyhounds, renowned for their quiet, peaceably give up their mouthfuls of white bread,[60] contrary to the struggle predicted by the Pope's instructions. After so much brutality and carnage, it is difficult to see how Gowther could possibly deserve this gentle miracle. Mere days into his penance, noble animals wait upon him in the privacy of his own shady dell. He is peaceful, safe, and self-sufficient in a sort of paradise. Again, the story seems to cross from romance back to hagiography: animal benefactors feeding the holy are not uncommon in medieval saints' lives.[61]

Outrage and extremity have characterized the story to this point: even the Pope's instructions are horrifying. But the strange suspension of the romance at this point creates an unbearable tension. The peaceful moment brings the narrative to a jarring standstill, stepping so far out of its belligerent trajectory as to defy its own applicability. The violent romance seems to forget itself. In the quiet valley, Gowther rests in a state of unworldliness, disconnected from the terms of social existence. Even an aristocrat performs some modicum of service or labor—even if it is completely symbolic or nominal in nature—in order to justify the acquisition of food from his social inferiors. To work for food is the fate of humanity, a condition of being in the world. But here, in this strangely suspended and geographically unspecified wilderness, Gowther receives his food by miracle. Although the mechanism will be approximated later by the Emperor's daughter (429–34), there is nothing here to explain the wonder or place it into a chain of productive activity. Gowther eats simply by existing in this magical moment. During the three-day sojourn with the greyhounds, he is shown that his life can change for the better. His penitential mindset creates a different life just by reaching out to it. The scene also reveals to the demonic duke what actual, nonparasitic nurture feels like. He reverts back to an oral phase even more bizarre than his infancy, his mouth transformed from a tool of harm to a means of connecting him to other creatures. The passive dogs teach him that nourishment is a sociable act by which one builds relationships with others rather than injuring them.

Greyhounds, moreover, are products of human nurture; selected and refined by husbandry, their bestial natures are irrevocably altered through

---

60. In the Royal version, each dog carries a "barley lof" (302), several steps down in the hierarchy of bread.

61. David Salter cites the cases of Elijah the prophet and St. Paul the hermit, both fed by ravens, and St. Cuthbert, fed by an eagle (*Holy and Noble Beasts: Encounters with Animals in Medieval Literature*, 80).

human intervention. The result is an animal with the wild parts removed, drawn out of its natural environment, and put to service. The greyhound is a living tool, converted through humankind's long-term efforts so that it has become an "instrument of labor," which alters the beast bodily and metaphysically into a useful object.[62] Gowther, too, will be transformed and tamed by his penance, his animalistic thirst for violence restrained and refined until it too is another instrument put to the public good. He is naturally "full wylde" (61) as a creature, yet he can be disciplined, his bestial qualities well employed at long last. He can be changed from an antisocial monster into a sort of helpful beast, on his way to becoming a man.

Such a metamorphosis, however, cannot be completed in the wilderness. While he is alone, Gowther can only perform his penance according to its letter, but hardly in its intended spirit. He is surrounded by animals with which he cannot create any meaningful social or economic interaction. Dogs especially are removed from economic considerations, as Adam Smith remarks, "Nobody ever saw a dog make a fair and deliberate exchange of one bone for another with another dog."[63] Their commerce instead a competition of brute force, dogs represent a primal state of existence in their naked self-interest. However, this network of expected violence is suspended in the dogs' pacific gifts: Steel notes that their donation of bread "interrupts economy" in that there is "nothing he [Gowther] can give in return that would transform his reception of bread into a node of exchange, equal or otherwise."[64] Gowther experiences an unexpected new relationship with the animals, but their mute favor cannot project Gowther back into human realms. Without an agent to start the process of his nutrition by dropping food to the dogs, these canine benefactors are simply utensils of divine intervention. Gowther's cure requires him to suffer their bestial mediation in the presence of convivial society. He must master the tools of his environment publicly and wrest control of his world so that it will provide him with what he requires to thrive. The mysterious greyhounds are not competitors in the struggle for existence; they only keep Gowther alive until he travels back to civilization—they cannot relieve him of the burden of his sins. In his peaceful time with them, the grotesquerie of Gowther's penance hardly seems offensive. It does not have the power to horrify. For Gowther to experience the true mortifying power of his cure, he must have onlookers to shock and a social body to judge whether he belongs.

---

62. Marx, *Capital*, 1.286.
63. Adam Smith, *The Wealth of Nations* (1776), ed. Edwin Cannan, 14.
64. Steel, *How to Make a Human*, 239–40.

7. "IF IT WER GNAFFD AND MARD"

Whether displayed in graceful etiquette or in an atrocious parody of manners, appetite is a political phenomenon. It is a device that both constitutes the bodies of consuming subjects and drives their purposes as constituents of the larger social group. And so Gowther must locate the proper venue in which to satisfy his bodily needs and practice his terrible penance, somewhere in the public sphere where he can learn the lessons of the Pope and the conduct book. During the poem's strangely quiet interlude, the duke eats under mysterious circumstances in the wilderness, fed by peaceful greyhounds in a secluded dale. This satisfies the hagiographic impulse of the story, but it can only postpone the pressing urgency of political hunger. No human—defined by Aristotle as a "political animal" (*zōon politikon*)—exists for long outside the commensal sphere.[65] A convivial Gowther is a redeemable Gowther, and so he is compelled to abandon his holy isolation to search for a royal court or noble household that will help him through his transformation.

The final movement of the poem begins by blurring the terms of his penance with the requirements of a society that is both mannerly and warlike, a conflation necessary to emphasize the political nature of the story. As Gowther continues his penitence in a strange court, he also joins in its ongoing war with the Saracens, a dramatic series of encounters that span the fear of sin and the fear of the social outsider in the medieval imagination. The tale moves so quickly into and through its homegrown crusade that the narrator must occasionally stop to remind the audience that Gowther is still bound to his regime of atonement (such as at 519–21). This seemingly extraneous subplot, however, plays a key role in the redemption of the demonic duke, creating a political context for the penitential romance. Gowther's participation in the war shows that his sociopathic violence does not need to be eliminated; it only needs to be redirected for the duke to be gathered into the fold of human society. This reintegration is managed in two ways: first, by placing Gowther under the table of an illustrious court so that he may be educated in proper manners; and second, by giving him an opportunity to put his formidable skills at killing to good use. In other words, what has seemed like a religious and contemplative redemption turns active, political, and violent.

Gowther's penitential regime transforms the poem itself into a new kind of story. He does not have to search long to find the right setting for his correction, as a nearby castle contains the court of an Emperor. He must sit out-

---

65. Aristotle, *Politics*, Book 1.2, 1253a.

side the gates, despite the obvious fairness of his aristocratic body ("þof he wer wel wro3t" [308]). This fact is not invoked as idle formulaic filler; rather, it signals a transposition to a new type of romance. The focus on Gowther's beauty, which is remarkable to all who see him (324, 434), would be a familiar trope to contemporary readers of the "Fair Unknown" plots of romance, an ironic reminder that Gowther is far from unknown—his mysterious identity conceals not unrealized gentility, but absolute terror.[66] Now, far from his native land and unable to speak, he is granted a second chance to rewrite his demented life story into a proper romance, in which his actions accord with the etiquette of narrative convention. Gowther's penitential imperative transforms the poem itself into a new kind of story.

This reborn narrative becomes concerned with the happenings of the court. Gowther once ate "rych fode" (120) at his father's table, but there was no detail to indicate what that meant in terms of the social practices of the older Duke's household. Yet now the romance of *Sir Gowther* becomes suddenly interested in the practice of conviviality, chronicling the formalities of aristocratic eating as the audience becomes enfolded in their performance, particularly as the presence of Gowther strains the propriety of these practices. From the trumpeters blowing the call to dinner (309) to the catalogue of the servants of the castle (313–14), to the steward's insistence upon removing the mysterious and unwelcome guest (318–19)—the story now renders the noble household visible, right down to the pomp and circumstance of the Emperor's meal, which adapts itself to include Gowther:

> When þo Emperowr was seyt and sarvyd
> And kny3ttus had is breyd karvyd,
>   He send þo dompmon parte;
> He [*Gowther*] lette hit stond and wold ry3t non.
> Þer come a spanyell with a bon,
>   In his mothe he hit bare,
> Syr Gwother hit from hym dro3he
> And gredely on hit he gnofe.
>   He wold nowdur curlu ne tartte—
> Boddely sustynans wold he non,
> Bot what so he fro þo howndus wan
>   If it wer gnaffyd or mard.
> (333–44)

---

66. For romances that use the "Fair Unknown" theme, see *Lybeaus Desconus* (ca. fourteenth century), *Sir Perceval of Galles* (ca. first half fourteenth century), and the "Tale of Sir Gareth" in Malory's *Morte D'Arthur*.

The stanza begins with the image of cultural finesse, an orderly demonstration of political privilege that is an important goal of the banquet. Seated and served with all formality, his honored knights carving his trenchers (pieces of bread used as plates) before him, the Emperor dines according to an elaborate code of courtesy. This ritual displays his own power as well as organizing the hierarchical positions of all who share his board. His charitable offer to Gowther incorporates the mysterious "dompmon" as part of his political unit, and it is just as much a part of his demonstration of precedence. Its congruence is marked by the assonant relationship of the tail-rhyme to the preceding couplet (*sarvyd/karyvyd/parte*). This rhyme, continuing through the stanza, evenly falls between high table and sub-table lines: the "parte" given as alms to Gowther aligns with the "curlu ne tartte" that he will not eat. The image contrasts with the bone "bare" by the spaniel under the table—the shock of the sight conveyed by the broken rhyme—and the "gnaffyd or mard" (that is, gnawed and beslobbered by dogs) condition of the food the duke must consume. The disparity is dramatically established between the prepared dishes rejected by Gowther, such as the curlew (a game bird much in demand by noble eaters) and the "tartte" (a baked pastry usually filled with meat), with the shreds and leftovers that he may eat. Gowther not only eats in a debased fashion but also explicitly rejects the ostentation which is the sine qua non of noble cuisine, the dazzling display and pomp of the high table. Instead, he prefers the bones and scraps of meat tossed aside by the aristocratic eaters and left to the dogs. Like for de Certeau's "poachers," however, the glorious production of noble existence is still necessary to Gowther's spectacle: he could not scavenge underneath just any table. The orderly, decorous procession of the exalted court must go on around him in order for Gowther's penance to be truly effective.

There is a travesty of that polite display as well: to note that Gowther's food is "gnaffyd and mard" grotesquely mirrors the manner of service to which a lord would be accustomed. The position of carver was very important to aristocratic eating; it was an honorific duty held by a favored knight or squire, or else an important servant.[67] Stephanie Trigg lays out the stakes for this important banquet hall skill: "The art of carving is the art of the proper, the love of the right way to handle and serve the right meat at the right time of the year"; emphasizing that the practice of prandial decorum itself radiates from this

---

67. Squires are often depicted as carvers in the *Canterbury Tales*, from the Squire who carves before his father the Knight (I.99–100), to Damian in the *Merchant's Tale* (IV.1773), to Squire Jankyn who resolves the friar's dispute in the *Summoner's Tale* (III.2243–89). The verb "depart," found in *The Summoner's Tale* rubric at III.2242, humorously reflects the jargon of carving.

fundamental moment of its ritual.⁶⁸ Whoever filled this role had to be highly skilled, familiar with a rigid set of technical vocabulary—synonyms for the act of cutting up meat—as well as proficient at an elaborate performance of specific actions required to properly serve a meat course with its proper accompaniments. For example, to serve venison, one had to know its proper term: to "breke that dere" as Wynkyn de Worde lists it,⁶⁹ and then serve it according to its traditional setting:

> Towche not þe venisoun with no bare hand
> but withe þy knife; þis wise shall ye be doande,
> withe þe fore part of þe knife looke ye be hit parand,
> xij. draughts with þe egge of þe knife þe venisoun crossande.
> Than whan ye þat venesoun so haue chekkid hit,
> with þe fore parte of youre knife / þat ye hit owt kytt,
> In þe frumenty potage honestly ye convey hit.⁷⁰

"Breaking" the roasted deer by cutting it into cubes and laying them atop a bed of frumenty (a barley porridge made with milk, salt, and saffron)⁷¹ was the culinary expectation for a diner, the correct way to sate one's appetite in the context of the banquet. To incorrectly serve a course, however, was not just a breach of decorum. Any other way would court the creation of an alternate, boorish, and potentially harmful identity. The hunger of a lord for deer was confirmed as legitimate through its proper service; one was constituted as a noble eater by eating according to noble expectations.⁷² The carver is the courtly figure that most conspicuously announces the triumph of the lordly

---

68. Trigg, "Learning to Live," 468.

69. Wynkyn de Worde, *The Boke of Keruynge* (late fifteenth century), in Furnivall, *Babees Book*, 261–88. *The Boke of Keruynge* is a prose adaptation of John Russell's *Iohn Russells Boke of Nurture*, missing Russell's *chanson d'aventures* frame story. Many of these terms for carving also appear on fol. 62r of the Heege Manuscript under the title "A tryppe off deere" (see Hardman, ed., *Heege Manuscript*, 9).

70. Russell, *Iohn Russells Boke of Nurture*, in Furnivall, ed., *Babees Book*, 141. This instruction also occurs in *The Boke of Keruynge* (also in Furnivall, ed., 265). See Brears, *Cooking and Dining in Medieval England*, 461, for an image of this process.

71. See the recipe for "furmenty with venison" in Austin, *Two Fifteenth-Century Cookery Books*, 70. See also the modern version in Hieatt and Butler, eds., *Pleyn Delit*, no. 22.

72. Additionally, if the wrong sauce was served with the wrong meat there was a possibility of compromising the lord's health by disrupting the balance of his bodily humors. See Terence Scully, "Mixing It Up in the Medieval Kitchen," in *Medieval Food and Drink*, ed. Mary-Jo Arn, 1–26.

banquet over a tamed and edible world. Not even in the tournament or the hunt is aristocratic violence displayed more decorously.

The sanitized and bloodless rituals of carving and serving stand in neat contrast to the uncontrollable aggression of Gowther's youth, even though the jargon of service conceals just as much force and power. If Gowther were not a penitent beggar, he might even expect to wield the power to carve the Emperor's food himself. For now, he must learn by observation, watching the elegance of the court unfold from below. Gowther's table manners parody the politesse on the tabletop: his food is "carved" by the dogs—that is, manipulated into appropriately sized morsels—and then "sauced" by the dog's saliva. Gowther eats in a distorted reflection of the lord that he is, though he is lord now only in the submensary realm of his own creation.

Gowther's anti-manners, as the mirror image of the glistening surfaces of lordly practice, allow them to shine the more brightly in the public eye. The public aspect of the feast extends beyond merely making the private act of sustenance into an event of conspicuous consumption. Dependent on the tireless labor of the kitchen and its servants, the feast stands for the economic potential of the household, the forces of production and consumption that link the house to the world around it. Politically as well as economically, the feast is organized in a set of concentric circles, from its plenteous center at the high table, to the guests of status at the surrounding boards, to the servants repaid with helpings of the meal, to the indigent outside the gates, waiting for charitable leftovers. Even the dogs among which Gowther sits and feeds have their part to play in the banquet's grand dance.

8. "EYTE AND DRYNKE AND MAKE MERY"

The world of the table stands in for the broader realm around it, and a similar armature of center and periphery structures the final scenes of *Sir Gowther*. The Emperor finds himself under attack by the Sultan of Perse, who comes seeking the hand of the Emperor's mute daughter, who represents the ideal center of the household—an inaccessible maiden kept safe in a tower (363–79). The Advocates version of the poem at first connects Gowther with the daughter only through their shared inability to speak. The Royal version is more detailed: she sends meat in the mouths of dogs for him and apparently they are in love ("Ether of hem loved other right" [B.368]). In either manuscript, romantic affection becomes nutritive, and the daughter makes herself known and loved by Gowther by way of his need to sustain his massive potential for war-making. Her efforts mollify the degradation of the duke's penance and reduce his travails now that he is a more than a fool, but a Crusader instead:

Þo meydon toke too gruhowndus fyn
And waschyd hor mowþus clene with wyn
    And putte a lofe in þo ton;
And in þo todur flesch full gud;
He raft boþe owt with eyggur mode,
    Þat doȝthy of body and bon.
(429–34)

Once again the greyhounds ("fyn" or well-bred animals), similar to those encountered in the secret valley, intervene to ennoble the penitent and long-suffering Gowther. The daughter ameliorates their demeaning and unclean condition by washing out their mouths with wine, and the two dogs submit themselves to be passive receptacles for the duke's satisfaction, passing on their mouthfuls of bread and meat. Gowther, for his part, obeys the Pope's prescription by savagely seizing the food from his canine benefactors (he "reft" it from them "with eyggur mode"), indicating that he still is imbricated in the violent circle of his penance. This time, however, there is a human agent who can take responsibility for the gift, the Emperor's beautiful daughter who pulls the object of her affection out of the strangely mannered though undeniably brutal world of the feast hall. However, she is no sooner introduced as a potential object of desire for Gowther than the Sultan intervenes to stand between them.[73] Gowther's violence toward women, especially those that are cloistered, is displaced onto the Sultan; the desire to kill the Sultan rectifies Gowther's sexual desires. The Sultan becomes the "hethen hownd" outside the walls that domesticates the terrible dog beneath the table.[74]

Gowther's victory and heroism in the war are celebrated, despite the disturbing specters of his previous cruelty. Once a tyrant and murderer, he is now a hero through the use of exactly the same sort of overwhelming physical force that characterized his reign of terror over the hapless Duchy of Estryke. The battle scenes are filled with vivid descriptions of Gowther's belligerent power. He not only cracks helmets and skulls but also "dynggus down" [strikes

---

73. See Cohen, "Gowther Among the Dogs," 233.
74. Gowther's identification with dogs, as well as his fantastic power to obliterate his enemies, recalls another hound of medieval literature, Cú Chulainn, the hero of the *Táin Bó Cúailnge* (ca. thirteenth century) of the Old Irish Ulster cycle, who receives his name after being punished for hastily killing a giant hound and is subsequently sentenced to assume the dog's role in guarding its owner's cattle (*The Táin*, trans. Ciaran Carson, 42).

down] his opponents in the terms as his former fraternal victims (154, 467). He breaks the backs of their horses (as he does the mounts of his mother's retainers [151, 575–76]), cleaves shields, and lops off the heads of his Saracen enemies. Although the language of force is no different than before, the reader is meant to understand the new context: before, Gowther's vicious ways were psychopathic and dangerous to the very fabric of society. Here, directed at a foreign threat, they are heroic and appropriate, communicating great martial prowess. Gowther is redeemed through combat because he has targets that can be obliterated with propriety.

Gowther's massive capacity for war-making, however, is in the end another narrative dodge, a misdirection that obscures the convivial nature of his redemption. The war ends with Gowther's rescue of the captured Emperor and decapitation of the Sultan, as well as the new war hero's own wounding by a Saracen spear (606–17). At this same moment, the mute daughter falls out of her tower, signifying that she and Gowther are in a sense wedded—of one flesh, their destinies wound together. With the miracle of the daughter's resurrection, the story confirms that the terms of Gowther's penance have not only been about eating but also its public performance. The first words the revenant daughter speaks invite Gowther to the table at last:

> Ho seyd, "My lord of heyvon gretys þe well,
> And forgyffus þe þi syn yche a dell,
>   And grantys þe þo blys;
> And byddus þe speyke on hardely,
> Eyte and drynke and make mery;
>   þu schallt be won of his.
> (642–47)

In the terms of Gowther's penance, consumption must be paired with conviviality to signify the correct deportment of the aristocrat. Eating represents little without merrymaking—otherwise it is merely bare subsistence, an acknowledgment of the common, animal need to be fed. Even during wartime, the Emperor's court is convivial, dancing and reveling after meals (510–12). The Royal version of *Sir Gowther* emphasizes this decorum by repeating the refrain, "The Emperour wyssh and went to mete," each time the court dines after the day's battle. "Eat, drink and be merry" is Gowther's final lesson in his education in manners—and ours as well.[75] With the knowledge that his penance is finally over, Gowther is set free to become the homme d'esprit of

---

75. The phrase comes from Ecclesiastes 8:15: "Therefore I commended mirth, because there was no good for a man under the sun, but to eat, and drink, and be merry."

Brillat-Savarin's aphorism. Not only will he eat like a human but also—via the knowledge gained at the Emperor's court, and his reassumption of noble status—he will be able to properly demonstrate his right to eat well. Gowther is now free to perform the identity he was always meant to have. A dangerous man for a dangerous time, Gowther is nonetheless tamed and rendered a useful consumer in Christian society. He is shriven and forgiven, ready to be the human, husband, and lord.

Examining *Sir Gowther* by way of its food imagery exposes the deliberate contrast between its polished surfaces and the ugly roots from whence it derives narrative nourishment. This romance of manners can be skimmed along this gleaming superficiality, but only if one ignores or rationalizes the brutality of its anti-hero, and the irony of its uncomfortable manuscript relationship with the "Urbanitatis."[76] *Sir Gowther* is a grim conduct lesson indeed, in which the rules and practices of privileged living are written in blood. This contradiction threatens to tear apart the narrative—maybe even the genre of romance as a whole. Nothing can be the same after *Sir Gowther*'s jaded, acerbic repast.

Both literally and symbolically, Gowther has been a parasite, stealing food from another creature in order to thrive. Yet this fiendish dependency occludes the parasitism inherent to the social order. Like Havelok, the demonic duke is conditioned to eat what he does not labor to produce. Both the educational and penitential aspects of *Sir Gowther* reveal that the sovereign does indeed labor—but to be recognized by his subordinates, through the painstaking performance of table manners and other acts of social distinction. But this manifestation of manners must come into the world parthenogenically, fully formed and ready for display. Otherwise, the sovereign is a boor, and no one will recognize him as superior. Gowther's presence in the Emperor's court creates parallel worlds within the feast hall, one above and one below the table. While the surfaces of the narrative and the table maintain their luster, order, and magnificence, the monstrous presence underneath reminds the reader of awful remnants that have fallen out of sight, warred over by the hounds of the hall. A microcosmic version of the Emperor's battle with the Sultan plays out at every meal, struggling to pull power and satisfaction from the jaws of the enemy. As the lord below the table, Gowther's weird anti-manners reveal a viciousness that perpetuates the realm of refined behavior. His penitential

---

76. One indication that this superficial reading may not have been adequate or satisfactory to its target audience may be intuited from the scratchy drawing on the bottom of the first leaf of *Sir Gowther* in the Heege Manuscript, possibly by a child, of three grotesque faces in a row, mouths open and eyes bulging. There is much in this version of the story that might keep a child up at night.

regime mirrors the expropriation and force that characterize aristocratic relations with other social classes. Eating only the food that has been discarded from above, Gowther represents the relationship between aristocrat and his dominion in the most vulgar way possible.[77] Yet the banquet both within and without the romance continues above as if nothing were out of place. In fact, the knights and ladies of the court throw *more* food to their dogs so that their mute guest may have enough to eat (346–48), blissfully unaware of the grotesquely satiric fool beneath their feet.

---

77. Dogs fighting over a bone form a simile for the lovelorn aristocrats of Chaucer's *The Knight's Tale*, intimating the crudity at the heart of romantic competition (I.1175–80).

CONCLUSION

Cheese and Cannibals

> Un dessert sans fromage est une belle à qui il manque un œil.
>
> A dessert without cheese is like a beautiful woman who's missing an eye.
> —BRILLAT-SAVARIN, *The Physiology of Taste*

SIR GOWTHER'S violations of decorum are figured as extravagant violence: drained wet-nurses, a mother's severed nipple. The sensationalism of these sufferings and Gowther's oral, canine penance for inflicting them, however, recodifies the entire realm of Christendom, an ostentatious display of the enormous power of table manners to fashion a world. Yet these fierce political appetites endure. Four hundred years later, Brillat-Savarin evokes another gastronomic ideal while skirting the boundaries of outrage. A dinner party without its fit and proper conclusion is a lovely, yet disfigured body, a piteous spectacle that should evoke no pity from demanding, sophisticated guests. Clearly something much more than the love of cheese is at stake here: this uniquely French culinary gesture elevates the display of *savoir faire* to a matter of national importance. Frenchness itself hinges on the cheese course. A fine-tuned sequence of prandial acts affirms patriotic identity—especially if the half-blinded "belle" of the aphorism is Marianne, the symbol of the French Republic. *Gaucherie* becomes treasonous; dismembering dinner a crime against the state. Political gastronomy, in the *Physiologie du Goût,* savors of a uniquely French *terroir* that is not only intellectual but also material in its mannered use of delicious commodities, a set of practices inscribed upon the body. The horrific image of the beautiful woman, missing an eye, emblematizes a transgression of manners profoundly abhorrent to a nation of politically aware, politically active diners.

As Brillat-Savarin does, *Andreas,* the *Roman de Silence, Havelok,* and *Sir Gowther* reckon humanity itself as the conformance to culinary practices. Those who inhabit the strictures of decent behavior are fully human, and the realm of political action is reserved for the *hommes d'esprit* who alone know how to eat. Their courtesy empowers these high-status diners to police citizens' movements, postures, and positions, and to safeguard the borders of the state with constant vigilance. *Political Appetite*'s four courses track the progression of socially instantiating and politically experimental eating across seven centuries of medieval English romance, from the exorbitant hungers of *Andreas* to the surfeited bellyache of *Sir Gowther.* Poetry of the edible speaks the political. In these romances, food can realize political aspirations or make a tasty critique of the brutal structures of edible power. Their appetizing language is a vocabulary of the material, the terms in which social units are imagined and empowered. The medieval English romance mobilizes the persuasive allure of consumption to both fascinate and challenge readers accustomed to the politicized assemblage of gastronomic materials and performances.

Our investment in the edible world we struggle to digest is made legible through the romance's persistent attention to culinary detail. Their characters never eat in a political vacuum. This far-reaching truth extends all the way to twenty-first-century readers of these romances, as we face the potential catastrophes of polluted ecosystems and global food shortages. Just as we do not eat free from political entanglement, neither do these fictional counterparts. Food acts are always vital to the poems' design, never merely to satisfy rhyme or drive meter. Each and every edible signifier brings with it a host of interrelated concepts and implications. For these delicious romances to be comprehensible, each term must remain in fluid interrelation—one *point de capiton* among many, every one with its own political investments and relations, its own economic trajectories in time and space. A narrative form lodged deep in medieval consciousness, romance deploys a host of social rituals and requirements to explore acquisitive and consumptive behaviors at the foundations of political economies.

Almost two centuries after *Sir Gowther,* the romance continues to draw power from these convivial practices, still using these material referents to order political bodies. Edmund Spenser's *The Faerie Queene* concludes its 1596 second edition with the Legend of Courtesy, revealing that social interactivity is the ultimate emblem of inward excellence—not true belief, rigorous purity, or the zealous pursuit of right. The intricate patterns of performing civility culminates in Spenser's massive project to present the "twelue priuate morall vertues" needed to fashion the perfect English gentleman.[1] Though never a matter of simple etiquette or good manners, courtesy instead becomes a way of displaying social grace, an ethics of interaction rather than a finite set of practices, a quality its hero can achieve by hunting down the Blatant Beast.

Courtesy is the ideal virtue of a political body, elaborated through the form of English romance. Given the poem's affiliations with such a hungry genre, and the long history of linking mannerly behavior to the table, the staging of violative devoration is almost required, and so Spenser marshals the threat of a terrible feast in order to explore the full ramifications of his book's ethical prerogatives. Serena, hapless heroine of Book Six, wanders into a "saluage nation" of cannibals, who perpetuate a "monstrous cruelty gainst course of kynde" (6.8.36) in course of searching for something (or someone) to eat. In just about seven hundred years of romantic representation, we have come full circle back to the man-eating imagination of *Andreas*. Like the Mermedonians, this awful tribe violates ancient, sacred traditions of hospitality to strangers, ostensibly because they have nothing else to eat: no farms, no livestock, no trade (6.8.35). These viciously idle, predatory people foil the virtuous, community-minded heroes and heroines of the Legend of Courtesy. Their cannibalism is figured as the ultimate inversion of the courteous imperative. Their man-eating desires, however, bring together a perverted sort of fellowship, organized upon awful appetites and decidedly unbrotherly love:

> So round about her they them selues did place
>   Vpon the grasse, and diuersely dispose,
>   As each thought best to spend the lingering space.
>   Some with their eyes the daintest morsels chose;
>   Some praise her paps, some praise her lips and nose;
>   Some whet their kniues, and strip their elboes bare:
>   The Priest him selfe a garland doth compose
>   Of finest flowres, and with full busie care
> His bloudy vessels wash, and holy fire prepare.
> (6.8.39)

The cannibal reavers are the polar opposites of the gracious shepherds that will eventually embody Spenser's truest model of courtesy: the pastoral over-

---

[1]. From Spenser's "Letter to Raleigh," appended to the end of the 1590 edition of the first three books of *The Faerie Queene* (ed. A. C. Hamilton, 715). All citations of the poem are from this edition.

tones of the scene here can only be terrifying. The savage predators feel an affection for the beautiful Serena as she sleeps, but it is horrible and acquisitive, a recipe for shocking transgression of a gustatory kind. Their compendium of cannibal desire invokes a much different sort of consumable language: the medieval poetic device of *effictio* (a part-by-part description of the body), notably used by Petrarch and enormously popular among Elizabethan poets (including Spenser). As the anthropophagites stare at the lovely form of the sleeping Serena, they hungrily divide up her body and praise its toothsome "morsels." In this separation, Spenser correlates poetic delectation to acts of consumption, revealing an indigestible side to the amorous, titillating catalogue of the female form. The violence of *effictio* is amplified by anaphora; the repeated "some" weds the celebration of Serena's beauty to the more menacing deeds the "saluages" have in mind as they whet their knives and roll up their sleeves. The narrator eagerly participates in this sinister partitioning, remarking upon her body a few stanzas later, as the menace toward his heroine is more pronounced, especially praising "her goodly thighs, whose glorie did appeare / Like a triumphal Arch, and thereupon / The spoiles of Princes hang'd, which were in battel won" (6.8.42), drastically altering Serena from cannibal victim to monument of sexual conquest. Through poetic complicity, verse conventions and gendered representations conscript Spenser's readers into becoming consumers, not much better than cannibals themselves.

This Elizabethan invocation of romantic cannibalism, as it did in the much-earlier *Andreas,* deforms the cultural forces that produced the poetic image in the first place. Man-eating, as a political appetite *par excellence,* inverts and perverts the social order surrounding it—even its fictional presence both fascinates and endangers human communities built upon prerogatives of sovereign consumption and the (culinary) duty of host to guest. The violence inherent to human food practices, which slaughter and dismember animals, transform the environment, and create rigid distinctions between class-bound eaters, requires an absolute distinction between eater and eaten, a distinction that anthropophagy elides in ghastly fashion. Yet, the Mermedonians and the almost-pastoral cannibals of the Legend of Courtesy cannot be entirely banished from the ranks of humanity, their gustation terribly legible to a world of eaters. This is a world constructed by the "fear and dread" of prey animals, projected as far back as the Book of Genesis and confirmed by the consumptive regimens of Marx and Bataille—yet it is often a fragile dominion easily undone just by violating its taboos. However, this cultural dissolution is often a source of play and fantasy, as evidenced by the numerous ancient geographies such as Herodotus's *Histories* (ca. 440 BCE) and medieval travelogues like the *Divisament dou Monde* of Marco Polo (ca. 1300) that project cannibal peoples into the world's distant spaces, an imaginative though politically constitutive practice that finds its ultimate expression in the accounts of global explorers from the early modern era forward.

The presence of cannibals on the margins of historical writing reveals that history and romance are not located far apart. It is at their intersection that *Political Appetites* stakes its intervention, exploring, through these four medieval English romances, a new frontier of the genre's broadly social concerns. I have shown throughout this book that an array of food practices—including eating and cooking, production and distribution—not only expand the cultural impact of these imaginative stories but also license their exploration of vexing political questions. Food does not just make these narratives more real, it renders them more effective in mobilizing their outward ambitions to critique and alter the circumstances of their creation. My reading of these four texts, as well as suggesting others to be read in a similar manner, reaffirms modern critical conversations that push romantic power beyond the ability merely to amuse or thrill their readers. Food criticism of the romances refuses to relegate these dynamic texts to just social *specula* that celebrate noble values unreflectively, or else form the groundswell of a popular English consciousness. Instead, this book augments our sense of the romance's cultural power and justifies the perennial popularity of romantic forms ever since their inception in early European culture, forms that have descended to the present day.

These chapters have proposed new ways to read these fascinating romances (and have in some cases expanded romance's generic borderlines) and suggested the power that can be applied to others through detailed attention to food practice, though I project that there is still a lot of work to be done in this area. Although cannibalism has already been studied extensively in *Richard Coer de Lyon,* and a thorough survey already exists of food used humorously in Old French romance, food in other examples of the widespread genre, in both Middle English and the French of England, has gone unstudied for the most part. Perhaps I have been remiss in not including more of these texts in my exploration. There also have been too few opportunities in the progression of this book to engage the extensive para-literary archive concerned with food practices, including penitential manuals (in which Gluttony plays a surprisingly minor role), conduct books, cookbooks, as well as the documentary evidence of household expenditures, crop production, and animal husbandry, even laws designed to promote public health and orderly markets. Another topic that has been excluded here, perhaps unjustly, has been the allegorical and religious dimensions of food in medieval literature. Although theological and hagiographic resonances have been explored in Bynum's extraordinary

Holy Feast and Holy Fast, few studies have taken up her provocative challenge to see "food as food and plac[e] it in its cultural context."[2] I omit this realm of gustatory signification out of a predominating interest in the secular and political engagements of edible imagery, which is inspired by Mann's 1979 warning against relying too much on allegory to interpret medieval texts: "The material world is not merely a vehicle for expressing the immaterial, but on the contrary contains the heart of its meaning and its mystery."[3] Mann also went unanswered in most medieval criticism for many years, though material entanglements and perspectives are frequently studied in contemporary criticism.[4] Food, as a real as well as allegorical object, has been a topic of intense critical interest to scholars of the massive visionary epic *Piers Plowman* (ca. 1362–87). Yet strangely enough, for a poem whose central object is an agricultural worker and where Gluttony is the most relatable of the Seven Deadly Sins, no book-length exploration exists of its food resonances.[5] Eating and drinking also form an important component to the poetry of Geoffrey Chaucer, but only so far Kathryn Lynch has studied these appetizing images.[6] Another study left unexplored is the examination of the food practices of the Round Table as a political ideal of Arthurian legend from Wace and Laȝamon to Malory, which takes the setting of the table as a phenomenological array of objects (much like J. Allan Mitchell suggests) as well as a locus of the performance of social power.[7] I conceive *Political Appetites* not as a complete meal, but rather as a dinner bell, an invitation to an innovative banquet of diverse and spectacular academic fare and unique and wondrous *entremets*.

The potential for expanded gastronomic activity in the fertile fields of medieval criticism reveals the timely power and relevance of the questions that have driven *Political Appetites*. These are questions that can be illuminated by traditional avenues of medieval study such as codicology and source

---

2. Bynum, *Holy Feast and Holy Fast*, 301.
3. Jill Mann, "Eating and Drinking in *Piers Plowman*," *Essays and Studies* n.s. 32 (1979): 27.
4. See Kellie Robertson's "Medieval Materialism: A Manifesto," *Exemplaria* 22 (2010): 99–118, for an empowering discussion of the influence of long-enduring materialist philosophies on medieval thought and poetics.
5. For a sampling of this large bibliography, see Robert Adams, "The Nature of Need in *Piers Plowman* XX," *Traditio* 34 (1978): 273–301; Robert Worth Frank Jr., "'The 'Hungry Gap,' Crop Failure, and Famine: The Fourteenth-Century Agricultural Crisis and *Piers Plowman*," *YLS* 4 (1990): 87–104; John A. Alford, "Langland's Exegetical Drama: The Sources of the Banquet Scene in *Piers Plowman*," in *Literature and Religion in the Later Middle Ages*, ed. Richard G. Newhauser and John A. Alford, 97–117; Margaret Kim, "Hunger, Need, and the Politics of Poverty in *Piers Plowman*," *YLS* 16 (2002): 131–68; Jill Mann "The Nature of Need Revisited," *YLS* 18 (2004): 3–29.
6. See Lynch, "From Tavern to Pie Shop," among others.
7. Mitchell, *Becoming Human*, 149–62.

criticism, as well as opened up by theoretical approaches such as Marxism and psychoanalysis, and by the advent of posthumanist ideas including speculative realism, the New Materialisms, and animal studies. Together these interventions can help us understand the archaeology of our tenuous existence within the almost bottomless consumability of our contemporary world. Both the power and threat of our readiness to eat can best be felt in the excesses of industrialized agribusiness, which feeds billions worldwide, but which exploits its laborers, manipulates its consumers, and threatens the sustainability of the planetary ecosystem. Western civilization has to a large degree treated the world as its personal banquet table, the roots of this attitude traceable back to Genesis. Yet not all of human history celebrates that fact, and critique of the edible order has always been with us. Fictions that both mirror and shape the world around us have often lauded the glories of culinary politics as well as censured their inequities. The medieval English romance is a particularly apt stage for the imaginative exploration of the quotidian origins of social structures: the hunger to have and hold power and status, and the thirst to understand these aims. The heights of their fantasies remain grounded in the lived conditions, practices, and productions of everyday life. This mythological materiality remains a distinguishing feature of the genre as it evolves across the centuries, communicating in very human terms our fascination with an earthly realm we have long believed is ours to devour, even as we tremble in fear of its uncertain future.

BIBLIOGRAPHY

Abdou, Angela. "Speech and Power in Old English Conversion Narratives." *Florilegium* 17 (2000): 195–212.

Adams, Robert. "The Nature of Need in *Piers Plowman* XX." *Traditio* 34 (1978): 273–301.

Adamson, Melitta Weiss. *Food in Medieval Times*. Westport, CT: Greenwood, 2004.

Agamben, Georgio. *Homo Sacer: Sovereign Power and Bare Life*. Trans. Daniel Heller-Roazen. Stanford, CA: Stanford University Press, 1998.

———. *The Open: Man and Animal*. Trans. Kevin Attell. Stanford, CA: Stanford University Press, 2004.

Akbari, Suzanne Conklin. "Nature's Forge Recast in the *Roman de Silence*." In *Literary Aspects of Courtly Culture*, edited by Donald Maddox and Sara Sturm-Maddox, 39–46. Rochester, NY: Boydell and Brewer, 1994.

Alain de Lille [Alaunus Insulis]. *De Planctu Naturae*. In *The Anglo-Latin Satirical Poets and Epigrammatists of the Twelfth Century*, edited by Thomas Wright. *Rerum Britannicarum Medii Aevi Scriptores*, vol. 59, part 2, 429–522. London: Longman and Trübner, 1872.

———. *The Plaint of Nature*. Trans. James J. Sheridan. Toronto: Pontifical Institute, 1980.

Albala, Ken. *Eating Right in the Renaissance*. Berkeley: University of California Press, 2002.

Alford, John A. "Langland's Exegetical Drama: The Sources of the Banquet Scene in *Piers Plowman*." In *Literature and Religion in the Later Middle Ages*, edited by Richard G. Newhauser and John A. Alford, 97–117. Binghamton, NY: Medieval & Renaissance Texts & Studies, 1995.

The Alliterative Morte Arthure. Ed. Valerie Krishna. New York: Franklin, 1976.

Ambrisco, Alan J. "Cannibalism and Cultural Encounters in *Richard Coeur de Lyon*." *JMEMS* 29 (1999): 499–528.

Amos, Mark Addison. "'For Manners Make Man': Bourdieu, de Certeau, and the Common Appropriation of Noble Manners in the *Book of Courtesy*." In Ashley and Clark, *Medieval Conduct*, 23–48.

Andreas. *Andreas and the Fates of the Apostles*. Ed. Kenneth R. Brooks. Oxford: Clarendon, 1961.

Arendt, Hannah. *The Human Condition* (1958), 2nd ed. Chicago and London: University of Chicago Press, 1998.

Arens, William. *The Man-Eating Myth: Anthropology and Anthropophagy.* New York: Oxford University Press, 1979.

Aristotle. *Aristotle's Politics.* Trans. Carnes Lord. Chicago: University of Chicago Press, 1984.

Ashley, Kathleen, and Robert L. A. Clark, eds. *Medieval Conduct.* Minneapolis: University of Minnesota Press, 2001.

Asser, John. *Asser's Life of King Alfred: Together with the Annals of Saint Neots Erroneously Ascribed to Asser.* Ed. William Henry Stevenson. Oxford: Clarendon, 1904.

———. *The Medieval Life of King Alfred the Great: A Translation and Commentary on the Text Attributed to Asser.* Trans. and ed. Alfred P. Smyth. Hampshire, UK: Palgrave, 2002.

Auerbach, Erich. *Mimesis: The Representation of Reality in Western Literature.* Trans. Willard R. Trask. Princeton, NJ: Princeton University Press, 1953.

Bakhtin, Mikhail. *Rabelais and His World* (1965). Trans. Helene Iswolsky. Bloomington: Indiana University Press, 1984.

Banham, Debby. *Food and Drink in Anglo-Saxon England.* Stroud: Tempus, 2004.

Barron, W. R. J. *English Medieval Romance.* London: Longman, 1987.

Barthes, Roland. "Toward a Psychosociology of Contemporary Food Consumption." In *Food and Drink in History,* edited by Robert Forster and Orest Ranum, translated by Elborg Forster and Patricia M. Ranum, 166–73. Baltimore, MD: Johns Hopkins University Press, 1979.

Bartolomeus Anglicus. *On the Properties of Things* (1240). Trans. John Trevisa. Ed. M. C. Seymour. Oxford: Clarendon, 1975.

Bartolovich, Crystal. "Consumerism, or the Cultural Logic of Late Cannibalism." In *Cannibalism and the Colonial World,* edited by Francis Barker, Peter Hulme, and Margaret Iversen, 204–37. Cambridge, UK: Cambridge University Press, 1998.

Bataille, Georges. *The Accursed Share.* Vol. 3, *Sovereignty* (1949). Trans. Robert Hurley. New York: Zone, 1993.

Battle of Maldon. In *The Anglo-Saxon Minor Poems,* edited by Elliott Van Kirk Dobbie. New York: Columbia University Press, 1942.

Battles, Paul. "Dying for a Drink: 'Sleeping After the Feast' Scenes in *Beowulf, Andreas,* and the Old English Poetic Tradition." *Modern Philology* 112 (2015): 435–57.

Becker, Alexis Kellner. "Sustainability Romance: *Havelok the Dane*'s Political Ecology." *New Medieval Literatures* 16 (2016): 83–108.

Bell, Kimberly K. "Resituating Romance: The Dialectics of Sanctity in MS Laud Misc. 108's *Havelok the Dane* and Royal *Vitae.*" *Parergon* 25 (2008): 27–51.

Bell, Kimberly K., and Julie Nelson Couch, eds. *The Texts and Contexts of Oxford, Bodleian Library, MS Laud Misc. 108: The Shaping of English Vernacular Narrative.* Leiden: Brill, 2011.

Bennett, Jane. *Vibrant Matter: A Political Ecology of Things.* Durham, NC: Duke University Press, 2010.

Benoît de Saint-Maure. *Chronique des Ducs de Normandie.* Ed. Francisque Michel. 3 vols. Paris: Imprimerie Royale, 1836–44.

Beowulf. Klaeber's Beowulf and the Fight at Finnsburh, 4th ed. Ed. R. D. Fulk, Robert E. Bjork, and John D. Niles. Toronto: University of Toronto Press, 2008.

Berry, Craig A. "What Silence Desires." In *Translating Desire in Medieval and Early Modern Literature,* edited by Craig A. Berry and Heather Richardson Hayton, 191–206. Tempe, AZ: Arizona Center for Medieval and Renaissance Studies, 2005.

Blamires, Alcuin. "The Twin Demons of Aristocratic Society in *Sir Gowther*." In *Pulp Fictions of Medieval England: Essays in Popular Romance McDonald*, edited by Nicola McDonald, 45–62. Manchester: Manchester University Press, 2004.

Bloch, R. Howard. *Etymologies and Genealogies: A Literary Anthropology of the French Middle Ages.* Chicago: University of Chicago Press, 1983.

Blurton, Heather. *Cannibalism in High Medieval English Literature.* New York: Palgrave Macmillan, 2007.

Boenig, Robert. *Saint and Hero:* Andreas *and Medieval Doctrine.* Lewisburg, PA: Bucknell University Press, 1990.

Boenig, Robert, trans. *The Acts of Andrew in the Country of the Cannibals: Translations from the Greek, Latin, and Old English.* New York: Garland, 1991.

Bolduc, Michelle. "Images of Romance: The Miniatures of *Le Roman de Silence*." *Arthuriana* 12 (2002): 101–12.

———. "Silence's Beasts." In *The Mark of the Beast: The Medieval Bestiary in Art, Life, and Literature,* edited by Debra Higgs Strickland, 185–210. New York: Garland, 1999.

Bosworth-Toller. Joseph Bosworth and T. Northcote Toller. *An Anglo-Saxon Dictionary Based on the Manuscript Collection of the Late Joseph Bosworth, Edited and Enlarged by T. Northcote Toller: Supplement.* Oxford: Oxford University Press, 1898. Online resource: http://www.bosworthtoller.com/.

Bourdieu, Pierre. *Distinction: A Social Critique of the Judgement of Taste* (1979). Trans. Richard Nice. Cambridge, MA: Harvard University Press, 1984.

———. *The Logic of Practice* (1980). Trans. Richard Nice. Stanford, CA: Stanford University Press, 1990.

———. *Outline of a Theory of Practice* (1972). Trans. Richard Nice. Cambridge, UK: Cambridge University Press, 1977.

Bowers, John M. *The Politics of Pearl: Court Poetry in the Age of Richard II.* Cambridge, UK: D. S. Brewer, 2001.

Bradstock, E. M., "The Penitential Pattern in *Sir Gowther*." *Parergon* 20 (1978): 3–10.

Brahney, Kathleen J. "When *Silence* was Golden: Female Personae in the *Roman de Silence*." In *The Spirit of the Court: Selected Proceedings of the Fourth Congress of the International Courtly Literature Society (Toronto 1983),* edited by Glyn S. Burgess and Robert A. Taylor, 52–61. Cambridge, UK: D. S. Brewer, 1985.

Brears, Peter C. D. *Cooking and Dining in Medieval England.* Totnes, UK: Prospect, 2008.

Brewer, Derek. "Feasts in England and English Literature in the Fourteenth Century." In *Feste und Feiern im Mittelalter: Paderborner Symposion des Mediävistenverbandes,* edited by Detlef Altenburg, Jörg Jarnut, and Hans-Hugo Steinhoff, 13–26. Sigmaringen, DE: J. Thorbecke, 1991.

Brillat-Savarin, Jean Anthelme. *Le Physiologie de Goût, ou Meditations de Gastronomie Transcendante* (1826). Paris: Hermann, 1975.

Brillat-Savarin, Jean Anthelme. *The Physiology of Taste, or Meditations on Transcendental Gastronomy.* Trans. M. F. K. Fisher. New York: Knopf, 1971.

Brown, Carleton. *English Lyrics of the Thirteenth Century.* Oxford: Clarendon, 1932.

Burns, E. Jane. "Arthurian Romance in Prose." In *A New History of French Literature,* edited by Denis Holier, 66–70. Cambridge, MA: Harvard University Press, 1989.

Busby, Keith. *Codex and Context: Reading Old French Verse Narrative in Manuscript*. 2 vols. Amsterdam: Rodopi, 2002.

Bynum, Caroline Walker. *Holy Feast and Holy Fast: The Religious Significance of Food to Medieval Women*. Berkeley: University of California Press, 1987.

Cadden, Joan. *The Meanings of Sex Difference in the Middle Ages*. Cambridge, UK: Cambridge University Press, 1992.

Calder, Daniel G. "Figurative Language and Its Contexts in *Andreas*: A Study of Medieval Expressionism." In *Modes of Interpretation in Old English Literature: Essays in Honour of Stanley B. Greenfield*, edited by Phyllis Rugg Brown, Georgia Ronan Crampton, and Fred C. Robinson, 115–36. Toronto: University of Toronto Press, 1986.

Cannon, Christopher. *The Grounds of English Literature*. Oxford: Oxford University Press, 2004.

Casteen, John Thomas. "Mermedonian Cannibalism and Figural Narration." *NM* 75 (1974): 74–78.

Caxton, William. *The Book of the Order of Chivalry*. Ed. Robert Adams. Huntsville, TX: Sam Houston State University Press, 1991.

———. *Caxton's Book of Curtesye*. Ed. F. J. Furnivall. EETS e.s. 3. London: Trübner, 1868.

———. *Dialogues in French and English*. Ed. Henry Bradley. EETS e.s. 79. London: Kegan Paul, Tench, and Trübner, 1900 (Reprint: Milwood, NY: Kraus Reprint, 1973).

de Certeau, Michel. *The Practice of Everyday Life*, vol. 1. Trans. Steven Rendall. Berkeley: University of California Press, 1984.

Charbonneau, Joanne. "From Devil to Saint: Transformations in *Sir Gowther*." In *The Matter of Identity in Medieval Romance*, edited by Phillipa Hardman, 21–28. Cambridge, UK: D. S. Brewer, 2002.

Chaucer, Geoffrey. *The Riverside Chaucer*. Ed. Larry D. Benson. Boston: Houghton Mifflin, 1987.

Chen, Anna. "Consuming Childhood: *Sir Gowther* and National Library of Scotland MS Advocates 19.3.1." *JEGP* 111 (2012): 360–83.

Chrétien de Troyes. *The Complete Romances of Chrétien de Troyes*. Ed. and trans. David Staines. Bloomington: Indiana University Press, 1990.

Clark, Robert L. A. "Queering Gender and Naturalizing Class in the *Roman de Silence*." *Arthuriana* 12 (2002): 50–63.

Cohen, Jeffrey Jerome. "Gowther Among the Dogs: Becoming Inhuman c. 1400." In *Becoming Male in the Middle Ages*, edited by Bonnie Wheeler and Jeffrey Jerome Cohen, 219–44. New York: Garland, 1997.

Cole, Andrew. "The Sacrament of the Fetish, The Miracle of the Commodity." In *The Legitimacy of the Middle Ages: On the Unwritten History of Theory*, edited by Andrew Cole and D. Vance Smith, 70–93. Durham, NC: Duke University Press, 2010.

———. "What Hegel's Master/Slave Dialectic Really Means." *Journal of Medieval and Early Modern Studies* 34 (2004): 577–610.

Coleman, Joyce. *Public Reading and the Reading Public in Late Medieval England and France*. Cambridge, UK: Cambridge University Press, 1996.

Coleman, Joyce. "Aurality." In Strohm, *Middle English*, 68–85.

Cook, Albert Stanburrough. "Bitter Beer-Drinking." *MLN* 40 (1925): 285–88.

Cooper, Helen. *The English Romance in Time: Transforming Motifs from Geoffrey of Monmouth to the Death of Shakespeare*. Oxford: Oxford University Press, 2004.

———. "Romance After 1400." In *The Cambridge History of Medieval English Literature*, edited by David Wallace, 690–719. Cambridge, UK: Cambridge University Press, 1999.

Cosman, Madeleine Pelner. *Fabulous Feasts: Medieval Cookery and Ceremony*. New York: Brazilier, 1976.

Crane, Susan. *Insular Romance: Politics, Faith, and Culture in Anglo-Norman and Middle English Literature*. Berkeley: University of California Press, 1986.

Couch, Julie Nelson. "Defiant Devotion in MS Laud Misc. 108: The Narrator of *Havelok the Dane* and Affective Piety." *Parergon* 25 (2008): 53–79.

———. "The Vulnerable Hero: *Havelok* and the Revision of Romance." *Chaucer Review* 42 (2008): 330–52.

Curtius, E. R. *European Literature and the Latin Middle Ages*. Trans. Willard R. Trask. New York: Harper & Row, 1953.

Cynewulf. *Elene*. In *Cynewulf's Elene*, edited by Pamela Gradon. New York: Appleton-Century-Crofts, 1966.

Dante Aligheri. *The Divine Comedy*. Trans. Charles Singleton. Princeton, NJ: Princeton University Press, 1970.

Davis, Kathleen. *Periodization and Sovereignty: How Ideas of Feudalism and Secularization Govern the Politics of Time*. Philadelphia: University of Pennsylvania Press, 2008.

Dean, James M. *The World Grown Old in Later Medieval Literature*. Cambridge, MA: Medieval Academy of America, 1997.

Derrida, Jacques. "Eating Well, or The Calculation of the Subject: An Interview with Jacques Derrida." In *Who Comes after the Subject?*, edited by Eduardo Cadava, Peter Connor, and Jean-Luc Nancy, 96–119. New York: Routledge, 1991.

DeRoo, Harvey. "Two Old English Fatal Feast Metaphors: *Ealuscerwen* and *Meoduscerwen*." *English Studies in Canada* 5 (1979): 249–61.

Douglas, Mary. *Implicit Meanings: Essays in Anthropology* (1975), 2nd ed. London: Routledge, 1999.

Dyer, Christopher. "Did the Peasants Really Starve in Medieval England?" In *Food and Eating in Medieval Europe*, edited by Martha Carlin and Joel Rosenthal, 58–72. London: Hambledon, 1998.

———. "English Diet in the Later Middle Ages." In *Social Relations and Ideas: Essays in Honour of R. H. Hilton*, edited by T. H. Ashton, et al., 191–216. Cambridge, UK: Cambridge University Press, 1983.

Earl, James W. "The Typological Structure of *Andreas*." In *Old English Literature in Context*, edited by John D. Niles, 66–89. London: D. S. Brewer, 1980.

Economou, George. *The Goddess Natura in Medieval Literature*. Cambridge, MA: Harvard University Press, 1972.

Edwards, A. S. G. "Oxford, Bodleian Library, MS Laud Misc. 108: Contents, Construction, and Circulation." In *The Texts and Contexts of Oxford, Bodleian Library, MS Laud Misc. 108: The Shaping of English Vernacular Narrative*, edited by Kimberley K. Bell and Julie Nelson Couch, 21–30. Leiden: Brill, 2011.

Elias, Norbert. *The Civilizing Process: Sociogenetic and Psychogenetic Investigations*. Vol. 1 (1939). Trans. Edmund Jephcott. New York: Urizen, 1978.

Elliott, J. K., ed. *The Apocryphal New Testament: A Collection of Apocryphal Christian Literature in an English Translation*. Oxford: Clarendon, 2005.

Exodus. In *The Junius Manuscript,* edited by George Philip Krapp. New York: Columbia University Press, 1931.

Fabian, Johannes. *Time and the Other.* New York: Columbia University Press, 1983.

Faletra, Michael. "The Ends of Romance: Dreaming the Nation in the Middle English *Havelok.*" *Exemplaria* 17 (2005): 347–80.

Fasciculus Morum: A Fourteenth-Century Preacher's Handbook. Ed. and trans. Siegfried Wenzel. University Park: Pennsylvania State University Press, 1989.

Fee, Christopher. "Productive Destruction: Torture, Text, and the Body in the Old English *Andreas.*" *Essays in Medieval Studies* 11 (1994): 51–62.

Ferhatović, Denis. "Spolia-Inflected Poetics of the Old English *Andreas.*" *Studies in Philology* 110 (2013): 199–219.

Field, Rosalind. "Romance in England, 1066–1400." In *The Cambridge History of Medieval English Literature,* edited by David Wallace, 152–76. Cambridge, UK: Cambridge University Press, 1999.

Fildes, Valerie. *Wet Nursing: A History from Antiquity to the Present.* Oxford: Blackwell, 1988.

Finlayson, John. "Definitions of Middle English Romance." *Chaucer Review* 15 (1980): 44–62 and 168–81.

Fitzgerald, Christina M. "Miscellaneous Masculinities and a Possible Fifteenth-Century Owner of Oxford, Bodleian Library, MS Laud Misc. 108." In *The Texts and Contexts of Oxford, Bodleian Library, MS Laud Misc. 108: The Shaping of English Vernacular Narrative,* edited by Kimberley K. Bell and Julie Nelson Couch, 87–113. Leiden: Brill, 2011.

Fleta. Edited by H. G. Richardson and G. O. Sayles. Vol. 2. Publications of the Seldon Society. Vol. 89. London: Quaritch, 1955.

Foucault, Michel. *Discipline and Punish: The Birth of the Prison.* Trans. Alan Sheridan. New York: Vintage, 1977.

Frank, Robert Worth, Jr. The 'Hungry Gap,' Crop Failure, and Famine: The Fourteenth-Century Agricultural Crisis and *Piers Plowman.*" *YLS* 4 (1990): 87–104.

Franklin, Alfred. *La Vie Privée d'Autrefois.* Vol. 3. Paris: Plon, 1889.

Frantzen, Allen J. *Food, Eating, and Identity in Early Medieval England.* Woodbridge, Suffolk: Boydell, 2014.

Freedman, Paul. *Out of the East: Spices and the Medieval Imagination.* New Haven, CT: Yale University Press, 2008.

Freud, Sigmund. "Family Romance" (1909). In *Collected Papers.* Vol. 5, edited and translated by James Strachy, 74–78. London: Hogarth, 1950.

———. *Totem and Taboo* (1913). Trans. James Strachey. New York: Routledge, 2001.

Frye, Northrop. *Anatomy of Criticism: Four Essays.* Princeton, NJ: Princeton University Press, 1957.

Funk, Carol Hughes. *The History of Andreas and Beowulf Comparative Scholarship.* PhD diss., University of Denver, 1997.

Furnivall, F. J., ed. *The Babees Book: Meals and Manners in Olden Times,* EETS o.s. 32. London: Trübner, 1868 [Reprint: New York: Greenwood, 1969].

Gaimar, Geoffrei. *L'Estoire des Engleis.* Ed. Alexander Bell. ANTS 14–16. Oxford: Blackwell, 1960.

———. *Lestorie des Engles solum la translacion Maistre Geffrei Gaimar*. Ed. and trans. Sir Thomas Duffus Hardy and Charles Trice Martin, 2 vols. *Rerum Britannicum Medii Aevi Scriptores*. Vol. 91. London: Eyre and Spottiswoode, 1889.

Garber, Marjorie. *Vested Interests: Cross-Dressing and Cultural Anxiety*. New York: Routledge, 1992.

Garrison, Jennifer. *Challenging Communion: The Eucharist and Middle English Literature*. Columbus: The Ohio State University Press, 2016.

Gaunt, Simon. "The Significance of Silence." *Paragraph* 13 (1990): 202–16.

Geoffrey of Monmouth. *History of the Kings of Britain*. Ed. Michael D. Reeve. Trans. Neil Wright. Woodbridge, Suffolk: Boydell, 2007.

Geoffrey de Vinsauf. *Poetria Nova*. In *Les arts póetiques du XIIe et du XIIIe siècle*, ed. Edmond Faral, 109–93. Paris, Champion, 1924.

———. *Poetria Nova*. Trans. Margaret F. Nims. Toronto: Pontifical Institute, 1967; rev. ed, 2010.

Gilmore, Gloria Thomas. "*Le Roman de Silence*: Allegory in Ruin or Womb of Irony." *Arthuriana* 7 (1997): 111–28.

Godefroy, *Dictionnaire de l'Ancienne Langue Francaise du IXme au XVIme Siécle*. Online resource: http://www.lexilogos.com/francais_dictionnaire_ancien.htm.

Godlove, Shannon N. "Bodies as Borders: Cannibalism and Conversion in the Old English *Andreas*." *Studies in Philology* 106 (2009): 137–60.

Gordon, Sarah. *Culinary Comedy in Medieval French Literature*. West Lafayette, IN: Purdue University Press, 2007.

Great Chronicle of London. Ed. Robert Fabyan, A. H. Thomas, and Isobel Thornley. London: G. W. Jones, 1938.

Guibert of Nogent. *The Deeds of God Through the Franks*. Trans. Robert Levine. Woodbridge, Suffolk: Boydell, 1997.

Guillaume de Lorris and Jean de Meun. *Le Roman de la Rose*. Ed. Ernest Langlois. SATF. Paris: Firmin-Didot et Cie, 1914–24.

———. *The Romance of the Rose*. Trans. Charles Dahlberg. Princeton, NJ: Princeton University Press, 1971.

Hagen, Ann. *Anglo-Saxon Food and Drink: Production, Processing, Distribution and Consumption*. Hockwold cum Wilton, Norfolk: Anglo-Saxon Books, 2006 [originally published 1992 and 1995 in 2 volumes].

Hamilton, David. "*Andreas* and *Beowulf*: Placing the Hero." In *Anglo-Saxon Poetry: Essays in Appreciation for John C. McGalliard*, edited by Lewis E. Nicholson and Dolores Warwick Frese, 81–98. South Bend, IN: University of Notre Dame Press, 1975.

———. "The Diet and Digestion of Allegory in *Andreas*." *Anglo-Saxon England* 1 (1972): 147–58.

Hanning, Robert W. "*Havelok the Dane*: Structure, Symbols, Meaning." *Studies in Philology* 64 (1967): 586–605.

———. *The Individual in Twelfth-Century Romance*. New Haven, CT: Yale University Press, 1977.

Harder, Henry L. "Feasting in the *Alliterative Morte Arthure*." *Studies in Medieval Culture* 14 (1980): 49–62.

Hardman, Phillipa, ed. *The Heege Manuscript*. Leeds: Leeds School of English, 2000.

Haskin, Dayton, S. J. "Food, Clothing and Kingship in *Havelok*." *American Benedictine Review* 24 (1973), 204–13.

Havelok. Ed. G. V. Smithers. Oxford: Clarendon, 1987.

Hegel, G. W. F. *Phenomenology of Spirit* (1807). Trans. A. V. Miller. London: Oxford University Press, 1977.

Heldris de Cornuälle. *Le Roman de Silence*. Trans. F. Regina Psaki. New York: Garland, 1991.

———. *Le Roman de Silence: A Thirteenth-Century Arthurian Verse-Romance by Heldris de Cornuälle*. Ed. Lewis Thorpe. Cambridge, UK: Heffer, 1972.

———. *Silence: A Thirteenth-Century French Romance*. Ed. and trans. Sarah Roche-Mahdi. East Lansing: Michigan State University Press, 1992.

Heng, Geraldine. *Empire of Magic: Medieval Romance and the Politics of Cultural Fantasy*. New York: Columbia University Press, 2003.

———. "The Romance of England: *Richard Coer de Lyon*, Saracens, Jews, and the Politics of Race and Nation." In *The Postcolonial Middle Ages*, edited by Jeffrey Jerome Cohen, 135–72. New York: St. Martin's, 2000.

Henisch, Bridget Ann. *Fast and Feast: Food in Medieval Society*. University Park: Pennsylvania State University Press, 1976.

Hermann, John P. *Allegories of War: Language and Violence in Old English Poetry*. Ann Arbor: University of Michigan Press, 1989.

Herzfeld, George, ed., *Old English Martyrology*, EETS, o.s. 116. London: Paul, Tench & Trübner, 1900.

Hesiod. *Theogony* and *Works and Days* in *Hesiod*, 2 vols. Ed. and trans. Glenn W. Most. Cambridge, MA: Harvard University Press, 2006.

Hibbard, Laura Loomis. *Mediæval Romance in England: A Study of the Sources and Analogues of the Non-Cycle Metrical Romances* (1924). New York: B. Franklin, 1963.

Hieatt, Constance B. "The Harrowing of Mermedonia." *NM* 77 (1976): 49–62.

Hieatt, Constance B., and Sharon Butler. *Pleyn Delit: Medieval Cookery for Modern Cooks*. Toronto and Buffalo: University of Toronto Press, 1976.

———, eds. *Curye on Inglysch: English Culinary Manuscripts of the Fourteenth Century (including the Forme of Cury)*. EETS s.s. 8. London: Oxford University Press, 1985.

Hill, Thomas D. "Figural Narrative in *Andreas:* The Conversion of the Mermedonians." *NM* 70 (1969): 261–73.

Hopkins, Andrea. *The Sinful Knights: A Study of Middle English Penitential Romance*. Oxford: Oxford University Press, 1990.

Holsinger, Bruce, and Ethan Knapp, eds. "The Marxist Premodern." *JMEMS* 34.3 (Fall 2004): 463–71.

Innocent III, Pope (Lotario dei Conti di Segni). *On the Misery of the Human Condition: De Miseria Humane Conditionis*. Trans. Donald Roy Howard. Indianapolis, IN: Bobbs-Merrill, 1969.

Irving, Edward B., Jr. "A Reading of *Andreas:* The Poem as Poem." *Anglo-Saxon England* 12 (1983): 215–37.

Jameson, Frederic. *The Political Unconscious: Narrative as a Socially Symbolic Act*. Ithaca, NY: Cornell University Press, 1981.

Jauss, Hans Robert. *Toward an Aesthetic of Reception*. Trans. Timothy Bahti. Minneapolis: University of Minnesota Press, 1982.

Jewers, Caroline A. "The Non-Existent Knight: Adventure in *Le Roman de Silence.*" *Arthuriana* 7 (1997): 87–110.

Judith. In *Beowulf and Judith,* edited by Elliott Van Kirk Dobbie. New York: Columbia University Press, 1965.

Kabir, Anaya, J. "Forging an Oral Style? *Havelok* and the Fiction of Orality." *Studies in Philology* 98 (2001): 18–48.

Kane, George. *Middle English Literature: A Critical Study of the Romances, the Religious Lyrics, [and] Piers Plowman.* London: Methuen, 1951.

Kantorowicz, Ernst. *The King's Two Bodies: A Study in Mediaeval Political Theology* (1957). Princeton, NJ: Princeton University Press, 1997.

Kay, Sarah. *The Chansons de Geste in the Age of Romance: Political Fictions.* Oxford: Clarendon, 1995.

Ker, W. P. *Epic and Romance: Essays on Medieval Literature.* London: Macmillan, 1908.

Kim, Margaret. "Hunger, Need, and the Politics of Poverty in *Piers Plowman.*" *YLS* 16 (2002): 131–68.

Kinoshita, Sharon. "Heldris de Cornuälle's *Roman de Silence* and the Feudal Politics of Lineage." *PMLA* 110 (1995): 397–409.

Kizer, Lisa J. "*Andreas* and the *Lifes Weg.*" *NM* 85 (1984): 65–75.

Knight, Stephen. "The Social Function of the Middle English Romances." In *Medieval Literature: Criticism, Ideology, and History,* edited by David Aers, 99–122. New York: St. Martin, 1986.

The Knightly Tale of Golagros and Gawane. Ed. Ralph Hanna. Scottish Text Society. Woodbridge, Suffolk: Boydell and Brewer, 2008.

Krueger, Roberta, ed. *Cambridge Companion to Medieval Romance.* Cambridge, UK: Cambridge University Press, 2000.

Küster, Hansjörg. "Spices and Flavourings." In *The Cambridge World History of Food.* Vol. 1, edited by Kenneth F. Kiple and Kriemhild Conée Ornelas, 435–37. Cambridge, UK: Cambridge University Press, 2000.

Labarge, Margaret Wade. *A Baronial Household of the Thirteenth Century.* London: Eyre & Spottiswoode, 1965.

Lasry, Anita Benaim. "The Ideal Heroine in Medieval Romances: A Quest for a Paradigm." *Kentucky Romance Quarterly* 32 (1985): 227–43.

Le Lai d'Haveloc and Gaimar's Haveloc Episode. Ed. Alexander Bell. London: Longmans, 1925.

Lecoy, Felix. "*Le Roman de Silence.*" *Romania* 99 (1978): 109–25.

Lévi-Strauss, Claude. "The Culinary Triangle." Trans. Peter Brooks. *Partisan Review* 33 (1966): 586–96.

Liber Niger. See Myers, A. R.

Lim, Gary. "In the Name of the (Dead) Father: Reading Fathers and Sons in *Havelok the Dane, King Horn,* and *Bevis of Hampton.*" *JEGP* 110 (2011): 22–52.

Liuzza, Roy Michael. "Representation and Readership in the Middle English *Havelok.*" *JEGP* 93 (1994): 504–19.

———. "The Tower of Babel: *The Wanderer* and the Ruins of History." *Studies in the Literary Imagination* 36 (2003): 1–35.

Le Livre des Proverbes Francais. Edited by M. LeRoux de Lincy. 2 vols. 2nd ed. Paris: Delahays, 1859.

Lumiansky, Robert M. "The Contexts of Old English '*ealuscerwen*' and '*meoduscerwen*.'" *JEGP* 48 (1949): 116–26.

Lydgate, John. *The Minor Poems of John Lydgate.* Part 2. Ed. Henry Noble McCracken. EETS o.s. 192. London and New York: Oxford University Press, 1934.

Lynch, Kathryn. "From Tavern to Pie Shop: The Raw, the Cooked, and the Rotten in Fragment 1 of Chaucer's *Canterbury Tales*." *Exemplaria* 19 (2007): 117–38.

Magennis, Hugh. *Anglo-Saxon Appetites: Food and Drink and Their Consumption in Old English and Related Literatures.* Dublin: Four Courts, 1999.

Malory, Sir Thomas. *The Works of Malory.* Ed. Eugène Vinaver. Oxford: Oxford University Press, 1971.

Mandeville, John. *The Travels of Sir John Mandeville.* Trans. C. W. R. D. Moseley. London: Penguin, 1983.

Mann, Jill. "Eating and Drinking in *Piers Plowman*." *Essays and Studies* n.s. 32 (1979): 26–43.

———. "The Nature of Need Revisited." *YLS* 18 (2004): 3–29.

Mannyng, Robert, of Brunne. *The Chronicle.* Ed. Idelle Sullens. Binghamton: State University of New York at Binghamton Press, 1996.

———. *Handlyng Synne.* Ed. Idelle Sullens. Binghamton: State University of New York at Binghamton Press, 1983.

Marco Polo. *The Travels.* Trans. Ronald Latham. London: Penguin, 1958.

Marx, Karl. *Capital: A Critique of Political Economy.* Vol. 1 (1867). Trans. Ben Fowkes. New York: Penguin, 1977.

Marx, Karl. *The German Ideology.* New York: Prometheus, 1998.

———. *Grundrisse: Foundations of the Critique of Political Economy.* Trans. Martin Nicolaus. New York and London: Penguin, 1973.

McCracken, Peggy. "'The Boy who was a Girl': Reading Gender in the *Roman de Silence*." *Romanic Review* 84 (1994): 517–36.

McDonald, Nicola, ed. *Pulp Fictions of Medieval England: Essays in Popular Romance.* Manchester: Manchester University Press, 2004.

McGregor, Francine. "The Paternal Function in *Sir Gowther*." *Essays in Medieval Studies* 16 (1999): 67–78.

Mead, W. E. *The English Medieval Feast.* London: Allen and Unwin, 1931.

Mehl, Dieter. *The Middle English Romances of the Thirteenth and Fourteenth Centuries.* London: Routledge & Kegan Paul, 1969.

Mennell, Stephen. *All Manners of Food: Eating and Taste in England and France from the Middle Ages to the Present.* 2nd ed. Urbana: University of Illinois Press, 1996.

Mertes, Kate. *The English Noble Household, 1250–1600: Good Governance and Politic Rule.* Oxford: Basil Blackwell, 1988.

Michelet, Fabienne L. *Creation, Migration, and Conquest: Imaginary Geography and Sense of Space in Old English Literature.* Oxford: Oxford University Press, 2006.

———. "Eating Bodies in the Old English *Andreas*." In *Fleshly Things and Spiritual Matters: Studies on the Medieval Body in Honour of Margaret Bridges*," edited by Nicole Nyffenegger and Katrin Rupp, 165–92. Newcastle upon Tyne: Cambridge Scholars, 2011.

The Middle English Dictionary. Online resource: http://quod.lib.umich.edu/m/med/.

Mitchell, J. Allan. *Becoming Human: The Matter of the Medieval Child.* Minneapolis: University of Minnesota Press, 2014.

Montanari, Massimo. *The Culture of Food.* Trans. Carl Ipsen. Oxford: Blackwell, 1994.

Morton, Timothy. *The Poetics of Spice: Romantic Consumerism and the Exotic.* Cambridge, UK: Cambridge University Press, 2000.

Muir, Bernard J., ed. *The Exeter Anthology of Old English Poetry: An Edition of Exeter Dean and Chapter MS 3501.* 2 vols. Exeter, UK: University of Exeter Press, 2000.

Myers, A. R, ed. *The Household of Edward IV: The Black Book and the Ordinance of 1478.* Manchester: Manchester University Press, 1959.

Nelson, Marie. "The Old English *Andreas* as an Account of Benign Aggression." *Medieval Perspectives* 2 (1987): 81–89.

Newman, Barbara. "Did Goddesses Empower Women?" In *Gendering the Master Narrative,* edited by Mary C. Erler and Maryanne Kowaleski, 135–55. Ithaca: Cornell University Press, 2003.

Nicholls, Jonathan. *The Matter of Courtesy: Medieval Courtesy Books and the Gawain-poet.* London: D. S. Brewer, 1985.

Olsen, Alexandra Hennessey. "The Aesthetics of *Andreas*: The Contexts of Oral Tradition and Patristic Latin Poetry." In *De Gustibus: Essays for Alain Renoir,* edited by John Miles Foley Jr., 388–410. New York: Garland, 1992.

Olsen, Karin. "The Dichotomy of Land and Sea in the Old English *Andreas.*" *English Studies* 79 (1998): 385–94.

Orosius, Paulus. *King Alfred's Orosius.* Part 1. Ed. Henry Sweet. EETS o.s. 79. London: N. Trübner & Co, 1883.

Ovid. *Metamorphoses.* Trans. Frank Justus Miller. Loeb Classical Library. Cambridge, MA: Harvard University Press, 1916.

The Oxford English Dictionary. Online resource: http://www.oed.com/.

Pearsall, Derek. "The Development of Middle English Romance." In *Studies in Medieval English Romances: Some New Approaches,* edited by Derek Brewer, 11–35. Cambridge, UK: D. S. Brewer, 1988.

Powell, Allison. *Verbal Parallels in Andreas and Its Relationship to Beowulf and Cynewulf.* PhD diss., Cambridge University, 2002.

Ramsey, Lee C. *Chivalric Romances: Popular Literature in Medieval England.* Bloomington: Indiana University Press, 1983.

Reading, Amity. "Baptism, Conversion, and Selfhood in the Old English *Andreas.*" *Studies in Philology* 112 (2015): 1–23.

Redon, Odile, Françoise Sabban, and Silviano Seventi. *The Medieval Kitchen: Recipes from France and Italy.* Trans. Edward Schneider. Chicago: University of Chicago Press, 1998.

Richard Coer de Lyon: Der mittelenglische Versroman über Richard Löwenherz. Ed. Karl Brunner. Leipzig: Braumüller, 1913.

Robert le Diable. Ed. E. Loseth. SATF. Paris: Firmin Didot, 1903.

Robertson, Kellie. "Medieval Materialism: A Manifesto." *Exemplaria* 22 (2010): 99–118.

Robson, Margaret. "Animal Magic: Moral Regeneration in *Sir Gowther.*" *Yearbook of English Studies* 22 (1992): 140–53.

Roche-Mahdi, Sarah. "A Reappraisal of the Role of Merlin." *Arthuriana* 12 (2002): 6–21.

Rogers, [James E.] Thorold. *Six Centuries of Work and Wages: The History of English Labour.* New York: Putnam & Sons, 1884.

Rouse, Robert. *The Idea of Anglo-Saxon England in Middle English Romance.* Cambridge, UK: D. S. Brewer, 2005.

Ryder, Mary Ellen, and Linda Marie Zaerr. "A Stylistic Analysis of the *Roman de Silence*." *Arthuriana* 18 (2008): 22–40.

Salter, David. *Holy and Noble Beasts: Encounters with Animals in Medieval Literature.* Cambridge, UK: D. S. Brewer, 2001.

Santich, Barbara. "The Evolution of Culinary Techniques in the Medieval Era." In *Food in the Middle Ages,* edited by Melitta Weiss Adamson, 61–81. New York: Garland, 1995.

Saunders, Corinne, ed. *A Companion to Romance.* Malden, MA: Blackwell, 2004.

Schaar, Claes. *Critical Studies in the Cynewulf Group.* New York: Haskell House, 1967.

Scheil, Andrew. *The Footsteps of Israel: Understanding Jews in Anglo-Saxon England.* Ann Arbor: University of Michigan Press, 2004.

Schmitt, Carl. *Political Theology: Four Chapters on the Concept of Sovereignty* (1934). Trans. George Schwab. Cambridge, MA: MIT Press, 1985.

Schmolke-Haselmann, Beate. *The Evolution of Arthurian Romance: The Verse Tradition from Chrétien to Froissart.* Trans. Margaret and Roger Middleton. Cambridge, UK: Cambridge University Press, 1998 [originally appeared as *Der arturische Versroman von Chrestien bis Froissart* (Tubingen: Niemeyer, 1980)].

Scully, Terence. *The Art of Cookery in the Middle Ages.* Woodbridge, UK: Boydell, 1995.

———. "The Mediaeval French Entremet." *Petits Propos Culinaires* 17 (1984): 44–56.

———. "Mixing It Up in the Medieval Kitchen." In *Medieval Food and Drink,* ACTA 21, edited by Mary-Jo Arn, 1–26. Binghamton, NY: Center for Medieval and Renaissance Studies, 1995.

———. "Tempering Medieval Food." In *Food in the Middle Ages: A Book of Essays,* edited by Melitta Weiss Adamson, 3–24. New York: Garland, 1995.

Shaner, Mary. "Instruction and Delight: Medieval Romances as Children's Literature." *Poetics Today* 13.1 (1992): 5–15.

Shaw, Brian. "Translation and Transformation in *Andreas.*" In *Prosody and Poetics in the Early Middle Ages: Essays in Honour of C. B. Hieatt,* edited by M. J. Toswell, 164–79. Toronto: University of Toronto Press, 1995.

Shuffelton, George, ed. *Codex Ashmole 61: A Compilation of Popular Middle English Verse.* TEAMS. Kalamazoo, MI: Medieval Institute Publications, 2008.

Sir Gawain and the Green Knight. In *The Poems of the Pearl Manuscript: Pearl, Cleanness, Patience, Sir Gawain and the Green Knight,* edited by Malcolm Andrew and Ronald Waldron. Exeter: University of Exeter Press, 2007.

Sir Gowther. Ed. Cornelius Novelli. PhD diss., University of Notre Dame, 1963.

———. Ed. Karl Breul. Oppeln: E. Franck, 1886.

Sisam, Celia, ed. *Early English Manuscripts in Facsimile.* Vol. 19. *The Vercelli Book.* Copenhagen: Roskilde and Bagger, 1966.

Smith, Adam. *The Wealth of Nations* (1776). Ed. Edwin Cannan. Chicago: University of Chicago Press, 1976.

Smith, D. Vance. *Arts of Possession: The Middle English Household Imaginary.* Minneapolis: University of Minnesota Press, 2003.

Southern, R. W. *The Making of the Middle Ages.* London: Hutchison, 1953.

Spenser, Edmund. *The Faerie Queene.* Ed. A. C. Hamilton. Harlow, UK: Longman, 2001.

Sponsler, Claire. *Drama and Resistance: Bodies, Goods, and Theatricality in Late Medieval England.* Minneapolis: University of Minnesota Press, 1997.

———. "Eating Lessons: Lydgate's 'Dietary' and Consumer Conduct." In Ashley and Clark, *Medieval Conduct,* 1–22.

Stanley, Eric Gerald. "Beowulf." In *Continuations and Beginnings: Studies in Old English Literature,* edited by Eric Gerald Stanley, 104–41. London: Nelson, 1966.

Steel, Karl. *How to Make a Human: Animals and Violence in the Middle Ages.* Columbus: Ohio State University Press, 2011.

Stein, Robert M. *Reality Fictions: Romance, History, and Governmental Authority, 1025–1180* Notre Dame, IN: University of Notre Dame Press, 2006.

Stock, Lorraine Kochanske. "'Arms and the (Wo)Man' in Medieval Romance." *Arthuriana* 5 (1995): 56–83.

Strohm, Paul, ed. *Middle English: Oxford Twenty-First Century Approaches to Literature.* Oxford: Oxford University Press, 2007.

Stuart, Christopher. "*Havelok the Dane* and Edward I in the 1290s." *Studies in Philology* 93 (1996): 349–64.

Sturges, Robert S. "The Crossdresser and the *Juventus:* Category Crisis in *Silence.*" *Arthuriana* 12 (2002): 37–49.

Szittya, Penn R. "The Living Stone and the Patriarchs: Typological Imagery in *Andreas,* Lines 706–810." *JEGP* 77 (1973): 167–74.

Táin Bó Cúailnge: The Táin. Trans. Ciaran Carson. New York: Penguin, 2007.

Taylor, Andrew. "'Her Y Spelle': The Evocation of Minstrel Performance in a Hagiographical Context." In *The Texts and Contexts of Oxford, Bodleian Library, MS Laud Misc. 108: The Shaping of English Vernacular Narrative,* edited by Kimberley K. Bell and Julie Nelson Couch, 71–86. Leiden: Brill, 2011.

Taylor, Joseph. "Sovereign Ecologies: Managing the King's Bodies in Anglo-Norman Historiography." In *The Politics of Ecology: Land, Life, and Law in Medieval Britain,* edited by Randy P. Schiff and Joseph Taylor, 179–209. Columbus: Ohio State University Press, 2015.

Thormann, Janet. "The Jewish Other in Old English Narrative Poetry." *Partial Answers: A Journal of Literature and the History of Ideas* 2 (2004): 1–20.

Trigg, Stephanie. "Learning to Live." In Strohm, *Middle English,* 459–75.

Trilling, Renée R. *The Aesthetics of Nostalgia: Historical Representation in Old English Verse.* Toronto: University of Toronto Press, 2009.

Turner, Jack. *Spice: The History of a Temptation.* New York: Knopf, 2004.

Turville-Petre, Thorlac. *England the Nation: Language, Literature, and National Identity, 1290–1340.* Oxford and New York: Clarendon, 1996.

———. "*Havelok* and the History of the Nation." In *Readings in Medieval Romance,* edited by Carol M. Meale, 121–34. Cambridge, UK: D. S. Brewer, 1994.

Two Fifteenth-Century Cookery Books. Edited by Thomas Austin. EETS o.s. 91. London: Oxford University Press, 1888.

Uebel, Michael. "The Foreigner Within: The Subject of Abjection in *Sir Gowther*." In *Meeting the Foreign in the Middle Ages*, edited by Albrecht Classen, 96–117. New York: Routledge, 2002.

de la Varenne, François Pierre. *Le Cuisinier François* (1651). Ed. Jean-Louis Flandrin, Philip Hyman, and Mary Hyman. Paris: Montalba, 1983.

———. *La Varenne's Cookery: The French Cook, the French Pastry Chef, the French Confectioner.* Trans. Terence Scully. Totnes, UK: Prospect, 2006.

Veblen, Thorstein. *A Veblen Treasury: From Leisure Class to War, Peace, and Capitalism*. Ed. Rick Tillman. Armonk, NY: M. E. Sharpe, 1993.

The Venerable Bede. *The Ecclesiastical History of the English People*. Ed. Judith McClure and Roger Collins. Trans. Bertram Colgrave. Oxford: Oxford University Press, 1994.

The Viandier of Taillevent. Ed. and trans. Terence Scully. Ottawa: University of Ottawa Press, 1988.

Vinaver, Eugène. *The Rise of Romance*. New York: Oxford University Press, 1971.

Walsh, Sister Marie Michelle. "The Baptismal Flood in the Old English *Andreas*: Liturgical and Typological Depths." *Traditio* 33 (1977): 137–58.

Warner, Richard. *Antiquitates culinariæ; or curious tracts relating to the culinary affairs of the old English*. London: R. Blamire, 1791.

Waters, Elizabeth. "The Third Path: Alternative Sex, Alternative Gender in *Le Roman de Silence*." *Arthuriana* 7 (1997): 35–46.

Wells, Sharon. "Manners Maketh Man: Living, Dining, and Becoming a Man in the Later Middle Ages." In *Rites of Passage: Cultures of Transition in the Fourteenth Century*, edited by Nicola F. McDonald and W. M. Ormrod, 67–81. Woodbridge: York Medieval Press, 2004.

Wilcox, Jonathan. "Eating People Is Wrong: Funny Style in *Andreas* and Its Analogues." In *Anglo-Saxon Styles*, edited by Catherine E. Karkov and George Hardin Brown, 201–22. Albany: State University of New York, 2003.

Wilson, C. Anne. *Food and Drink in Britain: From the Stone Age to Recent Times*. New York: Barnes & Noble, 1974.

Woolf, Rosemary. "Saints' Lives." In *Continuations and Beginnings: Studies in Old English Literature*, edited by Eric Gerald Stanley, 37–66. London: Nelson, 1966.

INDEX

Abdou, Angela, 51n46
Agamben, Giorgio, 2n3, 104n22
Akbari, Suzanne Conklin, 76–77, 87
Alain de Lille (Alaunus Insulis), 76, 79, 81
Alfred the Great, King, 104n21
Alliterative Morte Arthure (romance), 21–23, 27
Amos, Mark Addison, 142
Andreas (hagiographic romance), 28, 29, 32–65, 169–70
animal studies, 2n1, 89n65
animality and humanity, 136, 156–57
anthropophagism (cannibalism), 24–25, 32–33, 41, 169–71; as food practice, 42–47; as political appetite, 46; as politics of time, 37–39, 47; and theophagy, 44; versus "cannibalism," 32n2
Arendt, Hannah, 3n6, 98, 134
Arens, William, 38
Aristotle, 29, 77, 81, 158
Ashley, Kathleen, 138
Asser, John, 104n21
Auerbach, Eric, 10

Bakhtin, Mikhail, 4
baking, 77–82
banquets, 14–15
Barron, W. R. J., 10
Bartolomeus Anglicus, 149n51
Bartolovich, Crystal, 39–40

Bataille, Georges, 103–5,113, 115–16, 120, 123, 129, 170
Battles, Paul, 57
Beasts of Battle, 6
Becker, Alexis Kellner, 125n62
Bede, the Venerable, 37–38, 64
Bell, Kimberly K., 130n66
Bennett, Jane, 4
Benoît de Sainte-Maure, 13, 107
Beowulf (OE poem), 39, 49–51
Berry, Craig A., 71n13
Bible, The: Acts of the Apostles, 2; Book of Genesis, 2, 5, 170; Book of Revelations, 95; Ecclesiastes, 164n75; Gospel of Luke, 2n2, 32, 40–41; Gospel of Matthew, 136; Leviticus, 2
Blamires, Alcuin, 135–36
Blurton, Heather, 25n83, 33n4, 36
Boccaccio, Giovanni, 151
Boenig, Robert, 33n4, 36
Bolduc, Michelle, 83n46
Bourdieu, Pierre, 104n20, 139–40, 143
Bradstock, E. M., 135
Brahney, Kathleen J., 72
Brewer, Derek, 6
Brillat-Savarin, Jean Anthelme, 8, 116, 133, 167–68
Brooks, Kenneth, 57n57
Butler, Judith, 97
Bynum, Caroline Walker, 3, 171–72

INDEX

Cædmon, 64
cannibalism. *See* anthropophagism
Cannon, Christopher, 108
carving, 160–62
Caxton, William, 136
de Certeau, Michel, 8, 143, 146, 152, 160
Charbonneau, Joanne, 135
Chaucer, Geoffrey, 5, 6, 100n3, 118, 151, 166n77, 172
Chen, Anna, 135–36
Chevalier au Lion (Yvain), Le, 87n59, 120n57
children's literature, 4n11
Chrétien de Troyes, 13
Clark, Robert L. A., 73, 77, 138
coevality, 37, 54, 62–63
Cohen, Jeffrey Jerome, 153
Cole, Andrew, 104n19, 144n40
Coleman, Joyce, 15
commodity, 4, 118
conduct manual, 114n43, 138–41, 142–43, 144–45, 154–55
consumption: in edible world, 1; as identity, 7, 146, 152; as political critique, 24–28, 30–31; "productive consumption," 7–8, 144; as productive labor, 4, 7; sovereign, 1–2, 24–27, 30, 103–5, 107, 165, 170
conviviality, 6–7, 26–27, 48, 56–60, 65, 141, 144–45, 164
cooking: as labor, 30, 75; as prophecy, 94; as supersession of commodities, 118
Cooper, Helen, 12, 29
Couch, Julie Nelson, 111n37, 130
courtesy, 169
Crane, Susan, 10, 12, 100
cross-dressing, 73–74
Cú Chulainn, 163n74
cuisine, medieval, 18–24
culinary techniques, 19–21
"Culinary triangle," 75
culture as food production, 6

Dante Aligheri, 118n48
Davis, Kathleen, 38
Derrida, Jacques, 147
dieting and inedia, 4–5
Divisament dou Monde (Marco Polo), 42, 171
Donestre, 39

Douglas, Mary, 7n25, 46
Dyer, Christopher, 109n31

edible world, 1–3, 168
effictio, 170
Elene (OE poem), 13
Elias, Norbert, 141–42
entremet (or *soteltie*), 17–18
Erasmus of Rotterdam, 141–42
"Erþe toc of erþe" (13th century lyric), 5–6
Eucharist, 2–3, 52, 82
Exeter Book Riddle #27 (OE poem), 46

Fabian, Johannes, 37, 62–63
Faerie Queene, The (Spenser), 168–70
Faletra, Michael, 100
Fee, Christopher, 47n40
Ferhatović, Denis, 53n49, 56n54
Field, Rosalind, 15
Fildes, Valerie, 147n46
Finlayson, John, 11
fish, 112–13
food, as political theory, 99; as politics of time, 47
Foucault, Michel, 143
Franklin, Alfred, 19
Freedman, Paul, 24n81
Freud, Sigmund, 38, 152
Froissart, Jean, 151

Gaimar, Geoffrei, 100
Garber, Marjorie, 73
Gaunt, Simon, 72
Geoffrey of Monmouth, 83
Gilmore, Gloria Thomas, 84n48
Godlove, Shannon N., 41
Golagros and Gawane, The Knightly Tale of (romance), 25–27
Gordon, Sarah, 16n61, 74
Great Chronicle of London, 140
Guibert of Nogent, 25n83
Guthlac A (OE poem), 49n43

Hamilton, David, 42n28, 51n45, 52n47
Hanning, Robert W., 11, 102
Hardman, Phillipa, 137

Hartmann von Aue, 13
Haskin, Dayton, S. J., 102
Havelok the Dane (romance), 15, 28, 30, 97, 98–132, 133
"Hedgehogs" (*yrchouns*), 23
"Heege Manuscript" (Edinburgh, National Library of Scotland MS Advocates 19.3.1), 137–38
Hegel, G. W. F., 24n82, 104n19, 120
Heißhunger, 40
Heng, Geraldine, 12
Hermann, John P., 35–36, 53
Herodotus, 170
Hesiod, 5, 38
Hill, Thomas D., 35
Hopkins, Andrea, 135
humanity: marked by culinary practice, 168; as "political animals," 29
humors, bodily, 86
hunting, 150–52

Innocent, Pope, III, 148
Irving, Edward B., Jr., 44

Jameson, Frederic, 13
Jauss, Hans Robert, 13
Jean de Meun, 76–77, 79, 81
Jewers, Caroline A., 73
Judith (OE poem), 39

Kane, George, 11–12, 135
Kantorowicz, Ernst, 108n29
King Horn (romance), 115
Kay, Sarah, 7
Ker, W. P., 10
Kinoshita, Sharon, 72
kitchen, 116–20, 131
Knight, Stephen, 11

Labarge, Margaret Wade, 119, 119n56
labor, 3–4, 68–69, 98, 149
laborer as expanded bourgeois, 3–4
Lai d'Haveloc (Anglo-Norman romance), 114
Lasry, Anita Benaim, 72
Laval-Middleton manuscript (Univ. of Nottingham MS Mi.LM.6), 71

Lévi-Strauss, Claude, 74
Liber Niger, 140–41
Lim, Gary, 106n23
Liuzza, Roy M., 56, 112–13
Lynch, Kathryn, 100n3, 172

Magennis, Hugh, 36, 59n60
Malory, Sir Thomas, 14
Mandeville, Sir John, 42
Mann, Jill, 172
manners, table, 134–35, 139–41, 143, 158, 159–60, 162
Mannyng, Robert, of Brunne, 107, 108n30
Marco Polo, 42, 171
Marx, Karl, 1, 3n5, 8, 40, 68, 113n40, 118n52, 143–46, 152, 157, 170
McCracken, Peggy, 72
McDonald, Nicola, 12
Mead, W. E., 19
Mehl, Dieter, 11
Mennell, Stephen, 109n31, 138
Michelet, Fabienne L., 43, 46
Mitchell, J. Allan, 134, 142, 144, 146–47, 172
Montanari, Massimo, 110n33

"Nature" vs. "Noureture," 30, 67–69, 85, 88–93, 136
Neville, George, Archbishop of York, 18
Newman, Barbara, 78, 80

Octavian (romance), 103n18
Olsen, Alexandra Hennessey, 48
Orosius, Paulus, 42
Ovid, 5
Oxford Bodleian Library MS Ashmole 61, 138n21
Oxford Bodleian Library MS Laud Misc. 108, 101

Pearsall, Derek, 100
penitence, 135–36, 153–54
Perneys, Henry, 101
Physiologie du Goût, Le (Brillat-Savarin), 167–68
Piers Plowman, 172
politics of time, 47, 51–54, 55–56, 62

Ramsey, Lee C., 10, 99
Reading, Amity, 51n46
Richard Coer de Lyon (romance), 14, 24–25, 27, 85n51, 107, 171
Robert le Diable (OF romance), 149n48, 152n54
Robertson, Kellie, 172n4
Robson, Margaret, 153
Rogers, Thorold, 109n31
romance, medieval (genre): codified 9–14; as exploration of consumption, 172; and history, 171; history of genre, 34–35; as mixture, 69–70; as political statement, 31, 168
Roman de la Rose (Guillaume de Lorris and Jean de Meun), 13, 76–77, 79, 81
Roman de Silence (OF romance), 28, 29–30, 65, 66–97, 131
Round Table, the, 172
Rouse, Robert, 106n23
Ruin, The (OE poem), 6
Russell, John, 161
Ryder, Mary Ellen and Linda Marie Zaerr, 88

salt, 85–86
Salter, David, 156n61
Scheil, Andrew, 36
Schmitt, Carl, 104n22
Schmolke-Hasselman, Beate, 16n61, 27n86, 70–71
Scully, Terence, 95
Shaw, Brian, 46
Sir Gawain and the Green Knight (romance), 16–18, 27, 151
Sir Gowther (romance), 28, 30–31, 131, 133–66, 167
Sir Isumbras (romance), 103n18
Smith, Adam, 157
Smith, D. Vance, 9, 12, 102, 118n52
Soul and Body 2 (Exeter Book lyric), 6

Southern, R. W., 11
sovereignty, 99, 103–5, 107–8, 113–14, 115–16, 117, 119–20, 123–26, 129, 131
Spenser, Edmund, 168–70
spices, 20–21, 23–24
Sponsler, Claire, 139–40, 142, 143
Stanley, Eric Gerald, 35n8
Steel, Karl, 136n13, 157
Stein, Robert, 7n24, 11
St. Lawrence, 33
Stock, Lorraine Kochanske, 83n44
strawberries, 20
Stuart, Christopher, 100, 119n56
Sturges, Robert S., 73

Tale of Gamelyn (romance), 103n18
Taylor, Andrew, 101
Taylor, Joseph, 125n62
teeth, 19
terroir, 10, 167
Trigg, Stephanie, 160
Trilling, Renée R., 56

Uebel, Michael, 135
"Urbanitatis" (conduct manual), 138–39, 141, 154–55, 165

Veblen, Thorstein, 7n22
Viandier of Taillevent (cookbook), 17
Vinaver, Eugène, 11, 70

Wace, 13
Warner, Richard, 18
Waters, Elizabeth, 72
Wells, Sharon, 16
Wilcox, Jonathan, 36
Wonders of the East (OE travelogue), 39, 42
Woolf, Rosemary, 35n8, 50n44
Wynkyn de Worde, 161

INTERVENTIONS: NEW STUDIES IN MEDIEVAL CULTURE
Ethan Knapp, Series Editor

Interventions: New Studies in Medieval Culture publishes theoretically informed work in medieval literary and cultural studies. We are interested both in studies of medieval culture and in work on the continuing importance of medieval tropes and topics in contemporary intellectual life.

Political Appetites: Food in Medieval English Romance
  AARON HOSTETTER

Invention and Authorship in Medieval England
  ROBERT R. EDWARDS

Challenging Communion: The Eucharist and Middle English Literature
  JENNIFER GARRISON

Chaucer on Screen: Absence, Presence, and Adapting the Canterbury Tales
  EDITED BY KATHLEEN COYNE KELLY AND TISON PUGH

Chaucer, Gower, and the Affect of Invention
  STEELE NOWLIN

Fragments for a History of a Vanishing Humanism
  EDITED BY MYRA SEAMAN AND EILEEN A. JOY

The Medieval Risk-Reward Society: Courts, Adventure, and Love in the European Middle Ages
  WILL HASTY

The Politics of Ecology: Land, Life, and Law in Medieval Britain
  EDITED BY RANDY P. SCHIFF AND JOSEPH TAYLOR

The Art of Vision: Ekphrasis in Medieval Literature and Culture
  EDITED BY ANDREW JAMES JOHNSTON, ETHAN KNAPP, AND MARGITTA ROUSE

Desire in the Canterbury Tales
  ELIZABETH SCALA

Imagining the Parish in Late Medieval England
  ELLEN K. RENTZ

Truth and Tales: Cultural Mobility and Medieval Media
  EDITED BY FIONA SOMERSET AND NICHOLAS WATSON

Eschatological Subjects: Divine and Literary Judgment in Fourteenth-Century French Poetry
  J. M. MOREAU

Chaucer's (Anti-)Eroticisms and the Queer Middle Ages
  TISON PUGH

Trading Tongues: Merchants, Multilingualism, and Medieval Literature
　　Jonathan Hsy

Translating Troy: Provincial Politics in Alliterative Romance
　　Alex Mueller

Fictions of Evidence: Witnessing, Literature, and Community in the Late Middle Ages
　　Jamie K. Taylor

Answerable Style: The Idea of the Literary in Medieval England
　　Edited by Frank Grady and Andrew Galloway

Scribal Authorship and the Writing of History in Medieval England
　　Matthew Fisher

Fashioning Change: The Trope of Clothing in High- and Late-Medieval England
　　Andrea Denny-Brown

Form and Reform: Reading across the Fifteenth Century
　　Edited by Shannon Gayk and Kathleen Tonry

How to Make a Human: Animals and Violence in the Middle Ages
　　Karl Steel

Revivalist Fantasy: Alliterative Verse and Nationalist Literary History
　　Randy P. Schiff

Inventing Womanhood: Gender and Language in Later Middle English Writing
　　Tara Williams

Body Against Soul: Gender and Sowlehele *in Middle English Allegory*
　　Masha Raskolnikov

www.ingramcontent.com/pod-product-compliance
Lightning Source LLC
Chambersburg PA
CBHW032100300426
44116CB00007B/826